The Complete **Fawlty Towers**

The Complete
FAWLTY TOWERS

John Cleese and **Connie Booth**

Methuen London

This edition published in Great Britain in 1988
and reprinted 1988 (twice)
by Methuen London Ltd
Michelin House, 81 Fulham Road, London SW3 6RB
Copyright © 1977, 1979, 1988 John Cleese, Connie Booth,
Waterfall Productions Ltd

Photoset by Rowland Phototypesetting Ltd
Bury St Edmunds, Suffolk

Printed in Great Britain
by Richard Clay Ltd, Bungay, Suffolk

British Library Cataloguing in Publication Data

Cleese, John
    The complete Fawlty Towers.
    1. Fawlty Towers (Television program)
    I. Title   II. Booth, Connie
    791.45'7   PN1992.77.F3/

    ISBN 0-413-18390-4

Lines from 'I Cain't Say No'
(composer: Richard Rodgers; author:
Oscar Hammerstein II) © 1943
Williamson Music Limited are
reproduced by permission.

Contents

List of Illustrations

These photographs are reproduced by kind permission of BBC Enterprises.

The Complete Fawlty Towers

A Touch of Class

First of first series, first broadcast on 19 September 1975, BBC2.

Basil Fawlty John Cleese
Sybil Fawlty Prunella Scales
Manuel Andrew Sachs
Polly Connie Booth
Major Gowen Ballard Berkeley
Miss Tibbs Gilly Flower
Miss Gatsby Renée Roberts
Lord Melbury Michael Gwynn
Danny Brown Robin Ellis
Sir Richard Morris Martin Wyldeck
Mr Watson Lionel Wheeler
Mr Wareing Terence Conoley
Mr Mackenzie David Simeon

The Fawlty Towers reception lobby. The main entrance is at the back, with the stairs to the right. The entrance to the dining room is in the right wall; on the left, the reception desk running along the left wall, with the entrance to the office behind it. The entrance to the bar is beyond the desk.

Basil	*(on the phone)* One double room without bath for the 16th, 17th and 18th . . . yes, and if you'd be so good as to confirm by letter? . . . thank you so much, goodbye. *(puts the phone down)*
Sybil	*(bustling in)* Have you made up the bill for room twelve, Basil?
Basil	No, I haven't yet, no.
Sybil	Well, they're in a hurry. Polly says they didn't get their alarm call. And Basil, please get that picture up – it's been there for a week. *(goes into office)*
Basil	It's been there since Monday, Sybil . . . Tuesday . . . Wednesday . . . Thursday . . . *(to passing guests)* Good morning . . . Friday . . . Sat – *(realizes Sybil is no longer there; goes across to Manuel who has come in carrying three breakfast trays)* Manuel! There – is – too – much – butter – on – those – trays.
Manuel	*Qué?*
Basil	There is too much butter **on those trays.** *(he points to each tray in turn)*
Manuel	No, no, no, *Señor!*
Basil	What?
Manuel	Not 'on– those– trays'. No, sir – '*uno, dos, tres.*' *Uno . . . dos . . . tres.*
Basil	No, no. *Hay mucho burro allí!*
Manuel	*Qué?*
Basil	*Hay . . . mucho . . . burro . . . allí!*
Manuel	Ah, *mantequilla!*
Basil	What? *Qué?*
Manuel	*Mantequilla. Burro* is . . . is . . . *(brays like a donkey)*
Basil	What?
Manuel	*Burro . . . (does more donkey imitations)*
Basil	Manuel, *por favor . . .*
Manuel	*Si, si . . .*
Sybil	*(coming back in)* What's the matter, Basil?
Basil	Nothing, dear, I'm just dealing with it.
Manuel	*(to Sybil)* He speak good . . . how you say . . . ?

Sybil	English!
Basil	*Mantequilla . . . solamente . . . dos . . .*
Manuel	*Dos?*
Sybil	*(to Basil)* Don't look at me. You're the one who's supposed to be able to speak it.

Basil angrily grabs the excess butter from the trays.

Basil	Two pieces! Two each! *Arriba, arriba!!*

He waves his hand towards the bedrooms and Manuel runs off.

Sybil	I don't know why you wanted to hire him, Basil.
Basil	*(sitting at typewriter)* Because he's cheap and keen to learn, dear. And in this day and age such . . .
Sybil	But why did you say you could speak the language?
Basil	I learnt classical Spanish, not the strange dialect he seems to have picked up.
Sybil	It'd be quicker to train a monkey.

Misses Tibbs and Gatsby come down the stairs.

Sybil	*(turning on the charm)* Good morning Miss Gatsby, morning Miss Tibbs.
Basil	*(imitating the charm ironically)* Good morning, good morning.
Sybil	Basil!
Basil	Yes, dear?
Sybil	Are you going to hang the picture?
Basil	Yes I am, dear, yes, yes . . .
Sybil	When?
Basil	When I've, when I've . . .
Sybil	Well, why don't you do it now?
Basil	Well, I'm doing this, dear *(indicating typewriter)* . . . I'm doing the menu.
Sybil	You've got all morning to do the menu. Why don't you hang the picture now? . . . Well?
Basil	*(jumping up)* Yes, all right, I won't do the menu . . . I don't think you realize how long it takes to do the menu, but no, it doesn't matter, I'll hang the picture now. If the menus are late for lunch it doesn't matter, the guests can all come and look at the picture till they are ready, right? *(he starts to hang the picture to the right of the dining-room door)*

Sybil	Lower . . . *(he lowers it)* . . . Lower . . . up a bit . . . There! *(she disappears)*
Basil	Thank you, dear. Thank you so much. I don't know where I'd be without you . . . in the land of the living, probably.

He holds the picture in position. A young couple, the Mackenzies, come hurriedly down the stairs and ring the reception bell.

Basil	Yes?
Mr Mackenzie	Er . . . could we have our bill please?
Basil	Well, can you **wait** a minute?
Mr Mackenzie	Er . . . I'm afraid we're a bit late for our train – we didn't get our alarm call.

Basil glowers at them, then puts the picture down and strides back to the typewriter.

Basil	Right. I was up at five, you know, we do have staff problems, I'm so sorry, it's all done by magic.

He starts typing the bill. Sybil looks in from the office.

Sybil	*(accusingly)* Basil, are you doing the menu?
Basil	No, I'm not doing the menu, dear. I am doing the bill for these charming people who are in a hurry.
Mr Mackenzie	*(to Sybil)* I'm sorry to cause all this trouble, but the reason we're late is we didn't get our alarm call.
Sybil	Oh dear, I *am* sorry. *(sweetly)* Basil, why didn't they get their alarm call?
Basil	Because **I forgot!** I am so sorry I am not perfect! There you are, there's the bill. Perhaps you'd pay my wife, I have to put the picture up . . . if there aren't any dustbins to be cleaned out . . .

He walks towards the picture again. A newspaper boy comes in and puts his papers on the tables.

Newspaper boy	Newspapers!

Basil turns after him aggressively, tapping his watch – the boy exits rapidly. The Mackenzies leave; Basil's farewell smile lacks integrity.

Basil	Goodbye. See you again!
Sybil	Don't forget the picture, Basil.

Basil	I won't, dear, leave it to me.
Sybil	I'm going out now. I expect it to be up when I get back. *(she leaves)*
Basil	*(through his teeth)* Drive carefully, dear . . .

He takes the papers into the dining room, and, ignoring the other guests, gives one to Major Gowen.

Basil	Ah, good morning, Major.
The Major	Morning, Fawlty.
Basil	I do apologise for the tardiness of the arrival of your newspaper this morning, Major. I will speak to them again, see if **something** can be done.
The Major	Ah, more strikes . . . dustmen . . . Post Office . . .
Basil	It makes you want to cry, doesn't it. What's happened to the old ideal of doing something for your fellow man, of service? I mean, today . . .
Mr Watson	*(from his table)* Mr Fawlty?
Basil	Yes, I'm coming, I'm coming! *(to the Major, quietly)* They treat you like dirt, you know . . . of course it's pure ignorance, but with the **class** of guests one gets nowadays . . .
The Major	Ah! D'Olivera made a hundred!
Basil	Did he? Did he really? Good for him, good old Dolly. Well, well, well . . . *(Polly arrives with a cup of tea; he takes it, and gives her the other papers)* Thank you, Polly.
Mr Watson	We're only staying till Sunday!
Basil	Right, thank you . . . *(he picks up some food from the sideboard and goes through the lobby into the office; he has just sat down when he hears Sybil coming and hurriedly pushes his snack out of sight)* Ah, I thought you were going out, dear.
Sybil	*(holding out a copy of* Country Life*)* What's this?
Basil	I decided, Sybil, to advertise. I . . .
Sybil	How much did it cost?
Basil	Oh . . . I haven't . . . fifteen?
Sybil	Forty.
Basil	*(vaguely)* . . . Forty . . .
Sybil	I have **told** you where we advertise.
Basil	Sybil, I **know** the hotel business.
Sybil	No you don't, Basil.
Basil	Sybil, we've got to try to attract a better class of person.
Sybil	Why?

Basil	Well, we're losing **tone**.
Sybil	We're making money.
Basil	Yes, yes . . .
Sybil	Just.
Basil	Yes, but now we can try to build up a higher class of clientele! . . . Turn away some of the riff-raff.
Sybil	So long as they pay their bills, Basil.
Basil	Is that all that matters to you, Sybil? Money?
Sybil	This advertisement is a waste of forty pounds. *(turns to leave)*
Basil	One moment! One moment, please! *(proudly hands her a letter from the desk)* Well?
Sybil	. . . Well?
Basil	My dear woman, Sir Richard and Lady Morris, arriving this evening. For two nights. You see, they saw the advertisement in *Country Life*.
Sybil	I wish they were staying a week.
Basil	Well, so do I . . .
Sybil	Might pay for the ad then. *(makes to leave again)*
Basil	Sybil, look! If we can attract this class of customer, I mean . . . the sky's the limit!
Sybil	Basil, twenty-two rooms is the limit!
Basil	I mean, have you **seen** the people in room six? They've never even sat on chairs before. They are the commonest, vulgarest, most horrible, nasty . . .

But Sybil has gone. The reception bell rings. Basil goes to the reception desk; standing there is a very non-aristocratic-looking cockney, Danny Brown.

Danny	'Allo! *(Basil stands appalled)* Got a room?
Basil	. . . I beg your pardon?
Danny	Got a room for tonight, mate?
Basil	. . . I shall have to see, sir . . . single?
Danny	Yeah. No, make it a double, I feel lucky today! *(smiling appreciatively at Polly, who is passing)* 'Allo . . .
Polly	*(smiling nicely)* Good morning.

Danny watches her as she leaves. He turns back to Basil who is staring at him with loathing.

Danny	Only joking.
Basil	No we haven't.
Danny	What?

Basil	No we haven't any rooms. Good day . . .
Sybil	*(coming in)* Number seven is free, Basil.
Basil	What? . . . oh . . . Mr Tone is in number seven, dear.
Sybil	No, he left while you were putting the picture up, Basil . . . *(to Danny)* You have luggage, sir?
Danny	Just one case. *(to Basil, pointedly)* In the car . . . the white sports.

Basil closes his eyes in agony. Sybil rings the bell.

Sybil	Fill this in, would you, sir?
Basil	*(quietly)* If you can.
Sybil	I hope you enjoy your stay *(looking at register)*, Mr Brown.

Manuel arrives.

Basil	*(slowly)* Er, Manuel, would you fetch this gentleman's case from the car outside. Take it to room seven.
Manuel	. . . Is not easy for me.
Basil	What?
Manuel	Is not easy for me . . . *entender.*
Basil	Ah! It's not easy for you to understand. Manuel . . . *(to Danny)* We're training him . . . he's from Barcelona . . . in Spain. *(to Manuel) Obtener la valisa . . .*
Manuel	*Qué?*
Basil	*La valisa en el,* er, *auto bianco sportiv . . . y . . . a la sala . . . siete . . . por favor. Pronto.*
Manuel	Is impossible!
Basil	What?
Manuel	Is impossible.
Basil	Look, it's perfectly simple!
Danny	*(fluently)* Manuel – *sirvase buscar mi equipaje que esta en el automovil blanco y lo traer a la sala numero siete.*
Manuel	*Señor habla Español!*
Danny	*Solo un poco, lo siento. Pero he olvidado mucho.*
Manuel	*No, no, habla muy bien. Muy muy bien. Formidable!*
Danny	*Gracias, gracias.*
Manuel	*Lo voy a coger ahora. (runs off to get the case)*
Basil	. . . Well, if there's anything else, I'm sure Manuel will be able to tell you . . . as you seem to get on so well together. *(goes into the office)*
Danny	*(calling after him)* Key?

Basil comes back, takes the key from the hook and slams it down on the desk. Returning to the office he sits down, and switches on a cassette of Brahms. He settles back in rapture, but hears Sybil coming and rushes back to the picture in the lobby.

Basil	Hallo dear . . . just doing the picture.
Sybil	Don't forget the menu.
Basil	. . . I beg your pardon?
Sybil	Don't forget the menu.
Basil	I thought you said you wanted . . . Right! *(puts the picture down)* I'll do the menu.
Sybil	You could have had them both done by now if you hadn't spent the whole morning skulking in there listening to that racket. *(goes out)*
Basil	Racket? That's **Brahms**! Brahms's Third Racket!! . . . *(to himself)* The whole morning! . . . I had two bars.

In the dining room, Polly is taking Danny's order.

Polly	Ready to order?
Danny	Er, yeah. What's a gralefrit?
Polly	Grapefruit.
Danny	And creme pot . . . pot rouge?
Polly	Portugaise. Tomato soup.
Danny	I'll have the gralefrit. Now – balm carousel . . . lamb?
Polly	Casserole.
Danny	Sounds good. Does it come with a smile?
Polly	It comes with sprouts or carrots.
Danny	Oh, smile's extra, is it?
Polly	You'll get one if you eat up all your sprouts. *(exits)*
Danny	*(half registering a figure on the other side of the room)* Waiter!

Basil freezes and then comes balefully towards Danny.

Basil	. . . I beg your pardon?
Danny	Oh, 'allo. Can I have some wine please?
Basil	The waiter is busy, sir, but I will bring you the *carte des vins* when I have finished attending to this gentleman. *(indicates the table he has just left)*
Danny	Oh, fine – no hurry.
Basil	*(muttering on his way to the other table)* Oh, good, how

nice, how very thoughtful . . . *(at the other table)* I trust the beer is to your satisfaction, sir?

Mr Watson   . . . Yes, fine.

Basil   Ah, good. May I wish you *bon appétit. (snaps his fingers)* Manuel! *(Manuel runs in)* Would you fetch the wine list, please?

Manuel   *(not moving) Si, señor.*

Basil   . . . The **wine** list. The wine . . . *vino. (Manuel starts to move)* No, no. The list! There, there, the list! *(points to it – it is on another table)* The list, there! The red . . . there! . . . There!!

He picks up the list, hands it to Manuel, then gets Manuel to hand it to him so that he can give it to Danny.

Danny   'Ave you got a half bottle of the Beaujolais?

Basil   Yes.

Danny   Oh, fine.

Basil withdraws the wine list with a flourish, knocking the grapefruit out of Polly's hand as she approaches the table.

Basil   Right! Never mind! Never mind! Manuel – another grapefruit for table twelve please . . . Manuel! *(pointing at the grapefruit on the floor – to other guests)* I do beg your pardon . . . I'm so sorry . . .

Manuel picks up the grapefruit and cleans it. He is about to replace it on the table.

Basil   . . . No! . . . Throw it away.

Manuel   *Qué?*

Basil   Throw . . . it . . . away!

Manuel   Throw . . . it . . . away?

Basil   *(miming a throw)* Throw it away!! **Now!!!**

Manuel throws it away; it lands on another table. Basil retrieves it, grabs Manuel, and runs with him out of the room.

Basil   *(to the other tables as he passes)* Sorry! . . . Sorry! . . . Sorry!

They disappear into the kitchen. There is the sound of a slap and a yelp from Manuel. Polly appears bearing Danny's new grapefruit.

Polly	Sorry about that.
Danny	No, I like a bit of cabaret. *(picks up Polly's sketch pad from the table)* You left your sketch.
Polly	Oh! Sorry.
Danny	It's very good. Do you sell any?
Polly	Enough to keep me in waitressing. *(she leaves as Basil reappears with the Beaujolais)*
Basil	One **half** bottle of Beaujolais. *(he is about to open the bottle when the reception bell rings)* . . . Sybil!
Sybil	*(popping her head round the door)* Someone at reception, dear. *(she vanishes)*

(Basil hurries bad-temperedly into the lobby. Melbury is standing there.)

Basil	Yes, yes, well, yes?
Melbury	. . . Er, well, I was wondering if you could offer me accommodation for a few nights?
Basil	*(very cross)* Well, have you booked?
Melbury	. . . I'm sorry?
Basil	Have you booked, have you booked?
Melbury	No.
Basil	*(to himself)* Oh dear!
Melbury	Why, are you full?
Basil	Oh, we're not full . . . we're not **full** . . . of course we're not **full**!!
Melbury	I'd like, er . . .
Basil	One moment, one moment, please . . . yes?
Melbury	A single room with a . . .
Basil	Your **name**, please, could I have your name?
Melbury	Melbury.

The phone rings; Basil picks it up.

Basil	*(to Melbury)* One second please. *(to phone)* Hello? . . . Ah, yes, Mr O'Reilly, well it's perfectly simple. When I asked you to build me a wall I was rather hoping that instead of just dumping the bricks in a pile you might have found time to cement them together . . . you know, one on top of another, in the traditional fashion. *(to Melbury, testily)* Could you fill it in, please? *(to phone)* Oh, splendid! Ah, yes, but **when**, Mr O'Reilly? *(to Melbury, who is having difficulty with the register)* there – there!! *(to phone)* Yes, but when? Yes, yes . . . ah! . . .

the flu! *(to Melbury)* **Both** names, please. *(to phone)* Yes, I should have guessed, Mr O'Reilly, that and the potato famine I suppose . . .

Melbury I beg your pardon?

Basil Would you put **both** your names, please? . . . *(to phone)* Well, will you give me a **date**?

Melbury Er . . . I only use one.

Basil *(with a withering look)* You don't have a first name?

Melbury No, I am **Lord** Melbury, so I simply sign myself 'Melbury'.

There is a long, long pause.

Basil *(to phone)* Go away. *(puts phone down)* . . . I'm **so** sorry to have kept you waiting, your lordship . . . I **do** apologize, **please** forgive me. Now, was there something, is there something, anything, I can do for you? Anything at all?

Melbury Well, I have filled this in . . .

Basil Oh, please don't bother with that. *(he takes the form and throws it away)* Now, a special room? . . . a single? A double? A suite? . . . Well, we don't have any suites, but we do have some beautiful doubles with a view . . .

Melbury No, no, just a single.

Basil Just a single! Absolutely! How very **wise** if I may say so, your honour.

Melbury With a bath.

Basil Naturally, naturally! *Naturellement! (he roars with laughter)*

Melbury I shall be staying for one or two nights . . .

Basil Oh please! Please! . . . Manuel!! *(he bangs the bell; nothing happens)* . . . Well, it's . . . it's rather grey today, isn't it?

Melbury Oh, yes, it is, rather.

Basil Of course usually down here it's quite beautiful, but today is a real old . . . er . . . rotter. *(another bang on the bell)* Manuel!!! . . . Still . . . it's good for the wheat.

Melbury Yes, er, I suppose so.

Basil Oh yes! I hear it's coming along wonderfully at the moment! Thank God! I love the wheat . . . there's no sight like a field of wheat waving in the . . . waving in . . . **Manuel!!!!** *(he bangs the bell as hard as he can; no result)* . . . Well, how are you? I mean, if it's not a

	personal question. Well, it **is** a personal . . . *(he dashes from behind the desk)* Let me get your cases for you, please allow me . . .
Melbury	. . . Oh, thank you very much, they're just outside.
Basil	Splendid. Thank you so much. I won't be one moment . . .

He sprints off, collects the cases, and returns to find Sybil talking to Lord Melbury at the counter.

Basil	. . . Ah, Lord Melbury. May I introduce my wife?
Melbury	Yes, we have met.
Basil	My wife, may I introduce your lordship.
Sybil	Thank you, Basil, we've sorted it out.
Basil	Splendid, splendid.
Melbury	I wonder, could I deposit this case with you . . . it's just a few valuables?
Basil	Valuable, of course. Please let me take it now. I'll put it in the safe straight away. Sybil, would you put this in the safe, please?
Sybil	I'm just off to the kitchen, Basil.
Basil	*(muttering angrily)* Yes, well, if you're too busy . . .
Sybil	Nice to have met you, Lord Melbury. I hope you enjoy your stay. *(she leaves)*
Melbury	Thank you so much.
Basil	Yes, well I'll do it then, then I'll do the picture . . . *(suddenly polite again)* I'll put this away in one moment, your lord. *(to Manuel, who has appeared at last)* Manuel, will you take these cases to room twenty-one.
Manuel	. . . *Qué?*
Basil	Take . . . to room . . . twenty-one. *(he surreptitiously signals the number with his fingers)*
Manuel	. . . *No entender.*
Basil	*Prenda las casos en* . . . oh, doesn't matter. Right! I'll do it, I'll do it. Thank you, Manuel. *(picks up the cases)*
Manuel	I take them. *(grabs cases)*
Basil	*(not letting go)* No, no, go away!
Manuel	*Qué? (they struggle)*
Basil	Go and wait!
Manuel	Wait?
Basil	*(indicating the dining room)* In there! Go and wait in **there**! Go and be a waiter in there*! (Manuel runs off; to Melbury)* I **do** apologize, your lordship. I'm afraid he's

only just joined us. We're training him. It'd be quicker to train a monkey, ha ha ha!

Basil's laugh freezes as Melbury does not react. Then he goes upstairs with the cases, reappearing a moment later.

Basil   Do please follow me . . . I mean, if you're ready. There's no hurry . . .

Melbury   Oh yes, yes, fine. *(follows Basil upstairs)*

The dining room. Guests are eating peacefully until Basil rushes in and goes to the window table where Mr and Mrs Wareing and their son are eating.

Basil   Excuse me, I'm so sorry to bother you. Would you mind moving to that table?

Mr Wareing . . . What?

Basil   Could I ask you please to move to that table over there?

Mr Wareing But . . .

Basil   I'm so sorry to trouble you.

Mr Wareing *(getting up, protesting)* We're halfway through . . .

Basil   Thank you so much.

Mr Wareing Yes, but . . .

Basil   This is Lord Melbury's table, you see.

Mr Wareing What?

Basil   Lord Melbury. When he stays with us he always sits at this table.

Mr Wareing Well, why did they put us here?

Basil   Ah, an oversight . . . on my wife's part. I'm so sorry. He's just arrived, you see. Would you mind? – Polly! – Would you help these people to that table? Thank you, thank you so much.

The family get up very unwillingly. Polly, slightly puzzled, starts moving the dishes. Mrs Wareing is particularly slow . . .

Basil   Come on! **Come on!!** . . . Thank you. *(they move; Basil grabs a vase of flowers from another table and puts it on Melbury's; Melbury enters)* Ah, Lord Melbury! Do please come this way . . . your lordship . . . I have your table over here by the window . . . as usual . . . *(gives Melbury a slight wink, but gets no reaction)* Just here . . . thank you so much.

Melbury	Thank you, thank you very much . . .

Basil holds Melbury's chair, but moves it back just as Melbury sits down. Melbury falls, knocking the table over. Basil clouts Manuel, who happens to be passing.

Basil	I'm so sorry! Oh my Lord! Oh my God!!
Mr Wareing	*(to his wife)* I think he's killed him!
Basil	Get on with your meals!!! Thank you so much. *(he starts trying to make amends)*

In reception: Basil is at the desk doing the pools. Melbury comes out of the dining room wiping himself down with a handkerchief.

Basil	Lord Melbury, I really must apologize again for . . .
Melbury	Please, please, think nothing of it.
Basil	But it was so . . .
Melbury	Please! It was the smallest of accidents. It could have occurred anywhere.
Basil	Yes, but . . .
Melbury	No, no, no, I've forgotten all about it.
Basil	That's most . . . you're really . . . er, your lordship, would you allow me to offer you dinner here tonight . . . as our guest?
Melbury	That's extremely kind of you. Unfortunately I have an engagement tonight . . .
Basil	*(mortified)* Oh!
Melbury	Oh actually . . .
Basil	Yes?
Melbury	There is one thing.
Basil	Good! Good!
Melbury	I was wondering . . . can you cash me a small cheque? I'm playing golf this afternoon.
Basil	Oh, delighted!
Melbury	And I'd rather not go into the town . . .
Basil	Absolutely . . . I mean, er, how much? . . . er, if it's not a rude question.
Melbury	Er well . . . er . . . could you manage . . . fif . . . *(looks in his wallet)* Oh! . . . a hundred?
Basil	*(stunned)* A . . . h . . . hundred? *(recovering)* Oh absolutely . . . Oh yes, I mean, will a hundred be enough? . . . I mean a hundred and fifty . . . two . . . two

	. . . er, a hundred and sixty?
Melbury	. . . Let's see, that's, er, dinner tonight . . . few tips . . . oh, and it's the weekend, isn't it . . . is two hundred all right?
Basil	*(momentarily shattered)* Oh! *(extravagantly)* Oh! Please! Yes! Oh, ha, ha! – oh, tremendous! Oh . . . I'm so happy! I'll send someone to the town straightaway and have it for you here when you get back.
Melbury	Yes, well, that would be splendid.
Basil	Thank you, thank you, your lordship.
Melbury	Thank you so much.
Basil	Oh, not at all, my privilege . . . *(Melbury exits)* . . . What breeding . . . sheer . . . ooh! *(he starts to write the cheque, but Sybil walks in; he hides the book hurriedly and gives her a peck on the cheek)* Hallo, dear.
Sybil	What are you doing?
Basil	I'm kissing you, dear.
Sybil	Well, don't.
Basil	Just thought it might be nice to . . .
Sybil	I heard about lunch.
Basil	What? . . . Oh, that! Oh, think nothing of it.
Sybil	What?
Basil	It was the smallest of accidents. Could have occurred anywhere.
Sybil	Anywhere? First you move that nice family in the middle of their meal, and then you attack Lord Melbury with a chair!
Basil	Look, Sybil, I've had a word with Lord Melbury about it. He was quite charming . . . Oh, it's delightful to have people like that staying here . . . sheer class, golf, baths, engagements, a couple of hundr . . . h,h,horses . . .
Sybil	Well, I've never seen such tatty cases.
Basil	Of **course** you haven't. It's only the true upper class that **would** have tat like that . . . It's the whole point! . . . Oh, you don't know what I'm talking about . . .
Sybil	No I don't. But don't ever move guests in the middle of a meal again . . . and get that picture up. *(she goes into the office)*
Basil	. . . Sour old rat. *(Polly comes in)* Ah! . . . Polly . . . would you do me a favour? When you're down in town this afternoon . . . just between ourselves, don't

mention it to my wife . . . pop into the bank and just . . . *(writing the cheque . . .)*

In the town. Polly leaves the bank, crosses the street, and walks past a parked car. She checks, looks into it and is surprised to see Danny Brown sitting in it with another man. Danny sees her, motions her urgently to get into the car; she does so. He shows her an official-looking card and points to a jeweller's shop. At that moment Lord Melbury comes out of the shop, looks round furtively and hurries down the street. Danny nods in the direction of a waiting colleague who follows Melbury. Danny and Polly watch . . .

In reception: Basil is holding the picture against the wall, marking the position with a pencil. The phone rings.

Basil   . . . Could somebody answer that, please? *(it goes on ringing.)* . . . Hallo! Is there nobody who can answer that? There must be **someone** . . . *(Manuel runs in and heads for the phone)* Not you. *(Manuel goes away; Basil puts down the picture)* . . . I'll never get it up. I'll cancel my holiday . . . do it then. *(picks up the phone)* Hallo, Fawlty Towers . . .

The ringing continues. Sybil comes in and answers the other phone.

Sybil   Hello, Fawlty Towers . . . Oh, hello, Brenda . . . *(to Basil)* Basil, it's six o'clock.

Basil puts down his receiver wearily as Sybil continues her conversation. Polly comes in.

Basil   *(whispers)* Ah, Polly . . . did you cash it?
Polly   Yes, er . . . Mr Fawlty . . .
Basil   Good, good.
Polly   *(urgently)* Could I have a word with you? *(hands him the money in an envelope)*
Basil   What?
Polly   Could I speak to you in the office for just a minute . . .
Basil   Not **now** Polly!
Polly   It's very important, I . . .
Basil   Later! Later!

Sybil	Basil!
Basil	I'm just going, dear. Thank you, thank you so much, Polly.

He rushes into the bar. From behind the counter he hears someone come in. As it is exactly six o'clock he doesn't need to see who it is.

Basil	Ah, good evening, Major.
The Major	Evening, Fawlty.
Basil	The usual?
The Major	*(looking at his watch)* Er . . . er . . . oh, why not, indeed, why not? . . . I've just been watching one of those nature films on television.
Basil	Oh yes?
The Major	Did you know that a female gibbon gestates for seven months?
Basil	Seven months? Well I never . . . there you are, Major . . . seven . . . my word . . . *(the Wareing family have come in)* Ah, good evening, Mr Wareing.
Mr Wareing	*(coldly)* A gin and orange, a lemon squash and a scotch and water please.
Basil	Certainly.
Mr Wareing	Is there any part of the room you'd like us to keep away from?
Basil	What? . . . *(false jollity)* Oh, ha ha ha.
Mr Wareing	*(curtly)* We'll be over there, then.
Basil	*(to the Major)* Seven! Well, well . . .
Melbury	*(entering)* Evening, Fawlty.
Basil	Ah, good evening, Lord Melbury.
Mr Wareing	*(makes his point again)* Anywhere?
Basil	Yes, anywhere, anywhere . . . Your lordship, may I offer you a little aperitif . . . as our guest?
Melbury	That's very kind of you . . . dry sherry if you please. *(he wanders off)*
Basil	*(to the Major)* . . . What else? . . . Such . . . oh, I don't know what . . .
The Major	*Je ne sais quoi?*
Basil	Exactly! Exactly! *(Sybil enters)* Ah, there you are, Sybil. *(he departs lord-wards with the sherry)*
Sybil	Good evening, Major.
The Major	Evening, Mrs Fawlty.

Melbury is glancing at some coins in a display case. Basil brings him his drink.

Basil	There you are, your lordship.
Melbury	Ah, thank you very much.
Basil	I see my little collection of coins tickles your interest.
Melbury	What? Oh, yes, yes.
Basil	All British Empire of course. Used to be quite a hobby of mine . . . little investment too . . .
Melbury	Quite . . . oh . . . talking about, er . . . did you manage to . . .
Basil	Oh yes. Here you are, your lordship.

Meanwhile Polly runs out of the hotel front door and signals to Danny, who is sitting in a car; he flashes his lights in acknowledgement. Back in the bar . . .

Melbury	. . . Oh yes, you know, these sorts of things, their value's soared this last couple of years.
Basil	Have they really?
Melbury	Yes, yes. You take my advice. Get them revalued, and insure them for the full amount.
Basil	Yes, yes, I will.
Melbury	Can't take any risks nowadays, I'm afraid.
Basil	No, no, quite.
Melbury	Well, I must be off.
Basil	Thank you, thank you, your lordship. I'll certainly . . .
Melbury	*(leaving)* Goodbye.
Sybil	Basil!
Basil	Yes, yes, I was just talking to Lord Melbury, dear . . .
Mr Wareing	A gin and orange, a lemon squash, and a scotch and water please!
Basil	I do apologize, I was just talking to Lord . . .
Melbury	*(coming back in)* Fawlty!
Basil	*(leaving the Wareings in mid-sentence)* Yes, Lord Melbury?
Melbury	. . . I was just thinking . . . I'm having dinner tonight with the Duke of Buckleigh . . . do you know him?
Basil	Not . . . personally, no.
Melbury	Oh . . . well, he's a great expert, you know, Sotheby's and all that . . .
Basil	Is he?
Melbury	Well, if you liked, I could take them with me, ask him

	to have a quick look at them and find out their current value.
Basil	*(overwhelmed)* Would . . . would you really?
Melbury	Yes, yes, certainly. Well, I'll be off in a few moments. *(he leaves)*
Basil	Well that's really . . . so incredibly . . . er . . .
Sybil	Basil!!
Basil	I'm talking to Lord Melbury!
Mr Wareing	*(slow and loud)* A . . . gin . . . and orange . . . a lemon squash . . . and a scotch and water **please**!
Basil	All right! All right!

The reception bell rings urgently; it is Polly. Basil runs out clutching the coins in a box.

Polly	Oh, Mr Fawlty . . .
Basil	Was that Lord Melbury? Has he gone?
Polly	I rang . . . Mr Fawlty, I **must** speak with you.
Basil	What? . . . can't you see I'm **busy**?
Polly	Please! It's very important – can we talk in there? *(indicating the office)*
Basil	I can't!
Sybil	*(calling from the bar)* Basil!!
Polly	It's very important!
Basil	*(shouting)* I'm just dealing with something important out here, Sybil, thank you. *(to Polly)* All **right**! *(they both go into the office)* Yes? Yes, right, well, yes, yes, what is it?
Polly	It's about Lord Melbury.
Basil	Yes?
Polly	He's not Lord Melbury . . . he's a confidence trickster.
Basil	. . . I beg your pardon?
Polly	Mr Brown told me.
Basil	*(contemptuously)* Haaa!
Polly	Mr Brown's from the CID. They've been watching Melbury because he's pulling some big con trick in the town. They're going to arrest him when he leaves the hotel so as not to cause you embarrassment. But he asked me to tell you . . .
Basil	*(not believing a word of it)* Oh, how **nice** of him!
Polly	Please, Mr Fawlty . . .
Basil	Oh, I don't know what other tales Mr Brown of MI5 has been impressing you with but . . .

Polly	He's a con man!
Basil	Oh of course. It stands out a mile, doesn't it. He's so **common** – unlike that cockney git whose ulterior motive will soon no doubt become apparent to you, poor innocent misguided child that you are.
Sybil	*(entering briskly)* Basil, what is going on?
Basil	Nothing, my dear, nothing at all.
Polly	Mrs Fawlty . . .
Basil	Now look!
Sybil	Yes, Polly?
Basil	I don't know what she's . . .
Sybil	Basil!!!
Polly	Mr Brown's from the CID.
Basil	Hah!
Polly	He showed me his identification. They're watching Melbury. He's a confidence trickster.
Sybil	. . . I see. *(she goes straight to the safe)*
Basil	What . . . what do you mean, you see?
Sybil	Let's have a look at these valuables . . .
Basil	What are you doing, Sybil? . . . Sybil, I forbid you to open the safe! *(she opens the safe)* Sybil, I forbid you to take that case out! *(she takes the case out)* Sybil, do not open that case! I forbid it! *(sits down in dismay; she opens the case)* I never thought I would live to see the day when a peer of the realm . . . entrusts to us . . . a case of valuables . . . in trust . . .

Sybil places the open case in front of him. He looks into it for a long time. Then he lifts out an ordinary house brick. Disbelievingly, he shakes it close to his ear, lifts out another and sniffs it, then clinks them together. He puts them down and emits a strange growl.

Sybil	I'll call the police.
Polly	They're here already, Mr Brown's outside. *(she leaves; the reception bell rings)*
Sybil	Someone at reception, Basil.

Basil rises slowly and goes into reception. Hoping it is Melbury, he has clenched his fist – but it is Sir Richard and Lady Morris.

Basil	. . . Ah! . . . all right . . . er . . . *(collects himself)* Good evening.

Sir Richard	I believe you were expecting us.
Basil	No, I was expecting somebody else. *(goes into another reverie)*
Sir Richard	Sir Richard and Lady Morris.
Basil	*(absently)* Yes, yes, them as well.
Sir Richard	I'm sorry?
Basil	How did you know?
Sir Richard	What?
Basil	Oh . . . **you're** Sir Richard and Lady Morris, I do beg your pardon. I was just think . . . er . . . *(he goes off again, thinking revenge; he comes to . . .)* Now, would you mind filling this out, please, we've given you room . . . *(Lord Melbury comes down the stairs)* Ah hah!
Melbury	Ah, Fawlty!
Basil	Mr Fawlty to you, Lord Melbury.
Melbury	I beg your pardon?
Basil	Oh, nothing, please, forget all about it.
Melbury	Oh . . . er . . . well . . . here's the cheque for two hundred pounds . . .
Basil	Ah, thank you so much. *(he bites the cheque and throws it away; the Morrises are transfixed)* Now, about my priceless collection of coins . . .
Melbury	Oh yes . . . er, do you still want . . .
Basil	Do I still want you to take them to be valued by the Duke of Buckleigh, my lord?
Melbury	Er . . . yes.
Basil	No, I don't. Because we've just heard that the Duke of Buckleigh is . . . dead! Yes, he got his head knocked off by a golf ball. Tragic! Tragic! *(a pause; he beams at Melbury)* Well, how are you, Lord Melbury? . . . 'Ow are yer then – all right, mate? *(pinches Melbury's cheek)* 'Ow's me old mucker? *(gives Melbury a friendly slap on both cheeks; the Morrises are totally bemused)* Any valuables to deposit, Sir Richard . . . any bricks?

Melbury rushes off in a panic. Sybil has come up beside Basil, looking anxious.

Basil	*(to Sir Richard)* I do apologise . . . *(shouts after Melbury)* You bastard!! . . . *(courteous again)* We've given you room twelve with the view overlooking the park . . . I'm sure you'll like it . . . we'll have your bags brought up . . .

Melbury rushes from the bar across the lobby to the dining room, pursued by a policeman.

Basil Hello, Lord Melbury! . . . BASTARD!!

More policemen rush about.

Basil *(to the Morrises)* Please think nothing of it.

Melbury runs out of the dining room as Polly, running from the bar, knocks the table into him and catches him in an uncomfortable place. As he doubles up, Manuel comes out of the dining room carrying a chair, the corner of which repeats the attack. Melbury doubles up in agony on the floor and is surrounded by the police. Basil walks across smiling politely.

Basil *(to police)* Do please excuse me one moment. *(he puts the boot in, then retrieves the envelope with his two hundred pounds)*

Sybil Basil, the Morrises are leaving.

Outside, the Morrises are getting into their car. Basil hurtles down the steps.

Basil . . . Where are you going? . . . Where are you going?
Sir Richard We're leaving!
Basil Oh, don't – please stay – you'll like it here.
Sir Richard I've never been in such a place in my life. *(they drive off)*
Basil *(shouting after them)* You snobs! You stupid . . . stuck-up . . . toffee-nosed . . . half-witted . . . upper-class piles of . . . pus!!

He walks disconsolately back up the steps, where he meets the police escorting Melbury out.

Basil *(begging for a chance to thump Melbury)* Just one! Just one!
Policeman *(restraining him)* Sorry, Mr Fawlty.
Basil Oh just one, please.

But the police remove Melbury. Basil gives up, and steps backwards into a tub of flowers; he threatens it with his fist. As he goes into the lobby he meets Danny.

Danny Sorry, Mr Fawlty.

Basil walks past him back into the lobby.

Basil	Well, I'd better put the picture up . . . Oh . . . thank you Polly for the . . . well done, Manuel.
Manuel	*Qué?*
Basil	Oh . . . *Olé.*
Danny	*(coming back in)* I'm sorry about that, Mr Fawlty . . . can I buy you a drink?
Basil	No, no, I'd better put this up, I suppose. *(picks up the picture)*

Sybil enters from the bar with Mr Wareing.

Sybil	Basil!
Mr Wareing	*(very loudly)* A gin and orange . . . a lemon squash . . . and a scotch and water **please**!!
Basil	Right! *(he slams the picture down)* Come on, then! *(and he frog-marches Mr Wareing into the bar)*

The Builders

Second of first series, first broadcast on 26 September 1975, BBC2.

Basil Fawlty   John Cleese
Sybil Fawlty   Prunella Scales
Manuel   Andrew Sachs
Polly   Connie Booth
Major Gowen   Ballard Berkeley
Miss Tibbs   Gilly Flower
Miss Gatsby   Renée Roberts
O'Reilly   David Kelly
Lurphy   Michael Cronin
Jones   Michael Halsey
Kerr   Barney Dorman
Stubbs   James Appleby
Delivery Man   George Lee

The hotel lobby. Polly is behind the desk sorting the mail. A guest approaches the desk.

Guest . . . Sorry, I forgot my key. *(Gives Polly the key and leaves.)*

Polly Oh, thanks. *(the phone rings; she answers it)* Hallo, Fawlty Towers . . . yes . . . yes . . . no, this afternoon, that'd be fine . . . no, it's **sixteen** Elwood Avenue . . . sixteen, that's it. Thank you.

She rings off. Basil comes down the stairs carrying two suitcases, followed by Sybil.

Basil I'll put these outside, shall I dear?

He goes out through main entrance. Sybil gives Polly a piece of paper.

Sybil Polly, this is where we'll be if you need us. There's the number. So if Mr Stubbs wants to know anything when he comes, just ring, but don't if you don't **have** to, love, it's the first weekend we've had off since Audrey had her hysterectomy.

Polly Not to worry. I know what they've got to do. Oh, and somebody called about a garden gnome.

Sybil Oh, yes.

Polly Well, it's in, and they're going to deliver it this afternoon.

Sybil Oh, good. *(to herself)* Golf shoes . . . *(the Major comes in)* Good morning, Major.

The Major Very well, thank you.

Sybil *(to Polly)* Now, does everyone know about dinner tonight?

Polly I think so.

Sybil But you'll be able to handle breakfast tomorrow, will you?

Polly Oh yes, there's just the ladies and the Major.

Sybil Now where are those shoes?

She makes for the drawing room (the door to which is in the rear wall to the left of the main entrance). Manuel enters from the dining room, practising English to himself.

Manuel One moment please. I will het your vill. I will . . . **hhhet** your vill.

Polly Manuel . . . <u>G</u>et your <u>b</u>ill.

Manuel I will het your bill?

Polly <u>G</u>et, guh, guh.

Manuel Get! Guh, guh, guh!

Polly	That's it.
Manuel	*(trotting off)* I will get your vill.

Sybil comes out of the drawing room with her golf shoes.

Sybil	Oh, Manuel – put these in the cases, will you?

She gives Manuel the shoes and goes into the office. Manuel looks at the shoes, confused. Basil comes back in.

Basil	Ah, now, Manuel! While we're away . . .
Manuel	*(proudly)* One moment please, I will get your bill! *(he bows)*
Basil	What?
Manuel	I will get your bill. *Si?*
Basil	What are you talking about?
Manuel	Listen, please . . . Today . . . we have veef, beal or sothahhhes!
Basil	What?!
Manuel	Bang . . . hhhers.
Basil	Shut up.
Manuel	*Qué?*
Basil	Shut up!
Manuel	Oh, *si, si* – 'Shut up'. Yes, I understand, yes.
Basil	Well, will you shut up, then?
Manuel	*Si, si,* I shut up.
Basil	*(very slowly)* . . . While we're **away** . . .
Manuel	Shut up.
Basil	**Shut up!** . . . While we're **away** . . . gone . . . **clean** the **windows.** *(Manuel nods blankly)* Ah . . . Look . . . *Quando nosotros somos* . . . what's 'away' in Spanish?
Manuel	*Qué?*
Basil	'Away' . . . You know . . . '*away*'. Away!
Manuel	Oh, *si, si. (starts to leave)*
Basil	No, not **you!** Us! *(catches him)* Clean the **windows!** *(Manuel stares; Basil points to the dining room)*
Manuel	Green?
Basil	No, look – **clean** . . . the windows . . . *(puts a handkerchief in Manuel's hand and circulates the latter)*
Manuel	*(continuing the circular movement uncomprehendingly)* Clean?
Basil	Go on, go on!! *(he picks Manuel up and carries him into the dining room, past the Major . . .)*
The Major	Morning, Fawlty.

Basil	Morning, Major. *(. . . and deposits him in front of the window)*
Basil	*(demonstrating)* The window! See . . . look – clean the windows!

Manuel continues to do so. Basil turns to leave but Miss Tibbs and Miss Gatsby have blocked his exit. They look playful.

Miss Tibbs	Mr Fawlty.
Basil	Ah, good morning, ladies.
Miss Tibbs	Ursula and I think you're a very naughty boy, don't we, Ursula?
Basil	*(to himself)* Oh God . . . *(with an attempt at charm)* Oh really?
Miss Tibbs	Going away for the weekend and leaving us all alone.
Miss Gatsby	Tch, tch, tch.
Basil	Ah, yes.
Miss Tibbs	Ah, but we know where you're going – the cat's out of the bag.
Miss Gatsby	*(coyly)* You and your wife!
Basil	Well, it's only Paignton.
Miss Tibbs	*(patting his arm)* Aah! Well, have a lovely time. It'll do you good. You need to get away from things.
Basil	Yes, well, we're going together . . .
Miss Gatsby	And don't you worry about us.
Basil	Oh! All right! Now . . . you know men are coming to do some work here?
Miss Tibbs	Oh, yes.
Basil	So you have to go to Gleneagles for your din-dins tonight? Yes? And Polly will be in charge if you need anything.
Miss Tibbs	Now, have a lovely weekend.
Miss Gatsby	And don't do anything **we** wouldn't do.
Basil	Just a little breathing, surely? *(he manages to get away from them)* Well, I must buzz off now. *(he goes into the lobby)*
Miss Tibbs	Buzz?
Miss Gatsby	Yes, you know, Abitha . . . bubbity-bumble.
Miss Tibbs	Oh, buzz, buzz, buzz . . .

In the lobby, Basil is going behind the reception desk when he notices, lying on it, a drawing of Polly's. She comes in from the office as he stares at it.

Basil	Polly, I've asked you please not to leave your strange

	drawings lying around . . . I'm sorry, but what is this supposed to be?
Polly	Oh, it's just a sketch. *(she reaches for it)*
Basil	*(keeping it away from her)* But what is it, what are you trying to do, this is a junk yard, isn't it?
Polly	Can I have it?
Basil	Well, why's it got a collar and tie underneath?
Polly	It's not finished.
Basil	It's very good . . . you know, old soup tins, broken-down car, dustbins and mattresses and hoovers . . . and a nice smart collar and tie underneath. I mean, what's it supposed to **be?**!
Polly	It's not important – can I have it back?
Basil	*(surrendering it grudgingly)* It's irritating. I mean, do you ever **sell** any of those?
Polly	I sell a few portraits now and again, thank you.
Basil	Choh!
Polly	*(quietly)* I haven't much hope for this one.
Basil	Would you give me the stapler, please. I mean, what is the point of something like that?
Polly	No point.
Basil	No **point?**
Polly	What's the point in being alive?
Basil	Beats me. We're stuck with it, I suppose. Will you give me the **stapler** please.
Polly	*(giving him the date stamper)* If you don't go **on** at me.
Basil	The stapler!
Polly	Sorry. *(gives him the stapler)*
Basil	What's the matter with you?
Polly	I didn't get much sleep last night.
Basil	We **are** leaving you in **charge.**

The telephone rings. Sybil bustles in from the office and answers it.

Polly	I didn't do it to spite you, I promise.
Basil	Oh good! Well, you won't feel so tired then, will you.
Sybil	*(to phone)* Fawlty Towers . . . *(to Basil)* Basil . . .
Basil	Who is it?
Sybil	*(not pleased)* It's Mr O'Reilly, Basil.
Basil	*(taking the phone)* That's odd. Must be about the garden wall . . . Hallo . . . O'Reilly? Now look! When are you coming to finish the wall? We are **sick** and **tired** of

	having that pile of bricks blocking . . . *(seeing that Sybil and Polly are now out of earshot)* Now listen, I **told** you not to call. You know my wife thinks Stubbs is doing the doors . . . Well what time will they be here? . . . Right, four o'clock . . . no, listen, if there are any problems get Polly to call me, you understand? *(hears Sybil coming back)* So next week's definite, is it? Oh good, that'll be nice, won't it – I mean, we've waited for that wall about as long as Hadrian. No, Hadrian. The Emperor Hadrian . . . oh, it doesn't matter, I'll explain it next week. Goodbye. *(rings off grandly)*
Sybil	*(unimpressed)* You don't believe all that, do you Basil? We've been waiting four months, why should he do it now?
Basil	Oh, I think he will this time, dear.
Sybil	If you'd used Stubbs . . .
Basil	We'd have had a huge bill.
Sybil	Look! You get what you pay for. O'Reilly's a cut-price cock-up artist.
Basil	Oh, Sybil!
Sybil	With Stubbs, we may pay a little more . . .
Basil	A **little** more?
Sybil	Yes, a little. But he does a really professional job, and he does it when he says he will. You'll see. When's he coming?
Basil	Oh, about four o'clock, I think, dear.
Sybil	And you're going to wear that jacket, are you?
Basil	Yes I am, thank you, dear, yes.
Sybil	You just haven't a clue, have you.
Basil	You wouldn't understand, dear – it's called 'style'.
Sybil	*(spotting her friends' car drawing up)* Yoo hoo!! They're here, Basil.
Basil	Oh, how fabulous!
Sybil	Do try and be agreeable this weekend, Basil. Now have I got everything?
Basil	*(pianissimo)* Handbag, knuckle-dusters, flick-knife . . .
Sybil	Come on, Basil, don't hang about. *(she goes out)*
Basil	I'm just coming, dear! . . . Quick, Polly! . . .
Polly	*(coming out of the office)* Yes?
Basil	Now Polly, the men will be here at four o'clock. You know what they're doing?
Polly	Well, they're putting a door through to the kitchen

	(indicating the right-hand wall beyond the dining room).
Basil	At the bottom of the stairs. And . . . ?
Polly	. . . And . . . ?
Basil	And blocking the **drawing-room door**.
Polly	. . . Blocking it?
Basil	Yes, **blocking it off**, girl! So we can get a bit of privacy away from the plebs. Don't you take anything in? Where's my cap? *(he is wearing it)*
Polly	It's on your . . .
Basil	*(casually)* Oh, and one other thing. They won't be Stubbs's, they'll be O'Reilly's. Where **is** that cap? *(he prowls off looking for it)*
Polly	What? . . . **O'Reilly?**
Basil	Yes, yes!
Polly	Does Mrs Fawlty know?
Basil	I don't know, probably not. I wouldn't mention it though, they don't quite hit it off.
Polly	But . . .
Basil	I had to change it. Stubbs has got a virus or something.
Polly	. . . She said you were never to use him again. I don't want to be responsible . . .
Basil	He's sending his best men, all you've got to do is take a quick look when they've finished. Any problems, call me. Right – have a nice weekend.
Polly	If she asks me, I'll tell her.
Basil	Oh, thank you, thank you Polly, so much. Yes, I've always been a great admirer of loyalty.

Basil exits. Manuel enters: he remembers something, rushes to the desk where he left the golf shoes.

Manuel	I forget.
Polly	Oh, it doesn't matter, Manuel . . . *de nada*.
Manuel	*(seeing the drawing)* Oh! Is Mr Fawlty!
Polly	Shh! Windows, *por favor!*

Manuel scampers off.

In the lobby, later that day. Manuel is posing for Polly.

Manuel	Oh, Polly, finish, I **tired**.
Polly	Oh, that's wonderful, Manuel – just hold it a second.
Manuel	*Qué?*
Polly	*Quiero ascender para dormir.*

Manuel	No, no – you must speak me English. Is good. I learn.
Polly	I want to go upstairs in a moment.
Manuel	*Qué?*
Polly	*(pointing)* I . . . go upstairs . . .
Manuel	*Si.* Is easy.
Polly	For a little sleep.
Manuel	Is difficult.
Polly	For siesta.
Manuel	Siesta . . . little sleep?
Polly	Yes.
Manuel	Same in Spanish.
Polly	When O'Reilly's men come, you must wake me.
Manuel	When Orrible men . . . ? *(looks alarmed)*
Polly	Now Manuel, listen. When men come here . . . Señor O'Reilly . . .
Manuel	When men come . . .
Polly	You come upstairs and wake me up . . . *despierteme.*
Manuel	Ah! When men come, I . . . *vendre arriba para despertartle en su cuarto.*
Polly	*Antes que ellos comienzan a trabajar aqui, si?*
Manuel	*Comprendo, comprendo.*
Polly	Finished!

She finishes the sketch and disappears upstairs. Manuel relaxes from his pose. He goes behind the reception desk and enjoys his new responsibility. He rings the desk bell in an imperious manner.

Manuel	Manuel! *(picks up the phone, although it has not rung)* Manuel Towers. How are you. Is nice today. Goodbye. *(rings off as he sees Bennion the delivery man arriving, complete with a rather large garden gnome)* Ah! Hallo. Good day! How are you?
Bennion	*(referring to delivery note)* Number sixteen?
Manuel	*(consulting the register)* Si, si, sixteen. But no eat.
Bennion	What?
Manuel	Sixteen is free. But not possible . . . *(mimes eating)*
Bennion	*(indicating the hotel generally)* Is this . . . number sixteen?
Manuel	No no, this . . . lobby. Sixteen upstairs, on right.
Bennion	Who's in charge here?
Manuel	No, no, charge later. After sleep.
Bennion	Where's the boss?
Manuel	Boss is, er . . . Oh! I boss!

Bennion	No no, where's the **real** boss?
Manuel	*Qué?*
Bennion	The . . . the *generalissimo*.
Manuel	In Madrid.
Bennion	Look, just sign this, will you?
Manuel	*(signing the note)* Si, si . . . er . . . sixteen?
Bennion	What?
Manuel	You want room sixteen.
Bennion	No, I **don't** want a room, mate, I'm just leaving **him**, right? *(points at the gnome and walks out)*
Manuel	You want room sixteen . . . for **him?**
Bennion	*(as he leaves)* Yeah, with a bath, you dago twit.
Manuel	*(calling after him)* You mad! You . . . **mad** . . . You pay for room first . . . He crazy! *(he picks up the gnome)* Room sixteen . . . No pay, no room sixteen.

He puts the gnome out of sight behind the desk. The phone rings; as he goes to answer it O'Reilly's men – Lurphy, Jones, and Kerr – enter.

Manuel	*(to phone)* Hallo, Fawlty Towers. How are you, is nice day . . . No, he not here . . . No, no, he **not** here, very very sorry, goodbye. *(rings off; to the men)* Hallo, men.
Lurphy	Good day, now. *(he is Irish)*
Manuel	You are men?
Lurphy	*(dangerously)* You what?
Manuel	. . . You are men?
Lurphy	*(threateningly)* Are you trying to be funny?
Manuel	What . . . ?
Lurphy	I said, 'Are you trying to be funny?'
Kerr	*(restraining him)* Not here, Spud, not here.
Manuel	But, you are men with Orelly?
Jones	. . . What?
Manuel	You are Orelly men?
Lurphy	*(menacingly)* What does **that** mean?
Manuel	You Orelly.
Lurphy	You watch it!
Manuel	. . . Where Orelly?
Jones	What's he going on about?
Kerr	He means O'Reilly.
Lurphy	*(understanding at last)* Oh yes, that's right, yes – we are Orelly men. *(to his companions)* Thick as a plank.

Manuel	You wait here, please, I go . . . *(indicates upstairs; the phone rings; he answers it)* You wait too, please.
	He puts the phone down, hurries upstairs and knocks on the door of Polly's room. There is no response; he knocks again. He opens the door quietly and looks inside. Polly is on the bed, fast asleep.
Manuel	*(whispering)* Polly . . . Polly . . .
	But she is in a very deep sleep so he decides to take care of things himself. Back in the lobby, the men are looking around. The phone is ringing; Manuel rushes down the stairs and answers it.
Manuel	Hallo, Fawlty Towers, how are you, is nice day . . . oh, you again! No, I say he is not here, very very sorry, goodbye. *(rings off)* Choh! Choh!
	The men are consulting the plan.
Manuel	You men know what to do?
Jones	Oh, I think so. This is the dining room?
Manuel	*(nods)* . . . You are certain you know?
Jones	It looks pretty straightforward. We've just got to block this one off.
	The phone rings again. Manuel answers it.
Manuel	Yes, yes, yes . . . Is you again! Listen! He not here! How many times? Where are your ears?! You great big . . . hhhalf wit, I tell you, he **not here**! Listen! *(he holds the receiver out so that the caller may register the lack of Basilic noises)* Now you understand? . . . *(sudden comprehension and horror)* Oh, Mr Fawlty! I very sorry!! I very sorry . . . is you . . . yes, is me, Mr Fawlty . . . No, no, Polly is . . . she very busy . . . Men? Yes, yes, the men are here . . . *(to men, imperiously)* You work, men . . . *(to phone)* Yes . . . Man with beard? *(to men)* Please, which one is man with beard?
	Lurphy, who is the only bearded one, thinks this over for a bit and then indicates himself.
Manuel	*(to phone)* . . . Yes . . . hid . . . o . . . angtang . . . tag . . . tang . . . si . . . one moment, please. *(puts the receiver on the desk and addresses Lurphy)* You are a hid . . . eous . . . orang . . . tang. *(he bows; Lurphy hits him)*

Basil's voice *(from the phone)* Well done, Manuel. Thank you very much. *(dialling tone is heard)*

The next morning; it is a lovely day. Outside the hotel birds are singing; moles frolic; weasels dance the hornpipe. Polly is still fast asleep in her room. Outside, Basil's car draws up. He leaps out and runs up the steps. He strides into the lobby.

Basil Polly!

He goes to the wall by the stairs where the new door to the kitchen should be . . . it isn't. He looks round to the door to the drawing room to see if it is blocked off. It isn't.

Basil Polly! Polly!!

He opens the new door at the foot of the stairs and is halfway up the flight when he registers that this is wrong. He comes back and examines the door with mounting fury.

Basil . . . Polly!! Polly!!! . . . **Manuel!!!**

He makes for the dining-room door . . . but there is now a blank wall there. Polly has just opened the stairs door and sees his apoplectic reaction. She tries to close the door quietly but he has seen her.

Basil What have you done with my hotel?! Polly!! . . . What have you done to my hotel?
Polly What?

He grabs her by the ear and shows her the stairs door.

Basil Look!
Polly Oh, it's nice. I like it there. *(he leads her, lobe first, to the late dining-room door)* Ow! You're hurting me. *(she escapes the ear-lock)*
Basil What have you done with my dining-room door? Where is it?
Polly I don't know.
Basil **Why** don't you know? I left you in charge.
Polly Oh . . . I fell asleep.
Basil You fell **asleep!!**
Polly It's not my fault.
Basil You fell **asleep**, and it's **not your fault!!?**
Polly He forgot to wake me.

Basil	Who forgot to wake you?
Polly	. . . It **is** my fault.
Basil	Manuel!!! I knew it!
Polly	Don't blame him.
Basil	Why not?
Polly	It wasn't really his fault.
Basil	Well, whose fault is it then, you cloth-eared bint – **Denis Compton's?!!!**
Polly	Well, you hired O'Reilly, didn't you?

A pause; Basil's eyes go oddly glazed.

Polly	We all warned you . . . who else would do something like this?
Basil	. . . I beg your pardon?
Polly	You hired O'Reilly . . .
Basil	. . . Oh! Oh, I **see**! . . . It's **my** fault, is it? . . . Oh, of course, there I was, thinking it was your fault because you had been left in charge, or **Manuel's** fault for not waking you, and all the time it was **my** fault! Oh, it's so obvious now, I've seen the light. Ah well, if it's my fault, I must be punished then, mustn't I? *(slaps his bottom)* You're a naughty boy, Fawlty! Don't do it again! *(he catches himself a real cracker across the head, staggers, and straightens up)* . . . What am I going to do? She'll be back at lunch time!
Polly	Now wait . . .
Basil	I'm a dead man, do you realize!
Polly	*(soothingly)* Easy! . . .
Basil	You're dead too. We're **all dead**!! *(he is quivering violently)*
Polly	Don't panic.
Basil	What **else** is there to do? *(starts crying)*
Polly	We'll call O'Reilly – he made this mess, he can clear it up! *(Basil has not taken this in; she shakes him)* Oh, just pull yourself together. *(shakes him again)* Come on! Come on!

But he is worse. She pauses, takes a step back, then slaps his face. He goes to hit her back, then realizes it has done him some good.

Basil	. . . Again! *(she slaps him, rather deferentially)* . . . Harder!! *(she slaps him really hard)* Right! I'll call O'Reilly. *(runs behind the reception desk and falls over something)* What is this? *(lifts up the gnome)* I mean, what is going on here?
Polly	Your wife ordered it. Call O'Reilly.

Basil	That golfing puff-adder . . . *(he places the gnome on the desk and starts strangling it)*
Polly	*(banging the phone)* Call O'Reilly!!!
Basil	What?
Polly	Shall I call him?
Basil	*(releasing the gnome)* No, I'll do it, I'll call him . . . *(dialling)* You go and see if the roof's still on . . . *(Polly is drawing him)* . . . What are you **doing**?
Polly	Stay there!
Basil	You can't do that now!
Polly	Hold it, hold it.
Basil	Go and see if they've started breakfast! . . . **Now!!**

Polly completes her lightning portrait and hurries off.

Basil	*(to phone, silkily)* Hallo, Mr O'Reilly, and how are you this morning? . . . Oh good, good, no rare diseases or anything? . . . Oh, I do beg your pardon, Basil Fawlty, you remember, the poor sod you do jobs for . . . Well now, how are things your end . . . Oh, good. Good, good, good. Well now, how would you like to hear about things my end? . . . Oh well, up to your usual standard I think I could say, a few holes in the wall, the odd door missing, but nothing you couldn't be sued for.
Manuel	*(trotting in)* Good morning.
Basil	*(to Manuel)* . . . I beg your pardon?
Manuel	Good morning!
Basil	*(to the phone)* One moment please. *(walks round desk to Manuel)* Did you say 'Good morning'?
Manuel	*Si.*
Basil	I see. Well, what are you going to do now, then?
Manuel	*Qué?*
Basil	What . . . you . . . do . . . now?
Manuel	I serve breakfast.
Basil	Ah! Let's see you, then.

Manuel looks for the dining-room door, without success.

Manuel	Where is door?
Basil	Ah ha!
Manuel	Door is gone. *(points to wall)* Door was here.
Basil	Where? *(picks Manuel up and slams his head against the wall in three different places)* Here? . . . or here? . . . or here?

Manuel droops. The Major enters and strolls up to them.

The Major	Morning, Fawlty.
Basil	Good morning, Major. I'm so sorry, I'm afraid the dining-room door seems to have disappeared. *(knees Manuel in the back)*
The Major	Oh yes, so it has. It used to be there.
Basil	Yes, well, I was silly enough to leave the hotel for a few minutes.
The Major	Well, these things happen, you know. Now, I wonder where it's got to? Don't worry – it's bound to turn up . . . Er, have the newspapers arrived yet?
Basil	No, not yet, no, Major. Manuel! – would you please show the Major how to get into the dining room via the kitchen?
Manuel	. . . Is difficult.
Basil	Major, will you please show Manuel how to get into the dining room via the kitchen?
The Major	Oh, yes, yes, of course . . . come here, come on . . . what's your name . . . Manuel. *(he leads Manuel off)*
Basil	*(back on the phone)* . . . Now look here, O'Reilly, I want my dining-room door put back in and the other one taken out by **one o'clock**, you understand? . . . No, no, I don't want a debate about it. If you're not here in twenty minutes with my door, I shall come over and insert a large garden gnome in you. Good day. *(rings off with panache)*

In the lobby, one hour later. O'Reilly is nearly at work on the dining-room door.

O'Reilly	Well, I'm sorry, Mr Fawlty, but my men won't work on a Sunday and that's the way it is. There's nothing I can do about it.
Basil	Well, how long's it going to take you?
O'Reilly	I'm working as fast as I can.
Basil	Well, it had better be fast enough. I mean, she is back in **four hours!**
Polly	*(coming through the main entrance with tea and biscuits)* Tea up!
Basil	What?!
Polly	Brewed a cuppa for him, guv.
O'Reilly	Lovely!
Basil	He hasn't got time to drink that now!

Polly	Biscuits?
O'Reilly	Oh, these look good.
Basil	Give them to me. *(he confiscates the biscuits)* Now, will you get on with it!
O'Reilly	Look, look – this lot here *(pointing to the dining-room door . . .)* an hour and a half. That one *(pointing to the stairs)* – easy. Lick of paint all round, one hour. What's the time now?
Basil	Ten to nine.
O'Reilly	All right. Ten to nine and two and a half hours is . . . is . . . plenty of time. Give us a biscuit.
Basil	No. You can have one when you've done that door. Polly, take them away. *(to O'Reilly, confiscating the cup of tea)* You can have that when you've finished the door, too.

Polly exits with the tea and biscuits.

O'Reilly	The trouble with you, Mr Fawlty, is that you **worry** too much. You keep it up like this, you'll have a stroke before you're fifty. Stone dead you'll be.
Basil	Suits me.
O'Reilly	Oh! That's a dreadful thing to say.
Basil	Not at all. Get a bit of peace.
O'Reilly	Don't be so morbid. The Good Lord made the world so that we could all enjoy ourselves.
Basil	Look, my **wife** enjoys herself. **I** worry.
O'Reilly	Well, let me tell you, if the Lord had meant us to worry, he would have given us things to worry about.
Basil	He **has**! My **wife**!! She will be back here in four hours and she can kill a man at ten paces with one blow of her tongue. How am I supposed not to worry?
O'Reilly	*(calmly)* Just remember, Mr Fawlty, there's always somebody worse off than yourself.
Basil	Is there? Well I'd like to meet him. I could do with a laugh.
O'Reilly	You'll have to worry for the both of us. I tell you, if the Good Lord . . .
Basil	Is mentioned **once** more, I shall move you closer to him. Now, **please** . . .
Polly	*(running in)* Mr Fawlty! . . . She's here!
Basil	What?
Polly	She's here!
Basil	Oh God.

> *Goes to main entrance and sees Sybil. She gets out of the car, sees O'Reilly's van, and strides furiously towards the entrance. Basil runs back into the lobby.*

Basil   Quick – hide!! Hide!! I'll try and get rid of her! Hide!!
O'Reilly   Where?
Basil   *(pointing towards the bar)* In there!

> *O'Reilly runs into the bar.*

Polly   Mr Fawlty!
Basil   I'll try and stall her . . . God help me! *(he strides into the forecourt)* Hallo, Sybil!
Sybil   *(coldly)* Hallo, Basil.
Basil   Well, you finished your golf early!
Sybil   We haven't started yet, Basil.
Basil   Where are you going, dear?
Sybil   Up these steps.
Basil   Oh, don't do that! – it's such a lovely day. Let's go for a walk. We haven't done that for years. *(she pushes past him)* Oh, Sybil, I nearly forgot! You're not going to believe this. *(he manages to get into the lobby ahead of her)* Let me show you! *(gestures dramatically at the construction fiasco)* There! . . . Look at that! That's Stubbs for you. Mind you, I warned you! But **still** . . . a reputable builder like that! Choh! Tch, tch, tch.
Sybil   . . . Stubbs?
Basil   Wicked. Tch!
Sybil   Where's O'Reilly, Basil?
Basil   *(to himself)* Criminal! . . . *(to Sybil)* Hmmm?
Sybil   Where's O'Reilly?
Basil   . . . **O'Reilly?**
Sybil   Yes, O'Reilly.
Basil   Sybil, you never cease to amaze me. Just because of this . . . you **automatically** assume that it has to be O'Reilly. You just **assume** that I have been lying all along! I mean . . . **Why** . . . O'Reilly?
Sybil   Because his van's outside.
Basil   Well, he's here now! Of course he's here **now**!! He's come to clear up this mess that your Stubbs has made. That's why his *(with passion)* VAN'S OUTSIDE!!! . . . on a Sunday. That's what I call service.
Sybil   I agree.

Basil	. . . You do?
Sybil	Yes. But if Stubbs has made this mess then I think he should come and clear it up.
Basil	Well, yes, but there's no point now that O'Reilly's here, dear. We want it done **straight away**.
Sybil	There's no point in paying money to Mr O'Reilly when Mr Stubbs would have to do it for free. I'll call him now.
Basil	He won't be there on a Sunday.
Sybil	Well, then I'll call him at home.

Basil is suddenly racked by a spasm of pain from his old war wound.

Basil	Aaaaaaaagh! Oooh! Getting a bit of gyp from the old leg this morning. Not to worry. Anyway, I've called him at home and he's not there.
Sybil	When did you call him?
Basil	Oh . . . first thing. Before I called O'Reilly.
Sybil	Wasn't that rather early? For a Sunday?
Basil	And I called him five minutes ago, just before you came in. There's nobody there. Aaagh! *(he flexes his leg; the telephone rings; he answers it)* Yes, hallo, Fawlty Towers, yes!? . . . Who? . . . Er, yes, I think you'd better have a word with my wife. *(offers her the receiver; matter-of-factly)* Ummm . . . somebody from Mr Stubbs's, dear.
Sybil	*(looks dubious but takes the phone)* Hallo, Sybil Fawlty? Oh yes . . . well, it **is** a complete mess. Well, could you come over straight away and put it right? . . . *(to Basil)* Would you like to deal with this, Basil?

She gives him the phone, smiles sweetly, and goes into the drawing room . . . where Polly, pinching her nose to disguise her voice, is providing the other end of the phone call.

Polly	So you see we couldn't possibly manage it for at least three weeks . . . so if you want it done straight away, you'd better try someone like . . . oh, what's his name?
Sybil	O'Reilly?

Polly winces and puts her tail between her legs. Sybil takes the phone.

Basil's voice	*(over phone)* Bravo, Polly. Well done, girl! But listen – where are you speaking from?

Sybil	She's in here with me, Basil. *(she replaces the receiver)*
Polly	Mrs Fawlty, it's partly my fault.
Sybil	No it isn't.
Polly	Well, I should have told you.

They go back into the lobby. Basil is shouting on the telephone.

Basil	Is that somebody there trying to pretend that they're from Mr Stubbs's Company?!! . . . What sort of game do you think you're playing?!! I mean, **really!!** *(slams phone down; to Sybil)* Would you believe what some of these people will do, Sybil?
Sybil	I am going to make you regret this for the rest of your life, Basil.
Basil	Well, fair enough, I suppose. But I think Stubbs is partly to blame . . .
Sybil	*(screaming)* BASIL!!!
Basil	. . . Yes, dear?
Sybil	Don't you **dare!!!** Don't you dare give me any more of those . . . pathetic lies!!
Basil	Oh! Right.
Sybil	What do you **take** me for? Did you really think that I would believe this shambles was the work of professional builders, people who do it for a living?
Basil	. . . No, not really, no.
Sybil	Why did I **trust** you, Basil?! **Why** did I let you make the arrangements?! I could have **seen** what was going to happen. *Why* did I **do** it?
Basil	. . . Well, we all make mistakes, dear.
Sybil	*(slapping him hard)* I am **sick to death** of you!!! You never learn, do you?! You **never, ever, learn!!!** We've used O'Reilly three times this year, and each time it's been a **fiasco!!** That wall out there is **still** not done!! You got him to change a washer in November and we didn't have any running water for two weeks!!
Basil	*(reasonably)* Well, he's not really a plumber, dear.
Sybil	Well, why did you **hire** him?! . . . Because he's **cheap!**
Basil	Oh, I wouldn't call him cheap, Sybil.
Sybil	Well, what **would** you call him, then?
Basil	Well . . . cheap . . . **ish** . . .
Sybil	And the reason he's 'cheap-ish' is he's **no bloody good!!** *(kicks Basil's shin)*

Basil	*(hopping about)* Oh, Sybil, you do exaggerate. I mean, he's not **brilliant** . . .
Sybil	Not brilliant!?!?!? He belongs in a **zoo**!!! *(kicks his other shin)*
Basil	*(in some discomfort)* Sybil, you never give anyone the benefit of the doubt.

O'Reilly, refreshed by a quick drink in the bar, emerges into the lobby.

Sybil	He's **shoddy**, he doesn't care, he's a **liar**, he's **incompetent**, he's **lazy**, he's nothing but a **half-witted thick Irish joke!!!**
Basil	Hallo, O'Reilly . . . How funny! We were just talking about you . . . and then we got on to **another** Irish builder we used to know – Oh, God, he was awful!
Sybil	I was talking about **you**, Mr O'Reilly.
Basil	. . . **Were** you, dear? I thought you were . . . *(he puts his hand on Sybil's arm to calm her; she slaps it away)*
O'Reilly	*(turning on his gentle Irish charm)* Now, come, come, Mrs Fawlty . . .
Sybil	*(walking over to him)* I'm coming.
O'Reilly	*(winningly)* Oh dear me, what have I done now?
Sybil	*(pointing to his work)* That and that.
O'Reilly	Not to worry. I'm putting it right.
Sybil	. . . Not to worry?
O'Reilly	You've heard of the genius of the lamp, Mrs Fawlty? Well, that's me.
Sybil	. . . You think I'm joking, don't you?
Basil	*(more to himself than to O'Reilly)* Oh, **don't** smile.
Sybil	. . . Why are you smiling, Mr O'Reilly?
O'Reilly	Well, to be perfectly honest, Mrs Fawlty, I like a woman with spirit.
Sybil	Oh, **do** you? Is **that** what you like?
O'Reilly	I do, I do.
Sybil	Oh, good. *(she picks up a golfing umbrella)*
Basil	Now, Sybil! That's enough.

She hits him with it, steps up to the now apprehensive O'Reilly, and whacks him. He steps back.

Sybil	Come on, then – give us a smile.

She wallops him. He collapses under a flurry of blows, emitting a charming gentle Irish cry of distress. She lowers the umbrella and stands over him.

Sybil	O'Reilly, I have seen more intelligent creatures than you lying on their backs at the bottoms of ponds. I have seen better organized creatures than you running round farmyards with their heads cut off. Now collect your things and get out. I never want to see you or any of your men in my hotel again. *(starts dialling the phone)* Now if you'll excuse me, I have to speak to a **professional** builder. *(to phone)* Hallo, Mr Stubbs? . . . It's Sybil Fawlty here. I'm sorry to disturb you on a Sunday but we have a problem here with a couple of doors we'd like you to take care of. When do you think you could come round and take a look at them? . . . tomorrow morning at nine o'clock? That'd be fine. See you then. Thank you very much. Goodbye. *(rings off; to Basil, who protectively gets another twinge from his war wound)* Well, I think I shall go over to Audrey's now, and I shan't be back till the morning. *(she picks up her golf shoes, then sees the gnome)* Oh, Basil?
Basil	Yes, dear?
Sybil	What is **that** doing here?
Basil	It's a garden gnome, dear . . . isn't it nice?
Sybil	Well, don't you think it would be better in the garden?
Basil	Yes, dear. Good idea!
Sybil	No, no, Basil . . . put him back. On second thoughts, I think I'll leave him in charge. I'm sure he's cheap, and he's certainly better at it than you are. *(she turns on her heel and exits)*
Basil	*(calling after her)* Have a nice day, dear! Don't drive over any mines or anything. *(to himself)* Toxic midget. *(turns to see O'Reilly leaving)* . . . Where are **you** going, O'Reilly?
O'Reilly	Well, I . . .
Basil	Would you please take your tools back and continue with the work?
O'Reilly	Well, in view of what Mrs Fawlty was saying, I thought . . .
Basil	You're not going to take any of that seriously, are you?
O'Reilly	Well, I thought I might.
Basil	You **thought** you **might**?!! What sort of man are you, O'Reilly? . . . Are you going to let her speak to us like that?
O'Reilly	Well, she **did**, Mr Fawlty.
Basil	No, she didn't. She thinks she did, but we'll show her.

We're not just going to put this door back and take that one out, we're going to close that one off and put that one through as well. We're going to do the best day's work you've ever done, O'Reilly.

O'Reilly's enthusiasm is underwhelming.

The next morning. The lobby has been totally renovated. The dining-room door has been restored; the door across the stairs has gone; a new door has been created, leading to the kitchen; and the door to the drawing room has been blocked off. Everything has been made good and painted. Manuel is standing by the main door, looking outside.

Basil	Manuel! Any sign?
Manuel	*Qué?* No, no.
The Major	*(coming down the stairs)* Morning, Fawlty.
Basil	Morning, Major. Papers are here.
The Major	Ah, good.
Basil	Notice anything new, Major?
The Major	Another car strike!
Basil	. . . Never mind.
Polly	*(polishing the dining-room door)* Good morning, Major.
The Major	Good morning, er . . . *(looks closely at her)*
Polly	. . . Never mind.
The Major	Oh, right. *(noticing the door)* Ah, you found it! I knew you would. *(to Polly)* He lost it, you know. *(goes into dining room)*
Manuel	Mr Fawlty – she come! She come now!
Basil	Quick!

He puts his cassette recorder on the desk, playing 'The Dance of the Sugar Plum Fairy'. He disappears into the kitchen, Manuel and Polly into the dining room. Sybil strides in, turns off the cassette, then notices the new work . . . She looks closely at the dining-room door.

Basil	*(popping momentarily out of the kitchen)* Morning, dear!

She turns, but he has gone. She goes to the kitchen door and looks in; he pops playfully out of the dining-room door.

Basil	Did you have a pleasant evening, dear? *(sees Mr Stubbs arriving)* Ah, Mr Stubbs! My wife's just there. *(he disappears into the office)*

Stubbs	Good morning, Mrs Fawlty.
Sybil	*(embarrassed)* Oh, Mr Stubbs, this is most awkward . . . I'm afraid I have to apologize. My husband has put me in a rather embarrassing situation . . . once again. I **was** going to ask you to do some work here . . .
Stubbs	. . . Yes?
Sybil	But I was away last night and when I came back just now . . . well, it appears to have been done . . .
Basil	*(coming in from the office)* Everything all right, dear?
Stubbs	Oh, I see.
Sybil	I mean, it'll probably all fall down by lunch time . . .
Basil	Oh, do you think so, dear? Well, let's ask a real **expert**! Do **you** think it'll all fall down by lunch, Mr Stubbs?
Stubbs	No, no . . .
Basil	No, Mr Stubbs wouldn't agree with you on **that** one, dear.
Stubbs	*(peering)* . . . It's a very good job.
Basil	Oh, did you hear that, dear? . . . A very good job.
Sybil	Hmmmm?
Basil	Oh, none of us like to be wrong, dear. I certainly don't. *(to Stubbs)* And then we knocked this door here through, and closed this one off.
Stubbs	*(at kitchen door)* What did you use, an RSJ?
Basil	No, four by two. *(to Sybil)* Not bad, eh, dear? And **not** expensive.
Stubbs	No, I mean for the lintel. Did you use an RSJ? . . . you know, an iron girder? Or did you use a concrete lintel?
Basil	. . . No, a wooden one.
Stubbs	But that's a supporting wall!
Sybil	**What?!**
Basil	**Quite.** Well thanks very much for coming over this morning . . .
Sybil	Just a minute – you mean that isn't strong enough?
Stubbs	That's a supporting wall, Mrs Fawlty. It could give way any moment.
Sybil	Any moment?
Stubbs	Yes, God help the floors above! *(closes the kitchen door)* Look, keep this door shut until I can get a screwjack to prop it up, before the bloody lot comes in . . . I don't know, cowboys . . . *(hurries to the phone)*
Sybil	Basil! *(Basil has gone; she goes to the main entrance)* Basil!!! Where are you going?!!!

Basil is striding away from the hotel, carrying the garden gnome with its pointed cap foremost.

Basil   I'm going to see Mr O'Reilly, dear. Then I think I might go to Canada.

The Wedding Party

Third of first series, first broadcast on 3 October 1975, BBC2.

Basil Fawlty   John Cleese
Sybil Fawlty   Prunella Scales
Manuel   Andrew Sachs
Polly   Connie Booth
Major Gowen   Ballard Berkeley
Miss Tibbs   Gilly Flower
Miss Gatsby   Renée Roberts
Alan   Trevor Adams
Jean   April Walker
Mrs Peignoir   Yvonne Gilan
Mr Lloyd   Conrad Phillips
Rachel Lloyd   Diana King
Customer   Jay Neill

The hotel bar. It is about six o'clock in the evening. Sybil is sitting at the bar, deep in conversation with a customer – a conversation which is punctuated by her familiar laugh. Basil approaches the Major's table.

The Major   By jove, it's warm tonight, isn't it, Fawlty?
Basil   It certainly is, Major, yes.
The Major   Very warm, phew!
Basil   Oh! Can I get you another drink?
The Major   What? . . . Oh, well, why not indeed. What a nice idea.

At the bar, Sybil laughs.

Basil   Always reminds me of somebody machine-gunning a seal.
The Major   The heat?
Basil   . . . No, no, my wife's laugh.
The Major   Ah, yes.

Mrs Peignoir enters; she is attractive, slightly flirtatious, and a person of the French persuasion.

Basil   *(with much charm)* Ah, good evening, Mrs Peignoir.
Mrs Peignoir   Good evening. Thank you for your map, it was so useful. I had no idea how charming Torquay was.
Basil   *Enchanté.* May I ask – did you find anything of interest?
Mrs Peignoir   Mmm. A few pieces I liked very much, and one . . . oh! I **had** to have it.
Basil   Ah, formid**able**. I'm so pleased. May I introduce – Major Gowen, our longest standing resident – Mrs Peignoir.
Mrs Peignoir   How do you do, Major?
The Major   How do you do, Madam.
Basil   Mrs Peignoir is an antique dealer. She's down here for a few days, sniffing around for dainty relics.

Sybil lets out a real cackle. Basil looks round in disgust.

Basil   *(to Mrs Peignoir)* Please don't alarm yourself. That's only my wife laughing. I'm afraid her local finishing school was bombed.
Mrs Peignoir   Oh dear!
Basil   No, no, not really, just a thought. Well now, what can I get you?
Mrs Peignoir   Do you have any Ricard?
Basil   *(blankly)* I'm sorry?

Mrs Peignoir Any Ricard.
Basil   . . . We're **just** out of it, I think.
Mrs Peignoir A sherry, then.
Basil   But of course. *(smiling and bowing, he moves off)*
The Major   Tell me – are you by any chance – French at all?
Mrs Peignoir Yes, I am.
The Major   Good Lord!
Basil   *(at the bar, to Sybil)* Enjoying yourself, dear? . . . We
                  haven't put any nuts in the bowl, have we?
Sybil   Well, **I** haven't. I don't know about you.
Basil   Well, I'll do it then, shall I?
Sybil   That would be the simplest solution, dear.
Basil   *(thinking of an even simpler solution)* Where's Manuel?
Sybil   We've given him the evening off, dear, it's his birthday.
Basil   *(to himself)* Well, I mean, how old is he? Two and a half?
                  (another hearty laugh from Sybil and the customer) Excuse
                  me, there are no nuts here, Sybil.
Customer   No nuts!!! *(he and Sybil laugh)*
Sybil   *(to Basil)* You'll find them in the kitchen.
Basil   Oh, will I?
Sybil   Well, if you can bear to tear yourself away from Mrs
                  Peignoir you will. *(to customer)* Do go on.
Basil   *(bringing the Major and Mrs Peignoir their drinks)* Did you
                  ever see that film *How To Murder Your Wife?*
The Major   How to murder your wife?
Basil   Yes. Awfully good. I saw it six times. *(goes off in search of
                  nuts; to Sybil)* Very funny.

                  *Imitating Sybil's laugh, he meets Misses Tibbs and Gatsby in
                  the lobby.*

Miss Tibbs   Are you all right, Mr Fawlty?
Basil   What? Yes, yes, thank you very much. Are **you** all right?
Miss Gatsby   Yes.
Basil   Good, good. Well, we're all all right, then. *(goes into the
                  kitchen, once more imitating Sybil's laugh)*
Miss Gatsby   Must be the heat.
Miss Tibbs   Yes, he is getting taller, isn't he.
Miss Gatsby   I don't think he's very well, dear – I think we ought to
                  take care of him . . .

                  *They exit through the main door, passing Polly, who comes in
                  arm in arm with a young man, Richard.*

Polly	I think I left it somewhere . . . hang on. *(goes behind the reception desk, putting her sketch-pad on it)* Ah, here it is. *(holds up a book)* See you tonight.

They kiss across the desk. They are getting deeply into it when Basil enters.

Basil	Yes? *(they spring apart, startled)* A single for tonight, is it?
Polly	Er, no. Mr Fawlty, may I introduce Richard Turner?
Basil	*(who is not too broad-minded)* Sorry?
Polly	He's a friend of mine.
Basil	Oh, you know each other, do you? Just passing through, are you?
Polly	*(giving Richard the book)* There you go – see you tonight.
Basil	Oh, we've opened a library, have we? How nice! *(Richard leaves)* Please don't go on my account, Mr Turnip.
Polly	I'm sorry, Mr Fawlty.
Basil	Now look here, Polly . . .
Polly	We were just saying goodbye . . . no one was . . .
Basil	I mean, what sort of a place do you think this is, a massage parlour? I mean, we are running a nice, respectable, high-class . . . I'm sorry, did I say something funny?
Polly	*(trying not to laugh)* No, I was just looking . . .
Basil	No, no, obviously I've said something frightfully comic.
Polly	No, it's just the heat.
Basil	Well, so long as I amuse the staff, I mean, that's all I'm here for.
Polly	*(taking the bowl of nuts)* I'll just take these in, shall I?
Basil	*(registering her T-shirt)* And one other thing, Polly, I'm afraid we've abandoned the idea of the topless afternoon teas, so if you wouldn't mind changing before you go in where people might be trying to eat.
Polly	I was just going to. *(starts to leave)*
Basil	*(picking up her sketch pad)* Polly, would you come back here a moment, please?
Polly	*(to herself)* I'm on form tonight. *(to Basil)* Yes, Mr Fawlty?
Basil	I know these kind of drawings may be considered decent at Art School, but will you please not leave them lying around on display at reception.
Polly	I'll put them away when I've got some clothes on.

She leaves. Basil leafs through the drawings, which are obviously permissive.

Basil I mean, really . . . *(shaking his head)* Tch! *(the phone rings; he answers it)* Hallo, Fawlty Titties? Yes, yes . . . oh, it's you, Audrey. Yes . . . oh, he's left you again, has he? . . . Oh, dear . . . oh dear . . . *(he is not riveted)* How sad . . . hmmm. *(he invents a distraction)* Ah, good evening, Major – yes, I'll be with you in just one moment. *(to phone)* Yes, well, I'll ask her to call . . . mmm . . . yes . . . well, keep your pecker up. Bye. *(rings off; to himself)* Dreadful woman.

He stoops behind the desk with some papers. Alan and Jean, an attractive couple in their mid-twenties, come through the main entrance. They are laughing, cuddling and giggling.

Jean *(giggles)* Stop it, Alan!
Alan Woof! *(seeing Basil)* Hallo . . . we've booked a room.
Basil Have you?
Alan Yes. A double one. The name is . . .
Basil One moment, please. *(looks deliberately for the register)*
Alan *(quietly)* That's a nice suit.
Basil What? . . . I thought you said something.
Alan No.

Jean giggles.

Basil *(to her)* Are you all right?
Jean Yes, thank you. *(Alan pinches her bottom and she squeaks)*
Basil Are we ready?
Alan I think **we** are, yes!
Basil . . . Well, may I have your name, please?
Alan Yes, it's er . . . Bruce.
Basil Mr and Mrs Bruce.
Alan That's right.
Jean *(sexily)* Is it a double bed?
Basil I beg your pardon?
Jean Has our room got a double bed?
Basil A double bed?
Jean Yes.
Basil Well, we've only got **one** double bed . . . I mean, do you want that?
Alan Very much indeed, yes.

Basil	Tch! *(sighs heavily)* Well, I'll have to put you in twelve then.
Alan	All right.
Basil	Tch! *(gets the key, muttering)* I mean, why didn't you . . . never mind, all right . . .
Jean	Has it got a breeze?
Basil	Has it got a **breeze?**
Jean	Is it airy?
Basil	Well, there's air **in** it.
Jean	*(pointing at letter rack)* Oh, I think there's a letter for me.
Basil	What?
Jean	There's a letter for me. There.
Basil	No there isn't.
Jean	Yes. Jean Wilson.
Basil	*(getting the letter)* Jean Wilson. Is this you?

Alan laughs nervously. He and Jean have sensed that, unlike most, Basil will be looking for trouble.

Basil	*(handing the letter over)* Now, what's going on here? You're not married, is that it? . . . Well, I can't give you a double room, then.
Alan	Oh, look . . .
Basil	It's against the law.
Alan	What law?
Basil	The law of England. Nothing to do with me.
Alan	Nothing to do with you?!
Basil	Nothing at all. I can give you two singles if you like . . . um . . . *(busies himself)*
Alan	Shall we go somewhere else?

Jean is unwilling to go somewhere else. She is leaning on the reception desk, her elbows on some papers.

Basil	Excuse me. *(takes the papers away rudely)*
Mrs Peignoir	*(entering and putting her key on the desk)* Well there's my key, and now I'm off to paint the town red.
Basil	*(curtly)* Thank you so much.
Mrs Peignoir	*(slightly surprised)* Well . . . perhaps I'll see you later this evening.
Basil	Yes, my wife and I will be up till quite late tonight. Thank you. *(puzzled, Mrs Peignoir leaves)*
Alan	*(to Jean)* I don't believe a word of this. *(to Basil)* Excuse

	me, we'll have two singles then, please, if that's all right with the police.
Basil	Two singles. Certainly. Now . . .
Jean	*(intimately)* Next to each other.
Basil	Next to each other . . . Oh dear. We can't do that. What a shame . . .
Sybil	*(bustles in and takes an interest)* Good evening.
Alan & Jean	Good evening.
Basil	Um . . .
Sybil	A double, is it?
Jean	We'd **like** a double.
Basil	Two singles, dear. *(pianissimissiamo)* Not married.
Sybil	What?
Basil	Nothing, dear. I'm dealing with it, dear.
Sybil	Well, seventeen and eighteen are free. *(to Alan and Jean)* You'd have to share a bath.
Basil	Nooooo! Oh, Audrey called – *(quietly)* I'll handle it – and George has left her again.
Sybil	Oh, no.
Basil	*(to Alan and Jean)* Now, we've got one on the first floor and one right up at the top.
Sybil	Shall **I** deal with this, Basil?
Basil	I'm dealing with it, dear.
Sybil	No, dear, that's all right . . . Now, you wanted two singles?
Basil	I said I'd deal with it.
Sybil	Do you mind sharing a bathroom?
Basil	Look, I was here first.
Sybil	*(cheerfully)* Well it's my turn now, then.
Basil	I fought in the Korean war, you know. I killed four men . . . *(he leaves huffily)*
Sybil	He was in the catering corps. He poisoned them.

Basil goes into the office, shuts the door to the lobby and listens at it. There is a knock at the other door.

Basil	Yes? . . . Who is it?
Manuel	*(outside)* Is Manuel.
Basil	What do you want?
Manuel	Can I go now?
Basil	I thought you'd gone.
Manuel	*Qué?*
Basil	I thought you'd gone.

Manuel	No, no, I turned it off.
Basil	What?
Manuel	It was about so high . . .
Basil	No, I said I thought . . . *he creduto que* . . . oh, it doesn't matter.
Manuel	*Qué?*
Basil	It doesn't matter!
Manuel	. . . Oh, you think I gone!
Basil	Yes.
Manuel	No, no, I go now.
Basil	Wonderful.
Manuel	What? Is OK?
Basil	Is OK.
Manuel	Thank you. *(more knocking)*
Basil	Yes?!
Manuel	Before I go.
Basil	*(opening the door)* Yes, what *is* it?
Manuel	Is my birthday.
Basil	Yes, I know.
Manuel	*(beginning to read a prepared speech)* I want to thank you for your beautiful present *(he is carrying a new umbrella)* . . .
Basil	Oh, yes, right . . .
Manuel	. . . and for your much kindness to me since I come here.
Basil	Not at all, my pleasure.
Manuel	Since coming here from Spain, leaving my mother . . .
Basil	Outside.
Manuel	*Qué?*
Basil	Outside. *(he slams the door)* Thank you. *(returns to listen at the door to the lobby)*
Manuel	*(outside)* Since coming here from Spain, leaving my mother, my five brothers and four sisters.
Basil	*(opening Manuel's door again)* Give it to me . . . thank you. *(he tears up the speech and shuts the door; Manuel hovers outside; Sybil enters)*
Sybil	Can I have it, Basil?
Basil	What, dear?
Sybil	I want that key.
Basil	I've only got the key to room twelve, dear.
Sybil	That's the one.
Basil	Now look here, Sybil . . .
Sybil	BASIL!!!

Basil thrusts the key at her; she goes back into the lobby.

Basil   If you were my size . . .
Manuel   Since coming . . .

Basil opens the door and hits Manuel. Manuel scurries into the lobby.

Basil   Here we are, Manuel – number twelve please.
Manuel   *Si, si.*
Sybil   Basil . . . *(she and Basil go off, arguing)*

Manuel takes the bags upstairs. Alan and Jean follow; they meet Polly at the foot of the stairs.

Polly   Jean!!
Jean   Hello, Poll!!
Polly   What are you doing here?
Jean   We couldn't get in at the Bellevue.
Polly   Oh, no . . . Hello, Alan! *(they hug)*
Jean   It'll be fun. My parents arrive tomorrow.
Polly   What, here? I warned you!
Alan   Yes, we've already met the famous Fawlty!
Polly   Ssh! I'm not supposed to hob-nob. *(she motions them upstairs and they follow)*
Jean   Oh, I like your outfit.
Polly   I'll give you the pattern.

In the upstairs corridor, Manuel is holding their door open.

Jean   Are you going to be at Fiona's wedding?
Polly   I can't, but I'll be at the reception, in my very own Jean Wilson creation.
Jean   I want you to try it on later.
Polly   OK. How's that gorgeous stepfather?
Jean   Oh, I haven't seen him for a month. He's been in Singapore.
Alan   Oh, blast! I forgot to get those batteries for my electric razor. Is there anywhere still open, Poll?
Polly   Well, you might find a chemist.
Alan   Yes, well, I'd better take a look. Won't be long.

He goes back downstairs. Manuel offers round the bedroom key.

Jean   Is Richard coming tonight?
Polly   Mmmm . . . we'll be along about ten.
Jean   Great.

They go into the room. Manuel shrugs and tosses the key in after them. Downstairs in the lobby, Alan approaches the desk somewhat apprehensively as Basil is on duty . . .

Alan	Hello again.
Basil	. . . Well?
Alan	We managed to get it all sorted out with your wife.
Basil	Well, I wouldn't know about that. Is there something you want?
Alan	Yes, look, I know it's a bit late but do you know if there's a chemist still open?
Basil	*(drawing the wrong conclusion)* I beg your pardon?
Alan	Do you know if there's a chemist still open?
Basil	I suppose you think this is funny, do you?
Alan	Funny?
Basil	Ha ha ha.
Alan	No, I really want to know.
Basil	Oh do you, well I don't. So far as I know all the chemists are shut. You'll just have to wait till tomorrow. Sorry. Bit of a blow, I imagine.
Alan	What?
Basil	Nothing, you heard. Is that all?
Alan	Well . . .
Basil	Yes?
Alan	I don't suppose you've got a couple of . . .
Basil	Now look!! Just don't push your luck. I have a breaking point, you know.
Alan	I only want some batteries.
Basil	*(his imagination running riot)* . . . I don't believe it.
Alan	What?
Basil	Batteries, eh? Do you know something? You disgust me. I know what people like you get up to and I think it's disgusting.
Alan	What are you talking about? They're batteries for my electric razor. I want to shave.
Basil	Oh yes?
Alan	Look! I haven't shaved today. See? *(shows Basil his stubbly chin)*
Basil	An electric razor, eh?
Alan	Right.
Basil	. . . Well, I was referring to that when I said it was disgusting . . . It is of course **disgusting** that you haven't

shaved, but understandable. I mean sometimes I don't shave either and that's **disgusting** too, so I shall have a razor sent to your room straight away, thank you very much, goodnight.

Alan looks bewildered. Basil goes into the office and buries his face in his hands.

Evening; the Fawltys' bedroom. Basil and Sybil are in separate beds, both reading. Sybil is also eating chocolates. She emits three grating laughs at the contents of her magazine; Basil winces. The phone rings; Sybil answers it.

Sybil	Hello . . . Audrey! Any news? . . . Oh dear, he hasn't . . . ooh! I **know** . . . He doesn't deserve you, Audrey, really he doesn't . . . exactly . . . I know you have . . . *(all this is disturbing Basil's concentration)* I **know** . . . I **know** . . . oh I **know** . . .
Basil	Are you going to go on like that all night?
Sybil	What was that, Audrey? . . . oh I **know** . . . I **know** . . .
Basil	Well, why's she **telling** you then?
Sybil	I understand, dear, I really do.
Basil	Oh, I can't stand it any more. I'll go and clean the roof or something. *(gets out of bed; the front doorbell rings)* Ah! There's the front doorbell. Somebody's got back late.
Sybil	*(ignoring Basil completely)* Yes . . . yes . . .
Basil	I expect they forgot to get their pass key.
Sybil	. . . Oh, I **know** . . .
Basil	Somebody'd better go and let them in.
Sybil	. . . Yes! . . .
Basil	I'll go, then, shall I? *(nods several times)*
Sybil	. . . Mmmmm . . .
Basil	Yes, I agree. Right. I'll go, then . . . *(puts his dressing gown on; the bell goes again)* I mean, you know who that *is*, don't you. I mean, that's your pair. The Karma Sutra set. Good evening, welcome to Basil Fawlty Knocking Shops Limited . . .
Sybil	No, dear, it's only Basil.

He storms out, slamming the door. He comes crossly down the stairs into the lobby. The bell rings again.

Basil	I'm coming! I'm coming! *(unlocks the door angrily)* I suppose you know what time it is?

(But it is Mrs Peignoir. She is slightly and delightfully tipsy.)

Mrs Peignoir Oh, Mr Fawlty, I'm so sorry.

Basil *(immediately oozing charm)* Oh, no, it's only a quarter past eleven.

Mrs Peignoir Oh, I got you out of your bed.

Basil Oh, not at all, I just had a few little jobs to do and . . .

Mrs Peignoir Oh, you're so kind.

Basil Oh, well . . .

Mrs Peignoir Oh, I had just a lovely evening!

Basil Did you? How very nice!

Mrs Peignoir I saw some friends I hadn't seen for years and I had a little bit too much to drink, I'm afraid.

Basil Oh, no, I mean, what's life for if one can't get a bit . . . er . . .

Mrs Peignoir Blotto?

Basil Well, hardly blotto.

Mrs Peignoir Ah, Mr Fawlty, you're so charming.

Basil Ah well, one does one's best.

Mrs Peignoir I hope Mrs Fawlty appreciates how lucky she is.

Basil Well, I think probably not, in fact.

Mrs Peignoir *(dropping her purse)* Oh!

Basil is at once on his knees to recover it.

Basil Oh please, allow me . . . sorry . . . I beg your pardon . . . ah, there we are . . .

He collides with her, sinks to his hands and knees, and she inadvertently sits on his back, giggling. At this moment Alan and Jean come in. She gets up and collides with Alan.

Alan Sorry . . .

Basil *(scrambling to his feet)* Ah, there you are! Do come in.

Alan I'm awfully sorry, but we didn't realize . . .

Basil *(explaining loudly)* No, it was quite extraordinary, the front doorbell went just a moment or two ago and I thought to myself, I expect that'll be Alan and, er, and down I came and lo and behold it's not you at all, it was Mrs Peignoir – have you met? – Alan and, er, this is Mrs Peignoir, she's an antique dealer you know, I mean, she deals in antiques, she's not frightfully old or anything, ha ha ha, and so I let her in not ten seconds ago, hardly five, hardly time to say good evening, in she comes, drops her things, just like that, so down I go and over she goes, ha ha ha, and bless my soul there you are, golly, is that the time, my goodness, I was thinking it was a quarter past ten, my God, well, I'd better get to bed, I can't stand around here talking all night, got to get an early night, goodbye . . . sorry . . . *(disappears up the stairs)*

Alan   *(to Mrs Peignoir)* Are you all right?

Mrs Peignoir *(still laughing)* Yes, I am. Goodnight.

Alan   Jean, I'll just make that call.

Jean   Don't be too long. *(she follows Mrs Peignoir upstairs)*

In the Fawltys' bedroom, Sybil is now off the phone, back into her magazine and testing chocolates. Basil comes in, yawning noisily.

Sybil   . . . Well?

Basil   . . . Hmmmmm?

Sybil   Who was it?

Basil   It was your, er . . . pair . . . Huh! Tch! Caw!

He gets back into bed. From outside the door:

Jean's voice Good night.

Mrs Peignoir's voice *Bonne nuit.*

Sybil gives Basil a withering look.

Basil   Oh, and that . . . that woman . . . er?

Sybil   Mrs Peignoir.

Basil   Oh, something like that, yes . . .

Mrs Peignoir's voice *Dormez bien,* Monsieur Fawlty.

An uncomfortable pause.

Basil   How's Audrey?

Sybil   She's in a terrible state.

Basil   *(absently)* Ah, good, good.

There is a knock at the door. Basil tries to ignore it at first, but Sybil is looking pointedly at him.

Basil   *(loudly)* There's someone at the door, Sybil.

Sybil   Why are you shouting, Basil?

Basil   Was I shouting? Sorry, Sybil! *(totally unnerved, he gets out of bed and puts his dressing-gown on)* Well, I'd better see who that is, then, Sybil. I expect it's some key who forgot to get the guest for their door or some innocent

	explanation like that. Are you ready, Sybil?
Sybil	*(somewhat puzzled)* I'm ready, Basil.
Basil	Right. Well, I'll just see who that is, then, Sybil. Ready, Sybil? *(he opens the door about an inch; unable to see anyone, he moves out into the corridor)* Hallo?

Manuel, wearing a silly hat and some party streamers, and obviously somewhat tipsy, jumps out from round the corner.

Manuel	*Olé! (Basil jumps violently and falls over)* Oh, so sorry, Mr Fawlty . . . **poor** Mr Fawlty! *(stoops to help Basil up)*
Sybil's voice	Basil, are you all right?
Basil	No, I'm dying, but don't get out of bed.
Manuel	I hurt you, and you so wonderful, give me such beautiful present. Thank you . . .
Basil	You're drunk, Manuel.
Manuel	No, is beautiful, is my first one. Thank you, thank . . . *(Basil moans)* Oh, Mr Fawlty, so sorry, please . . .

Alan comes round the corner of the corridor behind them and sees Manuel and Basil grappling on the floor.

Manuel	Mr Fawlty, I love you, I love you, you so kind, you so good to me. I love you, I love you!

Alan hurries off, shaking his head.

Sybil's voice	Basil, I'm trying to read in here.
Manuel	Since I came here from Spain, leaving my five mothers and four aunties . . .

Basil's hands reach up and attempt to strangle Manuel.

The dining room, the next morning. Basil approaches Mrs Peignoir's table.

Basil	*Et maintenant – un peu de café?*
Mrs Peignoir	*Ah, oui, s'il vous plaît. Café au lait.*
Basil	*Café* what?
Mrs Peignoir	*Au lait.*
Basil	Ah! *Café . . . Olé!*

Manuel, looking terrible, appears with two cups of coffee. He sways to Alan and Jean's table and deposits the coffee, spilling some of it. He tries to mop it up but is overcome and helped back to the kitchen by Polly. Basil brings Mrs Peignoir her coffee.

Basil   There we are. *Voilà sommes nous. Café pour vous.*
Mrs Peignoir *'Vous'? Pas 'pour toi'?*
Basil   No, I'll probably have one later.
Mrs Peignoir *(laughs gaily)* Oh, that's very funny!
Basil   Oh, good, good.
Mrs Peignoir Oh, Mr Fawlty, I forget – the window in my bedroom – I
                       can't open it . . . er . . . could you . . . ?
Basil   Oh, certainly, I'll pop up and fix it, certainly.

> *He walks away. Manuel appears carrying two plates of food.*
> *The sight of them has a bad effect on him and he sinks to his*
> *knees. Basil appears behind him and rescues the plates.*

Basil   Thank you so much. *(puts them on Alan and Jean's table)*
                       Manuel?
Manuel   *(on floor)* Is terrible.
Basil   Manuel, would you go in the kitchen please.
Manuel   I can't.
Basil   Manuel! Go to the kitchen immediately.
Manuel   Oh, no, no, no.
Basil   Come on, Manuel.
Manuel   No, no . . . please, I die here, please.
Basil   *(to the guests)* Sorry about this. He's been working awfully
                       hard recently.
Polly   *(coming up)* Mr Fawlty, can I help?
Basil   I can manage this on my own, thank you, Polly. *(he tries to*
                       pick Manuel up but falls on the floor with him)
Alan   *(to Jean)* He's at it again.
Jean   Disgusting!
Basil   *(still on floor)* I beg your pardon?
Jean   Nothing!
Basil   I thought you said something.
Alan   No, no, no, carry on.
Basil   *(carrying Manuel out; to guests)* Get on with your meal!

> *In the lobby, two newcomers, Mr and Mrs Lloyd, are at the*
> *reception desk. Sybil is dealing with them.*

Sybil   Thank you, Mr Lloyd. This is just for tonight, isn't it?
Mr Lloyd   That's right.
Sybil   Will you be taking lunch?
Mr Lloyd   We won't have time, I'm afraid, we've got this wedding at
                       half past two . . .
Mrs Lloyd   I wonder, could I make a call?

Sybil	Oh, please, use that phone.
Mr Lloyd	Would it be possible to have some sandwiches sent up to our room?
Sybil	Certainly. Here's the key. I'll have your bags brought up in a moment.
Mr Lloyd	Thank you.

Mr Lloyd goes up the stairs. Mrs Lloyd starts dialling her number.

Sybil	*(going into the kitchen)* Would you like coffee with the sandwiches?
Mrs Lloyd	Oh, yes please.

Sybil disappears. Alan and Jean come out of the dining room.

Jean	Mum!
Mrs Lloyd	*(kissing her)* Hallo darling, hallo Alan.
Alan	Hallo, Rachel.
Jean	Where's Philip? Did he have a good trip?
Mrs Lloyd	Marvellous. He's upstairs. *(to phone)* Oh, could I speak to Mrs Brice, please?
Jean	I'll see you in a moment. *(she skips off upstairs)*
Alan	I'm just going to finish my breakfast. *(goes to dining room)*
Mrs Lloyd	Right ho, love.

Basil comes out of the dining room with Sybil, who indicates the cases.

Sybil	There they are.
Basil	Well, where's the key?
Sybil	He's already taken it up, Basil.
Basil	All right.
Mrs Lloyd	*(to phone)* Anne – it's Rachel Lloyd here . . . how's everything?
Basil	*(to Mrs Lloyd)* I'm going to take your cases upstairs.
Mrs Lloyd	*(to phone)* Yes, I **know** . . .

Basil sighs on hearing this familiar phrase and takes the cases upstairs. In the Lloyds' room, Jean is hugging Mr Lloyd.

Jean	Darling, it's **beautiful** . . . **thank** you.

She kisses him. Basil opens the door and sees this; he shuts it again in horror and runs downstairs.

Basil	Sybil! Sybil! *(he sees Mrs Lloyd in the lobby, and decides to*

	protect her from the goings-on upstairs) Ah! . . . Hello!
Mrs Lloyd	Hallo.
Basil	It's Mrs Lloyd, isn't it?
Mrs Lloyd	That's right.
Basil	Ah, how do you do. Fawlty. Basil Fawlty. *(shakes her hand)*
Mrs Lloyd	How do you do.
Basil	Oh, pretty well, really. Can't complain, ha ha ha.
Mrs Lloyd	*(not understanding all this)* Good.
Basil	Well . . . hah! *(indicates the kitchen door)* We . . . er . . . had this door knocked through recently . . . made rather a good job of it, don't you think?
Mrs Lloyd	Yes, yes, it's very nice.
Basil	Oh yes, marvellous, it's changed our lives, really. You know, we used to have to do the hundred yards through there and back again, but now we can just sort of open it . . . *(it is stuck)* Oh dear, it's not working as well as it usually does, ha ha ha . . . *(opens it)* . . . and go right in, just like that, it's marvellous. It's simple but effective. Would you like to have a go, see the kitchen and . . .
Mrs Lloyd	Well, I'd love to one day, but I think just now I'd better be getting upstairs. So I'll see you later . . .

She makes to leave. Basil suddenly grabs his thigh.

Basil	Aaaaargh! . . . Oooooh!
Mrs Lloyd	Are you all right?
Basil	Bit of trouble with the old leg. I'd better just sit down in here, just for a moment. *(he backs into the kitchen; she follows uncertainly)* Bit of shrapnel. Korean War. Still in there. Oh dear!
Mrs Lloyd	Can't they get it out?
Basil	Too deep. Too deep. Aaaaagh! . . . Well, this is the kitchen as you can see . . .
Mrs Lloyd	What . . .
Basil	The kitchen . . . Aagh! . . . Yes, we had it plastered about five years ago . . . we've got a few cracks up there now . . . *(Mrs Lloyd notices Manuel's feet sticking out of the laundry basket)* Oh, don't worry about him, he's just having a lie down. He's from Spain. Barcelona, you know. Sort of siesta. But he's fine. *(opens the lid to demonstrate this; Manuel groans; Basil closes the lid)* It was his birthday yesterday . . . so anyway, we got a few cracks up there but

nothing serious . . . so, as I say, it's not the Sistine Chapel, but we're very happy with it. *(he spots Jean crossing the lobby and stands up)*

Mrs Lloyd Are you sure he's all right?

Basil What? Oh yes, he's fine.

Manuel groans again.

Mrs Lloyd But he's groaning.

Basil Is he, is he?

Mrs Lloyd Can't you hear him?

More groans.

Basil So he is. Listen, I've just remembered I left your cases just outside your room by mistake – would you mind if I went and put them inside now . . . unless there's anything else you'd like to see?

Mrs Lloyd No, but . . . *(she looks at Manuel)*

Basil Oh, don't worry about him, my wife will deal with that. Sybil! So if you'd like to . . . come along, come along. *(ushers her out of the kitchen)*

In the Lloyds' bedroom; there is a knock at the door.

Mr Lloyd Come in.

Polly comes in with a tray.

Polly Your sandwiches, Mr Lloyd.

Mr Lloyd *(realizing after a moment who it is)* Polly!

Polly Hello!

Mr Lloyd How are you?

Polly Fantastic.

Mr Lloyd It's great to see you.

Polly You're still gorgeous.

They hug each other. Basil opens the door and sees this with disbelief. He closes the door hurriedly and wonders how to protect Mrs Lloyd.

Mrs Lloyd Is anything the matter?

Basil Mrs Lloyd . . . er . . . can I have a word with you?

Mrs Lloyd You are.

Basil *(thinking furiously)* Yes . . . there's something that I need to explain.

Mrs Lloyd Well?

Basil	*(opening the door to another room)* Could we go in here?
Mrs Lloyd	Oh, really, is it absolutely necessary?
Basil	I'm afraid it is.

Bewildered and thoroughly disconcerted, she follows Basil into the room.

Basil	Mrs Lloyd, I'm so sorry . . . but this is a much nicer room . . . than the one we've given you . . .
Mrs Lloyd	What . . . ?
Basil	I was saying that I was sorry that this room is so much nicer than yours . . . and I wanted to bring you in here now and show it to you . . . and to apologize . . . in case you found out about it later and got rather cross. Now, the point is . . . um . . . the point is . . . if it turns out you don't like your room, then we could always move you in here, but I don't think it's worth doing until you've definitely decided that you don't like that one as much as this one, and then we can sort of sit down round a table, discuss it, chew it over and . . . *(he looks out to see Polly leaving the Lloyds' room)* . . . and then it will be a piece of cake. Bob's your uncle. OK? Fine. *(ushers her back to her own room)* . . . Oh, sorry, sorry. *(he brings the cases into the Lloyds' room)*
Mr Lloyd	Oh, thank you, thank you very much. *(to his wife)* I wondered where you were, darling. *(Basil gives him a look of hatred and departs)* Darling . . . darling – are you all right?
Mrs Lloyd	But . . . this room is exactly the same as . . . that one . . .

Outside in the corridor, Basil stands fuming. Meanwhile in Alan's room Jean is massaging the back of Alan's neck while Polly tries on one of Jean's dresses.

Polly	Jean, it's absolutely smashing.
Jean	A bit tight over the bust.
Polly	Oh, I love it.
Alan	*(reacting to the massage)* Lower.
Jean	*(to Polly)* Are you sure?
Polly	Mmm. Can I pick it up tonight?
Alan	Lower . . . Oh, marvellous! That's it! Ooh!

Polly takes the dress off and puts her own back on. In the corridor, Basil can hear Alan's voice as the massage proceeds.

Alan's voice	Oh, that's amazing. That's amazing! Aaaah! Beautiful! Ooh! Oh baby, have you been taking lessons?
Polly's voice	So, see you tonight.

She opens the door; Basil crouches out of sight as she comes out.

Polly	For ten quid that's absolutely fantastic!

She makes off downstairs, still doing up the back of her dress. Basil is quite horrified.

Basil	No, no, no, nooooooo . . . *(he rushes down into the lobby, where he meets Polly)* Polly, I want to see you at reception in one minute in your hat and coat.
Polly	I'm sorry?
Basil	I want to see you at reception in one minute in your hat and coat.
Polly	Will they fit you?
Basil	Not . . . not . . . **you!** You! *(he speeds into the office, where Sybil is working)* They're going!
Sybil	What?
Basil	They're going!

He races off upstairs, knocks on the Lloyds' door and opens it abruptly.

Basil	I'm sorry, but you'll have to go. We made a mistake. All these rooms are taken. *(realizes that the room is empty)* Hallo?

The Lloyds, Alan and Jean are in Alan's room.

Jean	She was sitting on him!
Alan	Five minutes later, I saw him lying on the floor underneath the waiter!

The door opens; Basil looks in and stares at them.

Basil	. . . Ah, there you are . . . Yes, yes, I might have guessed, mightn't I? Yes, I see. Of course we're a bit behind the times down here in Torquay. Well, I'm sorry but you'll have to go. We made a mistake – all these rooms are taken. I'm so sorry. *(he goes; then he comes back)* Well, actually, I'm not sorry. I mean, you come here, just like that, and well, well, to be perfectly blunt, you have a very good time at our expense. I mean, I think you know what I

mean. Hah! I mean, you have had a **very, very** good time, haven't you? Well, not here you don't! Oh, no. Thank you and goodnight!

He slams the door and races off, leaving the occupants speechless. Downstairs, he storms into the office.

Basil	Well, that's taken care of that!
Sybil	Basil, **what** is going on? Why did you tell Polly to get her hat and coat?
Basil	Because she's going. Along with the Lloyds and that pair you let in. I've never seen anything like it in my life! **My God!!**
Sybil	Basil, what are you on about? Why are they leaving?
Basil	I'll tell you exactly why they're leaving. First of all, I go up there and I find that girl in his arms, in Lloyd's arms. Five minutes later Polly's in there!
Sybil	What girl?
Basil	That girl!
Sybil	She's his daughter.
Basil	What?
Sybil	She's Mr Lloyd's step-daugher. They're all one family.

There is a long, long pause while the implications sink in.

Basil	Well, what about Polly?
Sybil	She was at school with Jean. She's known them all for years.
Basil	For years, huh?
Sybil	For years.
Basil	. . . What have I done?
Sybil	What have you done?
Basil	I told them to leave.
Sybil	You've told them to **leave?**
Basil	Well, how was I supposed to know? Why didn't you tell me, you **half-wit?** Why didn't **they** tell me? You can't blame me for this!
Sybil	*(placidly)* Go and tell them they can stay.
Basil	. . . Why don't you go and tell them?
Sybil	*I* didn't tell them to go.
Basil	No, no, I suppose it's all my fault, isn't it?
Sybil	*(firmly)* Go and tell them! . . . Now!
Basil	No, I won't.
Sybil	You will.

Basil	No, no I won't.
Sybil	*(standing up)* Oh yes you will.
Basil	Oh yes I will. Right! That's right – leave it to me! Let me get you out of it. That's what I'm good for, isn't it? Basil Fawlty Limited. Other people's messes cleared up. By appointment to my wife Sybil . . . I mean, what am I going to say?!!
Sybil	Tell them you made a mistake.
Basil	Oh, brilliant. Is that what made Britain great? 'I'm so sorry I made a mistake.' What have you got for a brain – spongecake?

He hurtles out into the lobby. Polly is coming down the stairs in her hat and coat.

Basil	Er . . . very nice. Very nice. Take them off, get back to work. 'I'm so sorry I made a mistake.'

He hurtles past the dazed Polly, and rushes up the stairs too preoccupied to notice Mr Lloyd coming down.

Basil	*(to himself)* I'm so sorry I made a mistake.

Mr Lloyd looks oddly after him and starts back up the stairs. In the upstairs corridor, Basil hurtles to a stop.

Basil	*(to empty space)* I'm so sorry I made a mistake.

He knocks on Alan's door and opens it. The occupants turn to look at him.

Basil	I'm sorry . . . I'm so sorry, but my **wife** has made a mistake, I don't know how she did it, but she did, she's made a complete pudding of the whole thing as usual, it'll be perfectly all right for you to stay, I've sorted it all out, I'm frightfully sorry but you know what women are like, they've only got one brain between the lot of them, well not all of them but some of them have, particularly my wife, so please do stay and see you all later on, thank you so much. *(he spins round and sees Mr Lloyd; he is in no mood for shocks; he jumps and makes as if to hit Mr Lloyd for a split second, then pulls back, bows, and says with difficulty)* . . . I was just saying . . . please do stay . . . my wife made a most dreadful mistake. *(he exits, bowing)*
Mr Lloyd	Yes, I think she probably did.

The lobby. Late evening; it is quite dark outside. Basil is at the desk. Major Gowen appears.

The Major	Evening, Fawlty.
Basil	Ah, evening, Major.
The Major	Papers arrived yet?
Basil	Oh, yes. Sorry they're so late. *(hands one over)* Didn't get here till five. I'll have to have a word with them again.
The Major	Where's your lady wife this evening?
Basil	Oh, she's spending the night at Audrey's. George has walked out on her again so she's in the usual state.
The Major	Still, I suppose it must have upset her a bit.
Basil	Yes, but she makes such a song and dance about it.
The Major	You don't like Audrey very much, do you?
Basil	Oh, dreadful woman, dreadful.
The Major	Well, I think it's very decent of your wife to go round there and listen to all that rubbish.
Basil	Couldn't do without it, Major.
The Major	She's a fine woman, Mrs Fawlty.
Basil	No, no, I wouldn't say that.
The Major	No, nor would I. Well, goodnight, Fawlty.
Basil	Goodnight, Major.

The Major goes upstairs. Basil puts his recorder on; it plays Chopin. Mrs Peignoir comes in through the main entrance.

Mrs Peignoir	Ah, Mr Fawlty.
Basil	Oh. Good evening. Sorry. *(turns the recorder off)*
Mrs Peignoir	No, no, don't switch it off. I love Chopin.
Basil	Oh, really? Hah. There's your key. *(he switches the recorder back on)*
Mrs Peignoir	Ah, it's so romantic!
Basil	Exactly.
Mrs Peignoir	Are you romantic, Mr Fawlty?
Basil	No, good God, no! *(switches off the tape)*
Mrs Peignoir	Well, I think you are. I think beneath that English exterior throbs a passion that would make Lord Byron look like a tobacconist.
Basil	Oh, no. No way, no, sorry.
Mrs Peignoir	Oh, don't look so bashful. I won't try and sit on you again!
Basil	Ah! Ha ha ha!

They begin to climb the stairs.

Mrs Peignoir And where is your charming wife this evening?
Basil Oh, she's er . . . spending the night with a friend.
Mrs Peignoir *(naughtily)* Oooh!

They are now in the upstairs corridor.

Basil A girl . . . lady friend.
Mrs Peignoir While the cat's away, eh?
Basil Oh, hardly, no. There's too much to do. *(he glances at his watch)* Oh well, goodnight.
Mrs Peignoir *Bonne nuit* . . . oh! Mr Fawlty . . .
Basil . . . Yes?
Mrs Peignoir Did you fix my window?
Basil Oh, er . . . no . . . damn.
Mrs Peignoir If you could, please – it's so hot tonight.
Basil *(cautiously)* Yes, yes. OK. Right.

They move off upstairs. After a pause, Sybil comes in through the main entrance. Upstairs in Mrs Peignoir's bedroom, Basil has lifted the sash window.

Basil There we are.
Mrs Peignoir Ah, you're so strong.
Basil Well, I'm sure you are too . . . if you put your mind to it.
Mrs Peignoir Your wife shouldn't leave you alone with strange women.
Basil Oh, I wouldn't call you **that** strange.
Mrs Peignoir Oh, Mr Fawlty, you're so charming.
Basil Oh, only a little. *(he looks hard at his watch)*
Mrs Peignoir Oh, feel that breeze, isn't it wonderful?
Basil *(backing out)* It is nice, isn't it.
Mrs Peignoir I shall sleep *au naturelle* tonight.
Basil Good idea!
Mrs Peignoir Only it's not so much fun on your own . . .
Basil Oh well, one can always pretend. Agh! A twinge from the old leg. Better go and lie down. Goodnight!
Mrs Peignoir Goodnight.
Basil Damned shrapnel.

He closes the door, leaving Mrs Peignoir giggling, and goes to his bedroom, closing the door with a sigh of relief. Meanwhile in the lobby, Sybil switches off the light and makes for the stairs; but a loud bump and moan come alarmingly from the kitchen. Back in the Fawltys' bedroom, Basil is pottering. There is a knock at the door.

Basil   Er . . . who is it?
Mrs Peignoir's voice Oh, Mr Fawlty.
Basil   *(opening the door a fraction)* Oh, hello.
Mrs Peignoir I'm so sorry, but I have to leave early tomorrow. Could I
                  have a call at seven o'clock, please?
Basil   Oh, yes, marvellous, is that all, absolutely, seven o'clock.
Mrs Peignoir Please don't go yet.
Basil   What? *(he looks at his watch)*
Mrs Peignoir I think you've forgotten something.
Basil   Did I? Damn. Well, there you go.
Mrs Peignoir Your recorder. *(gives it to him)*
Basil   . . . Oh. Thank you.
Mrs Peignoir You left it in my room.
Basil   . . . Oh, thank you so much.
Mrs Peignoir You left it in my room so you could come and get it,
                  didn't you?
Basil   Ha ha ha!
Mrs Peignoir *(coquettishly)* I'm not having you knocking on my door in
                  the middle of the night!
Basil   *(falsetto)* Ha ha ha ha ha . . . I should coco!
Mrs Peignoir You naughty man! Goodnight.
Basil   Goodnight. *(he closes the door and locks it firmly)*

> *In the lobby, Sybil is listening to the strange noises from the
> kitchen. She hurries upstairs, and tries to open her bedroom
> door, but it is locked. She knocks. Basil makes snoring noises.
> She knocks again; he goes on snoring. She knocks again.*

Basil   (Oh, God!) Look, go to your room. I won't ask you again.
Sybil   *(outside)* Open the door.
Basil   Listen, I can't, my wife's just got back unexpectedly.
               She's in the bathroom. *(loudly, to an imaginary Sybil)*
               What, dear? I think you'll find it on the second shelf,
               Sybil darling.
Sybil   Let me in, Basil.
Basil   Look, you'll meet somebody else sooner or later. *(she
               hammers on the door)* Try to control yourself. Where do
               you think you are? Paris?
Sybil   Let me in!
Basil   Shut up, will you, you silly great tart! Go **away**! My wife
               will hear us.
Sybil   This **is** your wife.

Realisation dawns. There are no first-class explanations. He opens the door.

Basil	Oh, what a terrible dream!
Sybil	*(her mind elsewhere)* There's a burglar downstairs.
Basil	George got back, did he?
Sybil	There's a burglar downstairs. Quick!
Basil	What?
Sybil	**A burglar**!!! Quick!

Without bothering to put his trousers back on, Basil runs downstairs to the darkened lobby, failing to recognize Manuel as he comes out of the kitchen. Basil reaches into the kitchen for a frying-pan, creeps up behind Manuel and clouts him on the head with it. Manuel collapses face down. Basil sits astride him and is about to clout him again when the back of Manuel's head seems familiar. He takes a closer look.

Basil   Manuel?

The lights go on; it is the Lloyds, Alan, and Jean. Faced with the vision of Basil, in shirt and underpants, sitting across the prone Manuel, Jean is amused, Alan bewildered, and Mrs Lloyd slightly shocked.

Mrs Lloyd   . . . Goodnight.

She, Alan and Jean go upstairs. Mr Lloyd, slightly drunk, surveys the scene.

Mr Lloyd   **We've** been to a wedding!

He goes upstairs. Basil covers his face in his hand in mortification, and then draws back the frying pan for a revengeful clout . . .

The Hotel Inspectors

Fourth of first series, first broadcast on 10 October 1975, BBC2.

Basil Fawlty   John Cleese
Sybil Fawlty   Prunella Scales
Polly   Connie Booth
Manuel   Andrew Sachs
Mr Hutchison   Bernard Cribbins
Mr Walt   James Cossins
Major Gowen   Ballard Berkeley
Miss Tibbs   Gilly Flower
Miss Gatsby   Renée Roberts
John   Geoffrey Morris
Brian   Peter Brett

*Morning at Fawlty Towers. In the office, Basil is reading a
newspaper. At the reception desk, Sybil is on the phone. She
laughs – machine-gun plus seal bark.*

Sybil   . . . I know . . . well, it all started with that electrician,
didn't it . . . a real live wire he was, only one watt but
plenty of volts as they say . . .

*She laughs again. The noise rattles Basil, who puts a cigarette
in his mouth and looks in vain for a match.*

Sybil   . . . Well, anything in trousers, yes . . . or out of them,
preferably. *(she laughs)* Yes . . . um . . . no, just lighting up,
go on . . . I **know**, I'd heard that, with her mother in the
same room.

*Basil comes out and takes the matches; she takes them back
from him and gives him just one. Basil is disgruntled but spots
a guest coming and slips smartly back into the office.*

Sybil   No, no, of course I won't, go on. *(the new arrival, Mr
Hutchison, stops at the desk; Sybil sees him)* Basil!
Basil   *(in the office)* Yes, dear?
Sybil   Oh no! . . . Who saw them? . . . **Basil!**
Basil   *(trying to strike his match on the desk)* Yes, dear?
Sybil   Could you come and attend to a gentleman out here,
dear? *(to phone)* **nineteen?**
Basil   What, you mean out where you are, dear?
Sybil   Well, the last one was only twenty-two . . . he **was**!
Basil   Actually, I'm quite busy in here, dear . . . are you very
busy out there?
Sybil   I'm on the telephone, Basil. *(to Mr Hutchison)* My
husband will be with you in a moment.
Hutchison   Thank you.
Basil   So I'll stop work and come and help out there, shall I?
Sybil   No, no, no, the Maltese one.
Basil   Well, I'm glad that's settled, then. *(comes to the reception
desk reluctantly)*
Sybil   No, no, dear, **he** was an Arab.
Basil   Darling, when you've finished, why don't you have a nice
lie-down? *(to Mr Hutchison)* I'm so sorry to have kept you
waiting, sir. I had no idea my wife was so busy.
Hutchison   Fear not, kind sir, it matters not one whit.
Basil   . . . I beg your pardon?

Hutchison	*(loudly)* It matters not one whit, time is not pressing on me fortunately. Now some information please. This afternoon I have to visit the town for sundry purposes which would be of no interest to you I am quite sure, but nevertheless I shall require your aid in getting for me some sort of transport, some hired vehicle, that is, to get me to my first port of call.
Basil	Are you all right?
Hutchison	Oh, yes, I find the air here most invigorating.
Basil	I see . . . Well, did I gather from your first announcement that you want a taxi?
Hutchison	In a nutshell.
Basil	*(turning away)* Case more like. *(he picks up a minicab card; Sybil finishes her call and goes into the office)*
Hutchison	At two o'clock, please.
Basil	*(giving him the card)* Well, there's the number of the local firm.
Hutchison	Please, please – could you get it for me, because I never use the telephone if I can avoid it.
Basil	Why not?
Hutchison	The risk of infection . . . Now. I have a rendezvous at five o'clock at this address which I must reach from the Post Office in Queen's Square, so as the map is sadly inadequate I would be very grateful if you could draw me a diagram of the optimum route?
Basil	May I ask what's wrong with the map?
Hutchison	It's got curry on it.
Basil	. . . Look it's perfectly simple, you go to the end of Queen's Parade, bear left . . . *(Hutchison rudely waves the pen and paper in Basil's face)* . . . Look, just *listen*.
Hutchison	No, I just want a diagram.
Basil	It really is very simple.
Hutchison	Well, I'd rather have the diagram if it doesn't put you out.
Basil	It **does** put me out.
Hutchison	Well, I'd like it all the same!
Sybil	*(who has come back from the office)* Basil!!!
Basil	*(through clenched teeth)* . . . Right. *(he looks round for paper and pen)*
Hutchison	*(brandishing his pen at Basil)* Here we are, then.
Basil	We do have pens, thank you.
Hutchison	What?

Basil	We have actually got pens in the hotel, thank you so much . . . *(looks around vainly)* **Somewhere** . . . I mean, **where are** the pens . . . ? I mean, would you believe it?

As Basil looks around, Mr Walt, a smoothish-looking gentleman in his mid-forties, arrives at the desk; Sybil starts checking him in.

Basil	I mean, there are no **pens** here! *(to Mr Walt)* I mean, this is **supposed** to be a **hotel**.

Sybil is holding out a cardboard box which she has just picked up from the desk. She shakes it. It rattles.

Basil	. . . Well, what are they doing in there?
Sybil	I put them there.
Basil	Why?
Sybil	Just sign there, Mr Walt. Because you're always losing them, Basil.
Basil	I am not always losing them. People take them.
Sybil	Well, they don't take them from me.
Basil	They wouldn't dare . . . *(takes a pen and starts drawing the diagram, muttering)* Well, I'm sorry I didn't guess that you'd suddenly done that after twelve years, dear. I'm afraid my psychic powers must be a little bit below par this morning. *(pushing the diagram at Hutchison)* There we are.
Sybil	Don't be silly, Basil. It's written quite clearly on the top of the box. *(she gets Mr Walt's key)*
Basil	*(staring)* . . . 'Pens'? . . . It looks more like 'Bens' to me.
Sybil	Well, when Ben comes you can give it to him. Mr Walt's in room seven.
Basil	*(to Walt)* What do you think? Doesn't that look like 'Bens' to you?
Walt	. . . Not really.
Basil	Well, it does to me. Look, **that's** a 'P' . . .
Hutchison	*(studying his diagram)* I don't understand this, where is the Post Office?
Basil	It's there, where it says 'Post Office'. I'm sorry if it is confusing.
Hutchison	Oh. 'P.Off.' You've used the abbreviation.
Basil	Ah, the penny's dropped.
Hutchison	Well, I thought it said Boff.
Basil	Of course.

Hutchison	Yes. I thought Boff was the name of a locale . . . you know, the name of a district. That 'P' looks like a 'B', you see.
Basil	No it doesn't.
Hutchison	Yes it does . . . there's a little loop on the bottom of it . . .
Basil	*(taking the diagram and showing it to Walt)* Excuse me – would you say that was a 'P' or a 'B'?
Walt	. . . Er . . .
Basil	There. Does it say 'Boff' or does it say 'Poff'?
Walt	. . . Er . . .
Basil	There! There! It's a 'P', isn't it?
Walt	*(unwillingly)* I suppose so.
Basil	P. off.
Walt	. . . I beg your pardon?
Basil	P. Off. Not B. Off. Whoever heard of a Bost Office?

Manuel arrives.

Basil	*(to Walt)* Nine?
Walt	What?
Basil	Room nine?
Walt	Room seven.
Basil	Manuel, would you take these cases to room seven, please.
Manuel	*Qué?*

Basil takes some cards from below the desk. He shows Manuel a drawing of a suitcase.

Basil	*(to Walt, indicating Hutchison)* He thinks Boff is a locale . . .
Walt	He thinks what?
Basil	*(showing Manuel a vertical arrow)* You know, some zone, some province . . . in equatorial Torquay. *(he shows Manuel a number '7'; Manuel holds up a card saying 'OK')*
Basil	*(to Walt)* Manuel will show you to your room . . . if you're lucky.

Manuel takes Walt's cases and scurries upstairs; Walt follows.

Hutchison	Excuse me, excuse me – in how many minutes does luncheon commence, please?
Basil	Here, I'll write it down for you.

Hutchison	You won't forget the taxi, will you . . . two o'clock. And if anybody wants me, I shall be in the lounge.
Basil	. . . If anybody **wants** you?
Hutchison	I'll be in the lounge. *(goes into bar)*
Basil	*(calling after him)* Anyone in particular? . . . I mean, Henry Kissinger? . . . or just anyone with a big net? *(goes into the office, where Sybil sits filing her nails)* I don't know what it is about this place . . . I mean, some of the people we get here . . .
Sybil	What are you on about?
Basil	I wish you'd . . . **help** a bit. You're always . . . refurbishing yourself.
Sybil	What?
Basil	Oh . . . never mind! Never mind!!
Sybil	Don't shout at me. I've had a difficult morning.
Basil	Oh dear, what happened? Did you get entangled in the eiderdown again? . . . Not enough cream in your eclair? Hmmm? Or did you have to talk to all your friends for so long that you didn't have time to perm your ears?
Sybil	Actually, Basil, I've been working.
Basil	Choh!
Sybil	You know what I mean by 'working', don't you, dear? I mean getting things done, as opposed to squabbling with the guests.
Basil	I would find it a little easier to cope with some of the cretins we get in here, my little nest of vipers, if I got a smidgeon of co-operation from you.
Sybil	Co-operation – that's a laugh. The day **you** co-operate you'll be in a wooden box. I've never heard such rudeness.
Basil	Look, if you think I'm going to fawn to some of the yobboes we get in here . . .
Sybil	This is a hotel, Basil, not a Borstal, and it might help business if you could have a little more courtesy, just a little.
Basil	I suppose talking to Audrey for half an hour helps business, does it?
Sybil	It **was** about business for your information. Audrey has some news that may interest you.
Basil	Oh, really – this'll be good. Let me guess . . . The Mayor wears a toupée? Somebody's got nail varnish on their cats? Am I getting warm? . . .

Sybil	There are some hotel inspectors in town. *(she exits)*

Basil is stunned. After a moment he runs into the lobby after her.

Basil	What? What does she know?
Sybil	That's **all** she knows.
Basil	**How** does she know?
Sybil	*(calmly)* A friend of Bill Morton's overheard three men in a pub last night comparing notes on places they'd just been in Exeter.
Basil	Three men!? . . . I'll call Bill.
Sybil	You don't have to call Bill, Basil. Just try and exercise a little courtesy.

She exits into the kitchen. Basil picks up the phone on the reception desk and is dialling when the Major comes in from the bar.

The Major	Papers arrived yet, Fawlty?
Basil	No, not yet . . . not yet, Major, sorry, sorry . . .

The Major exits. Basil sees Hutchison approaching again. He pretends not to and starts dialling again. Hutchison, ignored, starts ringing the bell insistently.

Hutchison	Could you do that in a moment, please?
Basil	I'm on the telephone.
Hutchison	Well, you haven't finished dialling yet, have you? *(he puts his finger on the receiver rest, cutting Basil off; Basil slams the receiver down; Hutchison gets his finger away just in time)* Now listen . . . there is a documentary tonight on BBC2 on Squawking Bird, the leader of the Blackfoot Indians in the late 1860s. Now this commences at eight forty-five and goes on for approximately three-quarters of an hour.
Basil	I'm sorry, are you talking to me?
Hutchison	ndeed I am, yes. Now, is it possible for me to reserve the BBC2 channel for the duration of this televisual feast?
Basil	Why don't you talk properly?
Hutchison	I beg your pardon?
Basil	No, it isn't.
Hutchison	What?
Basil	It is not possible to reserve the BBC2 channel from the commencement of this televisual feast until the moment of the termination of its ending. Thank you so much. *(he*

starts to re-dial, but Hutchison puts his finger on the rest again)

Hutchison	Well, in that case, may I suggest you introduce such a scheme?
Basil	No. *(he brings the receiver down hard, missing the finger by a whisker)*
Hutchison	I'd just like to tell you that I have a wide experience of hotels and many of those of my acquaintance have had the foresight to introduce this facility for the benefit of their guests.
Basil	*(unimpressed)* Oh, I see, you have had a **wide** experience of hotels, have you?
Hutchison	Yes, in my professional activities I am in constant contact with them.
Basil	*(dialling again)* Are you. Are you really. *(he stops; he has registered a potential connection between Hutchison and 'hotel inspector')*
Hutchison	Well, then, is it possible for me to *hire* a television to watch the programme in the privacy of my own room?
Basil	*(playing for time)* . . . I beg your pardon?
Hutchison	Have you the facility to hire a television set to one of your guests?
Basil	Er . . . good point. I'm glad you asked me that. Not . . . as such.
Hutchison	Oh.
Basil	However, we do plan to introduce such a scheme in the near future.
Hutchison	Well, that's not much use to me tonight, is it?
Basil	No, but . . . I'll tell you what. Why don't I introduce **another** scheme straight away, along the lines that you've already suggested, by which I reserve the BBC2 channel for you tonight.
Hutchison	Now that's more like it.
Basil	Not at all. I mean, that's what we're here for, isn't it.
Hutchison	Yes . . .
Basil	Is there anything else, before I call your taxi?
Hutchison	Well, yes, there is. Someone in there mentioned that you have a table-tennis table.
Basil	Indeed we do. It is not . . . in absolutely mint condition. But it certainly could be used in an emergency.
Hutchison	Ah.

Basil	It is to be found in the South Wing, overlooking the courtyard, where there is of course ample parking.
Hutchison	What?

Polly has entered the main door.

Basil	Ah, Polly!
Polly	Yes, Mr Fawlty?
Basil	Mr Hutchison, may I introduce Polly Shearman, who is with us at the moment.
Hutchison	Oh . . . how do you do?
Polly	How do you do.
Hutchison	Wait a minute. We've met before, I think.
Polly	Yes, I served you at breakfast.
Hutchison	Oh yes. *(wagging his finger at her)* And you spilt the grapefruit juice, didn't you, you naughty girl?
Polly	*(charmingly)* And **you** moved the glass, didn't you?
Basil	*(quickly)* Thank you, Polly. *(she moves off)* Awfully nice girl. Very bright. She's a fully qualified painter, you know.
Hutchison	Oh, really?

Miss Tibbs and Miss Gatsby come down the stairs.

Basil	Ah, good morning . . . good morning, ladies.
Miss Tibbs & Miss Gatsby	Good morning, Mr Fawlty.
Basil	*(to Hutchison)* We do like to have girls of that calibre to help us out, it does add a certain . . . Well, would you care to partake of lunch now? *(he moves round to usher Hutchison into the dining room)*
Hutchison	Surely it's not yet . . .
Basil	Oh, goodness, we don't worry about things like that here. No fear – I mean, this is a hotel, not a Borstal!

He ushers Hutchison into the dining room. Sybil appears.

Sybil	Basil?
Basil	*(at the dining-room door)* Yes, dear?
Sybil	It's not half past yet.
Basil	I was just saying to Mr Hutchison, dear, this is a hotel not a Borstal, ha ha ha. *(he mouths the word 'inspector' at her)*
Sybil	Chef won't be ready, Basil.
Basil	Leave it to me, dear, leave it to me.
Sybil	Did you ring Bill?
Basil	No, dear, not necessary. *(still signalling)*
Sybil	What?

Basil	Explain later. *(winks)* But I must look after Mr Hutchison now. *(mouths 'inspector' again)*

In the dining room, Polly is taking Hutchison's order.

Polly	A Spanish omelette.
Hutchison	*(loudly)* And all on the plate, please, none on the tablecloth.
Polly	. . . Er, excuse me, you're not by any chance the Duke of Kent, are you?
Hutchison	No, no . . . oh no. You've got the wrong person there.
Basil	*(bustling up)* Ah, Mr Hutchison! You've ordered, have you?
Hutchison	Oh yes, I'm going to have your Spanish omelette.
Basil	Splendid.
Hutchison	Yes – I assume that all the vegetables within the omelette are fresh?
Basil	Oh, yes, yes.
Hutchison	Including the peas?
Basil	Oh yes, they're fresh all right.
Hutchison	They're not frozen, are they?
Basil	. . . Well, they're **frozen**, yes.
Hutchison	Well, if they're frozen, they're not fresh, are they.
Basil	Well, I assure you they were absolutely fresh when they were frozen.
Hutchison	Oh dear – there's a lot of this nowadays in hotels.
Basil	A lot of what?
Hutchison	Yes, I'll just have cheese salad, please.
Basil	What?
Hutchison	I eat only fresh vegetables, you see – I'll just have the cheese salad.
Basil	Well, we could do the omelette without the peas.
Hutchison	Oh, no, I always feel that the peas are an integral part of the overall flavour – might I suggest that in future you avail yourself of sufficient quantities of the fresh article?
Basil	. . . Now look! We've been serving . . . *(recovers himself)* Yes, yes, good idea . . . now, something to drink?
Hutchison	Yes, I'll have a ginger beer, please.
Basil	A ginger beer?
Hutchison	Yes, and a glass of fresh water.

The phone rings in the lobby.

Basil	. . . Fresh?

Hutchison	Water, yes.
Sybil	*(putting her head round the door)* Mr Hutchison -- a telephone call for you at reception.
Hutchison	Telephone? . . . Oh dear . . . oh dear . . . *(he takes out a clean handkerchief and exits)*
Basil	*(to himself)* . . . Clever . . . clever . . .

Basil goes into the kitchen. Mr Walt enters from the lobby and looks around, wondering where he should sit.

Walt	*(to Manuel, who is busily putting napkins on tables)* Good afternoon.
Manuel	No, is no sun. Is no good for me.
Walt	I beg your pardon?
Manuel	I homesick, yes?
Walt	Is there anywhere you'd like me to sit?
Manuel	*Qué?*
Walt	I'm in room seven.
Manuel	*(ushering Walt to door and pointing up the stairs)* Oh yes please, here . . . you go up . . . room seven.
Walt	No, no.
Manuel	Yes, please, I show you.
Walt	No, look, I want a table.
Manuel	A table?
Walt	For one.
Manuel	Ah! Table one. Oh, please – yes, table one – so sorry. *(indicates a table)*
Walt	. . . Thank you.

Manuel helps Walt to sit, then gets a menu and a piece of card. He gives Walt the menu.

Manuel	So sorry, but I think you say for room and I do it for I am myself not want to know it easily.
Walt	I'm sorry?
Manuel	No. Is my fault.
Walt	Well, I'll try the pâté . . . and the lamb casserole.
Manuel	*(looking at the card)* You . . . room ten?
Walt	No. Room **seven**.
Manuel	Seven? *Si.*
Walt	Yes.
Manuel	No, no, **this** is table **one**. Is Wednesday. Room seven is table five. Please. *(Walt moves patiently to Mr Hutchison's table)* So sorry . . . seven is what I think you say but one is

	for table not for this one so is *come se habla en Ingles pero puedo ver las nombres solamente quando estan delante de mi.*
Walt	*(stoically)* The pâté and the lamb.
Manuel	*Si.* Pâté . . . Lamb . . . *(he exits muttering into the kitchen)*
Basil	*(coming in and delivering the ginger beer and the glass of water down in front of Walt)* One ginger beer . . . and one glass of fresh water. *(he looks at Walt and jumps violently)* What are you doing there?
Walt	. . . I . . .
Basil	You can't sit there, it's **taken.** Come on.
Walt	Look, I've been moved once already.
Basil	Well, you're in room seven, aren't you?
Walt	Yes, but the waiter said table five.
Basil	Well, *this* isn't table five, is it? *(sees the plastic table number; it says 'five')* Tch. *(picks it up and moves to another table)* Would you come over here, please, this is table five. *(puts the 'five' down on the new table, takes an 'eight' off and pockets it)* . . . Come on!
Walt	Look, I did ask the waiter.
Basil	Well, he's hopeless, isn't he. You might as well ask the cat. Now, settle down, come on, come on.
Walt	. . . I beg your pardon?
Basil	Would you sit down please? *(Walt resignedly sits)* Thank you. *(moves off)*
Walt	I hate to trespass further on your valuable time, but might I look at the wine list?
Basil	Now?
Walt	Yes, please.
Basil	*(removing the Major's wine list from his grasp)* Excuse me . . . *(gives it to Walt)* Here we are. Are you happy now?
Walt	Could I have an ashtray, please? *(Basil produces an ashtray)* Thank you – I'll have a bottle of the Aloxe-Corton '65.
Basil	The what?
Walt	*(showing him)* The Aloxe-Corton '65.
Basil	*(registering the price)* Oh! The Cortonne. Yes, of **course,** my pleasure. *(he returns the wine list to the Major; Hutchison re-enters, wiping his ear with his handkerchief)* Ah, there you are, Mr Hutchison! Nice to have you back again. *(fawns after him)*
Hutchison	Not so close, please, not so close.
Basil	Oh, sorry . . . everything to your satisfaction?

Hutchison	Your earpiece was very greasy – I've wiped it out for you.
Basil	Oh, thank you so much. *(exits to kitchen)*
Hutchison	*(muttering)* Dreadfully greasy, it was . . . I don't know who's been using it. *(tastes his ginger beer)* Oh dear – that's **tepid!** *(Basil and Polly come in from the kitchen)* Have you got an ice bucket, please?
Basil	An ice bucket?
Hutchison	This ginger beer is distinctly warm.
Basil	Ah, Polly – an ice bucket for Mr Hutchison, please. Thank you. *(Polly looks dazed; Basil goes to Walt's table with the bottle)* There we are – the Cortonne '65.

Clearly performing for Hutchison, he inserts the corkscrew with panache and pulls. He struggles, gamely smiles, turns his back, struggles again and it comes. Triumphantly, he pours. Alas, no wine is forthcoming.

Basil	Ah . . . a bit still in there. Sorry.

He re-inserts the corkscrew, struggles, and pours again. Nothing happens. He pokes some pieces of cork out and pours. A dribble flows, followed by a torrent. Some goes in the glass.

Basil	Thank you so much. May I congratulate you on your choice.
Walt	*(tasting the wine)* Excuse me.
Basil	Yes?
Walt	I'm afraid this is corked.
Basil	I just uncorked it. Didn't you see me?
Walt	What?
Basil	*(shows him the cork on the end of the corkscrew)* Look.
Walt	No, no . . .
Basil	No, you see, I took it out of the bottle – that's how I managed to get the wine **out** of the bottle **into** your glass.
Walt	I don't mean that. I mean the wine is **corked.** The wine has reacted with the cork.
Basil	I'm sorry?
Walt	The wine has reacted with the cork and gone bad.
Basil	Gone bad? May I . . . ? *(he tastes the wine and turns into the corner to cover his reaction)* So you don't want it?
Walt	I'd like a bottle that's not corked.
Basil	Right! Right! That's cost me, hasn't it? Well never mind – I'll get another bottle. *(he takes the bottle; on his way out, he*

	addresses the guests) I do hope you're all enjoying your meals. *(no reaction)* I **said**, 'I do hope you're all enjoying your meals.' *(there is a bit of nodding)* Thank you, thank you. *(calls to Walt)* Excuse me . . . excuse me!! Table five!
Walt	. . . Er yes?
Basil	Are you having the lamb or the mackerel?
Walt	. . . The lamb.
Basil	I'll have another one standing by just in case. *(exits* con brio)

Sybil comes in, looks round for Basil, and exits. Polly comes in, followed by Basil with a fresh bottle.

Basil	Let's give this one a go, then, shall we? . . . Polly, would you get Mr Hutchison his main course, please. *(to Hutchison, fawning)* So sorry to keep you waiting, Mr Hutchison. It will be with you in just one moment. Thank you.
Sybil	*(looking in)* Basil.
Basil	Yes, dear? *(but she's gone; he leaves the replacement bottle on the sideboard behind Walt and goes into the lobby)*
Sybil	*(sweetly)* How are you getting along with your hotel inspector?
Basil	. . . Fine. Fine.
Sybil	He sells spoons.
Basil	. . . Sorry?
Sybil	I listened in on his phone call. He works for a cutlery firm. But he specializes in spoons.
Basil	You listened in?
Sybil	Yes.
Basil	You listened in on a private call to one of our guests?
Sybil	That's right, Basil.
Basil	. . . The little rat! I'll get him for that.
Sybil	Now, Basil . . .
Basil	Trying that on with me.
Sybil	Trying **what** on?
Basil	Pretending he's a hotel inspector . . . 'Do we hire television sets' . . . 'fresh peas' . . . 'ice buckets' . . .
Sybil	Basil, it was **your** mistake. You can't . . .
Basil	Now, you let me handle this!
Sybil	Basil!!! This whole inspector business was in your own imagination. It's nothing to do with him. There is no

	excuse for rudeness, do you understand? . . . **Do you understand?**
Basil	Yes!!!
Sybil	Good. *(she turns and walks away)*

Basil, planning revenge, enters the dining room and stalks the sitting Hutchison.

The Major	Papers arrived yet, Fawlty?
Basil	Not yet, Major, no. *(he stands behind Hutchison)* Spoons, eh?
Hutchison	I'm sorry?
Basil	Spppppppppppooooooons!
Hutchison	I beg your pardon?
Basil	I understand you're in the spoon trade.
Hutchison	Oh! Yes . . .
Basil	Ah, fascinating! Fascinating. How absorbing for you.
Hutchison	Yes, as a matter of fact . . .
Basil	So much more interesting than being a **hotel inspector!**

He leaves. Hutchison is puzzled. Polly arrives and places an omelette in front of him.

Hutchison	What . . . oh, thank you . . . *(looks at it)* No . . . Miss!! Miss!!
Polly	Yes?
Hutchison	I didn't order that.
Basil	*(from afar)* Is there something we can get you, Mr Hutchison? A tea cosy for your pepper pot, perhaps?
Hutchison	No, no. *(to Polly)* I changed the order, you see.
Basil	*(coming up, aggressively)* What seems to be the trouble?
Polly	Well, I thought Mr Hutchison ordered an omelette, but . . .
Basil	No, he went off it, Polly, so we changed the order. It's perfectly simple . . .
Polly	Well, I'm sorry, but I wasn't told.
Basil	Well, I told the chef, so he should have told you.
Polly	Well, he **didn't**.
Basil	Well, is that my fault?
Polly	No, is it mine?
Hutchison	No, it's his fault.
Basil	What?
Hutchison	It's the chef's fault.

Basil	I beg your pardon?
Hutchison	Well clearly in a case like this where the order has been changed and the chef's been informed it's obviously his responsibility.
Basil	You want to run the place?
Hutchison	What?
Basil	You want to come and run the hotel? Right! Mr Hutchison is taking over, Polly, so I'll have the omelette. *(trying to get Hutchison to his feet)* I'm sure with his natural charm and wide experience there'll be no more problems . . .
Hutchison	No, no . . .
Basil	Come on, then, you can't sit about all day, there's lots to be done. *(jiggling Hutchison's chair)* Come on!
Sybil	*(appearing from nowhere)* What is going on, Basil?
Basil	Hello, dear!
Sybil	Well?
Basil	*(jiggling the chair very slightly)* Is that better, Mr Hutchison?
Hutchison	What?
Basil	Is that better?
Hutchison	Thank you, yes . . .
Basil	Oh good. Well that's sorted out then. Good.
Sybil	Is there something wrong?
Hutchison	Yes, there is, yes . . . I have been given an erroneous dish.
Sybil	Thank you, Basil, I'll deal with this . . . thank you, Polly . . . *(Basil walks innocently away)* Now, Mr Hutchison.
Hutchison	Now, you see, I did order the omelette in the first place, but then I changed my mind.
Sybil	I see. Well I'll just go in the kitchen and find out what happened.
Hutchison	Thank you.

She heads for the kitchen. Meanwhile Basil is looking at the sideboard; the bottle has gone. He looks round and sees Manuel.

Basil	Manuel!
Manuel	*(running up)* Si?
Basil	*(indicating sideboard)* The bottle.
Manuel	Er . . . Yes!
Basil	Where is it?

Manuel	*Qué?*
Basil	*. . . donde es . . . ?*
Manuel	Oh, I take it. *(indicates kitchen)* I take it. I take it.
Basil	*(beckoning gently)* Come here. *(takes a spoon from the bowl Manuel is carrying)* You're a waste of space. *(raps him on the head with the spoon and hustles him into kitchen)*
Sybil	*(coming in from kitchen with some pâté)* There we are, Mr Hutchison.
Hutchison	No, no, no! Just a moment, please!
Sybil	Yes?
Hutchison	I did not order that.
Sybil	You didn't?
Hutchison	I did **not**.
Sybil	I'm sorry, there's an order for pâté for this table.
Hutchison	Oh dear me, things do seem to be going wrong today, don't they.
Basil	*(coming back with another bottle)* Hallo, Sybil, taking care of things, are you?
Sybil	Yes, thank you Basil.
Basil	Good . . . *(to Hutchison)* Everything all right, then?
Hutchison	Well it appears that . . .
Sybil	We're just sorting it out, thank you Basil.
Basil	That's funny . . . you didn't order 'pâté maison', did you, Mr Hutchison?
Hutchison	No I did not, I ordered . . .
Basil	Well, I'll leave you to deal with it, dear.

He goes to Mr Walt's table and starts uncorking the bottle. He has done so when he notices another bottle open on the table.

Basil	How did you do that?
Walt	What?
Basil	*(indicating Walt's bottle)* Where did you get it?
Walt	Where did I **get** it?
Basil	That's right! I mean, how did you get it?
Walt	The waiter opened it for me.
Basil	The waiter opened it for you!!??
Walt	. . . Yes!

Manuel, unaware of recent developments, arrives with Walt's pâté.

Basil	I've told you about him, haven't I!

Manuel starts to leave. Basil jabs him in the rear with the corkscrew. He leaves more rapidly. Meanwhile Polly is delivering a lamb casserole to Mr Hutchison.

Hutchison	Oh, no, no!! For goodness sake . . .
Basil	*(running up)* What is it, what is it?!!
Hutchison	I did not order a lamb casserole!
Basil	No, he didn't, he did not order one, Polly, so **why** . . . has . . . he . . . got . . . **one?**
Polly	Because Mrs Fawlty told me to **give** him one.
Basil	I know how she feels.
Polly	I've got an order for one for this table.
Basil	Who took the order?
Polly	*(valiantly)* . . . I don't know.
Basil	. . . Manuel!!
Hutchison	I mean, look, how can it be so difficult to get a cheese salad?
Basil	. . . You want to run the place?
Hutchison	No no, I . . .
Basil	Right, well shut up then.
Hutchison	I beg your pardon?!
Polly	I'll get you a cheese salad, Mr Hutchison.
Basil	*(to Polly)* And don't listen to anyone . . . just **get him a cheese salad.**

Manuel appears.

Manuel	*Si? (Basil hits him; he retires)*
Hutchison	Excuse me!! I've changed my mind . . . *(rising)* I do not want the cheese salad. I wish to cancel it. I am not used to being spoken to like that, Mr Fawlty, and I've no wish to continue my luncheon.
Basil	*(realising he went a bridge too far)* I do apologizc if what I said just now seemed a trifle . . . brusque.
Hutchison	Brusque? It was **rude**, Mr Fawlty. I said . . . **rude!**
Basil	Well, I'm deeply sorry if it came over like that. I mean, nothing could have been further from my mind . . .
Hutchison	You told me to shut up!
Polly	*(brilliantly)* No, no. He told **me** to shut up.
Hutchison	*(to Polly)* You what? He said it to me.
Basil	Ah, no, I was looking at you but I was talking to Polly. *(still looking at Hutchison)* Wasn't I, Polly?
Polly	*(straight to Hutchison)* Oh, yes.

Basil	*(still to Hutchison)* Ah! Did you notice then . . . that I was looking at you but talking to her?
Hutchison	What?
Polly	*(looking at Basil)* You see, he was looking at you but talking to me. *(to Basil)* Wasn't he?
Basil	*(to Polly)* Wasn't I?
Hutchison	*(not sure where to look)* What?
Polly	*(to Hutchison)* So you weren't being rude, were you Mr Fawlty?
Basil	*(to Polly)* Absolutely not. You see?
Hutchison	*(to Basil)* . . . Me?
Basil	*(to Hutchison)* Yes.
Hutchison	*(to Basil)* Well, if you say shut up to somebody, that's the one you want to shut up, isn't it?
Polly	*(to Basil)* Not necessarily.
Basil	*(to Hutchison)* . . . I'm sorry, were you talking to me?
Hutchison	*(to Basil)* Yes.
Polly	*(to Basil)* I beg your pardon.

A pause. Hutchison has now been successfully confused.

Basil	*(to Hutchison)* There! You see how easily these misunderstandings occur.
Hutchison	Er . . . yes, I do . . .
Basil	So . . . one cheese salad then please, Polly.
Polly	*(to Basil)* Certainly, Mr Hutchison. *(leaves)*
Basil	And if there's anything else please don't hesitate to ask.
Hutchison	*(after looking round for a moment to see if he is being addressed)* Yes, thank you.

Basil moves away. Manuel creeps up on Walt and removes his empty plate.

Walt	*(jumping)* Aaah!
Basil	*(to Manuel)* What are you **doing**? *(to Walt)* I'm so sorry. He's from Barcelona. I trust your pâté was satisfactory?
Walt	Yes, yes, thank you.
Basil	Oh, good, good. The chef buys it himself, you know.
Walt	Buys it?
Basil	Oh, insists on it. I imagine the Cortonne complemented it delightfully.
Walt	Yes. It's very good.
Basil	Ah! Excellent.

Walt	More like a '66 really.
Basil	Is it?
Walt	Well, lots of body.
Basil	*(picking up the bottle and expertly gauging its weight)* Quite right. It's always a pleasure to find someone who appreciates the boudoir of the grape. I'm afraid most of the people we get in here don't know a Bordeaux from a claret.
Walt	. . . A Bordeaux **is** a claret.
Basil	Oh, a **Bordeaux** is a claret. But **they** wouldn't know that. You obviously drink a lot . . . wine, I mean. Well, not a **lot,** a fair amount, the right amount for a connoisseur, I mean, that doesn't mean you're . . . does it, I mean some people drink it by the crate but that's not being a connoisseur, that's just plain sloshed. Oh, a Bordeaux's one of the clarets all right.
Walt	One?

Manuel creeps in with Walt's casserole and skulks off.

Basil	*(swiftly)* You're down here on business, are you?
Walt	*(dismissively)* Yes.
Basil	You're not in the wine trade by any chance?
Walt	No we're not.
Basil	**We're?**
Walt	*(anxious to start on his casserole)* . . . I am down here on business with a couple of colleagues and we are not in the wine trade.
Basil	Ah, it's just that you're obviously so expert.
Walt	No . . . I am not expert.
Basil	Oh, but you are.
Walt	I'm not.
Basil	Oh yes you are.
Walt	I am not an expert!
Basil	*(suddenly seizing Walt's shoulder)* **Three** of you?
Walt	*(astonished)* What?
Basil	Three . . . three of you?
Walt	Yes . . . there are three of us . . . well, the other two aren't here. They're staying at another hotel.
Basil	*(recovering his wits)* Quite! So . . . it's all all right, is it?
Walt	. . . What?
Basil	Well, I mean things in general . . . I mean, the wine's really good?

Walt	Yes.
Basil	And the pâté was all right?
Walt	Yes, I said so.
Basil	And the casserole?
Walt	I haven't tasted it yet.
Basil	*(sniffing the casserole admiringly)* Mmmmm!
Walt	I've not been given the chance.

There is an explosion of complaints from Hutchison.

Basil	*(to Walt)* Well, I'll leave you to your meal if I may . . . *bon appétit. (he hurtles towards Hutchison)*
Hutchison	*(fortissimo)* Oh, no, come on now, this is quite absurd. I'm sorry, but I **do not want an omelette**!!
Manuel	*(offering Hutchison an omelette)* Is nice!
Hutchison	I don't want the bloody thing. I've sent it back once!
Basil	*(whizzing up)* Here, give it to me.
Hutchison	I fail to see how this sort of thing can happen!
Basil	*(tearing up the omelette)* There. I've torn it up. You'll never see it again.

He deposits the remains on the Major's table. The Major gratefully tucks in.

Hutchison	*(still fortissimo)* I told you I wanted a cheese salad.

Polly arrives with it.

Basil	Thank you, Polly, one cheese salad, there we are, sir. I'm so glad everything is to your satisfaction.
Hutchison	No it is not! It is absolutely ridiculous! I mean, you are **supposed** to be running a **hotel**!
Basil	*(admiring the salad)* My, that does look good.
Hutchison	I've had the omelette, a prawn cocktail with a bloody silly name . . .
Basil	Look at that cheddar. Delicious!
Hutchison	. . . then I had a plate of stew and then the bloody omelette again!
Basil	Can we keep it down a little?
Hutchison	I mean, all I wanted was a cheese salad. It wasn't as though I'd ordered an **elephant's ear on a bun**, was it!
Basil	*(smiling vainly at Walt)* Thank you, thank you so much.
Hutchison	I mean the whole thing is absolutely ridiculous.
Basil	*(pushing him back in his chair)* Well, I'm glad we've sorted it all out now.

Hutchison	. . . I mean for a man who's supposed to be running a hotel, your behaviour is totally . . .

Basil laughs genially at the other guests and places a hand across Hutchison's mouth.

Basil	Well, I'm glad everything's to your satisfaction now . . .
Hutchison	*(muffled)* Let me go, let me go . . .
Basil	Is there anything else **at all** I can get you, sir?
Hutchison	*(struggling)* Let me go, I can't breathe!
Basil	*(merrily)* Ha ha ha ha ha! *(hissing)* Shut up, then.
Hutchison	I can't breathe!
Basil	Shut up and I'll let go.
Hutchison	You told me to shut up again!
Basil	Look at that **lovely** cheese! *(Hutchison starts threshing about in search of oxygen; Basil tightens his grip and assures the others)* It's all right, he's only choking. *(Hutchison leaps convulsively; Basil thumps him on the back)* Don't worry . . . bit of cheese went the wrong way. *(more convulsions and thumping; Basil beams and slips in a quick rabbit-punch; Hutchison slumps with his face in his salad)* Ah, never mind, he's fainted, poor chap. Manuel! *(to Walt)* Poor chap! Bit of cheese!
The Major	Yes, please.

Basil and Manuel pick up Hutchison and carry him into the lobby.

Sybil	What's happened?
Basil	He fainted, dear.
Sybil	**Fainted?**
Basil	. . . Got a bit of cheese stuck.

They carry Hutchison into the bar, followed by Sybil.

Sybil	. . . Basil, you do **not** faint from getting a bit of cheese stuck.
Basil	Well, I was giving him a bit of a pat on the back and he sort of . . . **moved**, just as I was . . .
Sybil	What have you **done**, Basil?
Basil	Nothing, he just moved as I . . .
Sybil	Oh my God! Call the doctor.
Basil	Look, I can handle this.
Sybil	Call the doctor!
Basil	I can handle it!!

Sybil   Call the doctor!!
Basil   Look, I can handle it . . . right, right, I'll call the doctor,
                   obviously I can't handle it . . . *(he goes into the lobby,
                   muttering)* I'm just a great stupid sabre-toothed tart so
                   we'll let my husband do it. *(picks up the phone but sees Walt
                   emerging from the dining room)* Ah! . . . I'm so sorry to have
                   left you, I trust you enjoyed your meal?
Walt   *(peremptorily)* Yes, yes, thank you. I was wondering . . .
Basil   The casserole was really good, was it?
Walt   . . . Well, it was adequate.
Basil   Oh, quite, yes, exactly, I'm afraid the chef at lunch today
                   is **not** our regular, but . . . incidentally, I'm sorry about
                   that poor chap choking himself like that.
Walt   I was wondering if you had a telephone I might use?
Basil   Oh, please, do use this one. *(hands him the receiver)* I don't
                   know how he managed to do it. Ah, here he is. Good.
                   (Hutchison emerges unsteadily from the bar) Ah, Mr
                   Hutchison! **There** you are . . . What a **frightful** shame
                   about that piece of cheese getting stuck in the old
                   windpipe like that. *(indicating the bar)* Would you like to
                   go in there and discuss it?
Hutchison   No, I'd prefer to come in **here** and discuss it.
Basil   *(retreating)* . . . Oh, fine, I'm afraid it's a little bit of a
                   mess . . .

                   *Hutchison comes behind the bar and hits him. Basil disappears
                   below the desk. After a pause he stands up and smiles warmly
                   at Hutchison.*

Basil   Well, that lie-down seems to have done you some good.

                   *Hutchison hits him again and Basil reels towards Walt's end of
                   the desk. Hutchison hits him twice more.*

Basil   *(to Walt)* Sorry about this.

                   Hutchison hits him a couple more times. He flops out of sight.

Hutchison   I am not a violent man, Mr Fawlty.
Basil's voice Yes you are.
Hutchison   No I'm not! But when I am insulted and then attacked, I
                   would prefer to rely on my own mettle than call the
                   police.
Basil's voice Do you? Do you really?
Hutchison   Yes, I do, now stand up like a man, come on.

Basil's voice	. . . Bit of trouble with the old leg, actually.
Hutchison	Come on!

He picks Basil up. Basil has found a stapler. He shows it to Walt.

Basil	Look what I've found!
Hutchison	I hope I've made my point.
Basil	Absolutely! *(to Walt)* I've been looking for that.
Hutchison	I would just like to say that this hotel is extremely inefficient and badly run, and that you are a very rude and discourteous man, Mr Fawlty.
Basil	*(happily)* Ah ha ha ha ha.
Hutchison	. . . Did I say something funny, Mr Fawlty?
Basil	. . . Well, sort of **pithy**, I suppose.
Hutchison	Oh really . . . well, here's the punch line. *(he elbows Basil in the stomach; Basil doubles up out of sight)* Now I am going to fetch my belongings, and I do not expect to receive a bill. *(he goes off upstairs)*
Sybil	*(comes in, leans over the desk and looks down at Basil)* You've handled that, then, have you, Basil?
Basil's voice	Yes dear, thank you, leave it to me.

She goes off. Walt finishes his call.

Basil	*(hauling himself into view)* Incidentally, I don't know if you realize, but he's a regular customer of ours . . . he loves it here, it's his second home. It's just that we always have to have this little . . . don't know why, but he seems to like it.
Walt	Really?
Basil	Yes, the only danger is, though, that somebody's going to think he **really** isn't satisfied about something or that the fighting's real, and tell people. You won't mention it, will you . . . we'd be delighted to offer you dinner here tonight as our guest, to show our gratitude.
Walt	. . . What?
Basil	Dinner tonight . . . would you . . . ?
Walt	*(puzzled)* No, I can't tonight, thank you.
Basil	**Tomorrow** night?
Walt	. . . I shall be leaving tomorrow. Sorry.
Basil	. . . All right. Fifty pounds, then!
Walt	I beg your pardon?
Basil	Fifty pounds not to mention it.
Walt	Fifty pounds?!!

Basil	. . . Sixty, then! . . . Not to write about it . . . you know, articles, books, letters . . . *(taking out his wallet)*
Walt	I'm afraid I really don't . . .
Basil	*(clutching him)* Please! Oh please! It's taken us twelve years to build this place up. If you put this in the book we're finished.
Walt	What book?
Basil	The hotel guide. Oh . . . I'm sorry, I shouldn't have mentioned it. *(emits a strangled high-pitched whine)* Oh, what have I done?
Walt	Look, I think you've got me confused with somebody else. I'm nothing to do with any hotel guide. I'm down here for the Exhibition – we sell outboard motors . . . all right?
Basil	*(now sobbing uncontrollably)* Outboard motors? . . . You're not an inspector?
Walt	No.
Basil	Not on the side or anything?
Walt	No.
Basil	*(grabbing him)* Swear to God.
Walt	I tell you, I've nothing to do with it!
Basil	Thank you, thank you, oh, thank you so much. I don't know how I can ever . . . *(he suddenly freezes; a pause)* Thanks.

He disappears into the kitchen. Walt leaves by the main doors. Three men walk into the hotel past him; they are the inspectors.

1st inspector	Twenty-six rooms, twelve with private bathrooms.
2nd inspector	Yes, well, why don't you have dinner here, and Chris and I can try the Claremont.
3rd inspector	OK. The owner's one Basil Fawlty.

They ring the bell. At that moment Hutchison comes downstairs. Manuel scampers up to him.

Manuel	Please, please! Mr Fawlty wants to say *adios*.

Basil strides out of the kitchen and firmly places a large squidgy pie in Hutchison's crotch and another in his face.

Basil	Manuel, the cream.

He opens Hutchison's briefcase and Manuel pours a pint of best quality cream into it. The Major comes up.

The Major	Papers arrived yet, Fawlty?
Basil	Not yet, Major, no, sorry.

The Major wanders off. Basil shakes the briefcase thoroughly and tucks it under Hutchison's arm.

Basil   Now go away. If you ever come back I shall kill you.

He propels the stunned Hutchison out of the main door, turns expansively and kisses Manuel on the forehead. He then strides triumphantly to the counter and beams at the new arrivals.

Basil   Good afternoon, and what can I do for you three gentlemen? *(a pause; then the terrible truth dawns)* Aaaagh!!!

Gourmet Night

Fifth of first series, first broadcast on 17 October 1975, BBC2.

Basil Fawlty   John Cleese
Sybil Fawlty   Prunella Scales
Manuel   Andrew Sachs
Polly   Connie Booth
André   André Maranne
Kurt   Steve Plytas
Colonel Hall   Allan Cuthbertson
Mrs Hall   Ann Way
Mr Twitchen   Richard Caldicot
Mrs Twitchen   Betty Huntley-Wright
Major Gowen   Ballard Berkeley
Miss Tibbs   Gilly Flower
Miss Gatsby   Renée Roberts
Mr Heath   Jeffrey Segal
Mrs Heath   Elizabeth Benson
Master Heath   Tony Page

The forecourt of Fawlty Towers. Basil is fiddling under the bonnet of his car, which is clearly a real mother of an old car. He makes a final adjustment and strides round to the driver's seat. He presses the starter twice, without results.

Basil   Oh come on, is it so difficult for you to start? . . . I mean it's so **basic**. If you don't go, there's very little point in having you.

He tries again, then gives up, goes round to the front and takes a delicious-looking savoury from a small pile on the engine, pops it in his mouth and starts fiddling again. The horn jams on; he clears it.

Basil   Now, just pull yourself together, right? Make the effort. *(he gets back in and presses the starter; it whines pitifully)* Come on . . . now look!

Manuel   *(running down the steps)* Mr Fawlty! Mr Fawlty! Telephone!!

Basil   What?

Manuel   Telephone . . . telephone. *(mimes a telephone)*

Basil   Oh . . . where's Sybil?

Manuel   . . . *Qué?*

Basil   Where's . . . *Sy* . . . *bil?*

Manuel   . . . Where's . . . the bill?

Basil   No! No! I own the place. I don't pay bills. Where's my **wife?**

Manuel   She not there.

Basil   She **is** there! *(Manuel looks helpless)* Oh, never mind, right, leave it to me, **I'll** do it! *(he strides towards the hotel)* I'll mend the car, **I'll** answer the telephone, then you can all handcuff and blindfold me and I'll clean the windows . . .

He steams into the lobby. Manuel gets ahead of him.

Manuel   In here.

Basil   Yes, I **know** it's in here!

Manuel   *(indicating telephone)* This way, please. *(he goes into the kitchen)*

Basil   Yes, I **know** it's this way, I **own** the place!

But just before he gets to the telephone, Sybil appears from the office and answers it herself.

Sybil   Hallo, Fawlty Towers . . . Oh, André, thank you for calling. Kurt's marvellous, we're absolutely delighted with him . . . really, André, he's wonderful . . .

Basil goes to the kitchen and leads Manuel back to the desk.

Basil   *(pointing to Sybil)* This Basil's wife. *(pointing to himself)* This . . . Basil. This . . . smack on head. *(demonstrates; Manuel slinks off)*
Sybil   Just one moment, André . . . Basil!
Basil   Yes, dear?
Sybil   Have you taken the car in yet?
Basil   Yes, I'm just dealing with it, dear.
Sybil   You're not trying to do it yourself, are you, Basil?
Basil   *(discovering a change of subject on the wall)* Have you seen this mark up here, dear?
Sybil   Did you hear what I said?
Basil   Yes I did, dear, it's a bit of a scratch . . .
Sybil   Take it into the **garage**, Basil.
Basil   *(absently)* Yes, yes, just having a look at it, dear.
Sybil   *(to phone)* I'm sorry, André, where was I? Oh yes. Well, he's the best chef we've ever had – we can't thank you enough for finding him for us . . . *(Basil checks that Sybil is not looking and slips into the kitchen)* Look, can you come and have dinner on Sunday? . . . there's something we want to ask your advice about . . . OK, lovely, see you then. *(she rings off; Polly comes in)* Hallo, Polly.
Polly   Can you come and have a drink, Mrs Fawlty?
Sybil   Drink?
Polly   I've sold a sketch!
Sybil   Really? I'd love to.

They go into the kitchen, where Kurt and Manuel are preparing food. Basil is lurking by another pile of savouries.

Polly   Hallo.
Kurt and Manuel Hallo.
Sybil   Kurt, André **can** come on Sunday. *(to Basil)* I thought you were taking the car in . . . *(he is popping another savoury into his mouth)* Are you at those again?

Basil	I just took one, dear.
Sybil	*(confiscating the plate)* I think you've had enough of those, Basil. Now will you deal with the car, please.
Kurt	*(seeing Basil still munching)* Good, Mr Fawlty?
Basil	Superb, Kurt.
Polly	*(gives Sybil a glass of wine; to Basil)* For you, Mr Fawlty?
Basil	Thank you, Polly.
Sybil	Are you going to do the car?
Basil	In a moment, my little piranha fish. *(to Polly)* What's all this, then?
Polly	I've just sold a sketch.
Basil	What, for **money?**
Kurt	I bought it, Mr Fawlty. She's very talented. *(Polly offers him a glass of wine)* Oh, no, Polly, I won't.
Polly	Oh, come on.
Kurt	No, thank you.
Polly	Oh, please, I bought it to thank you.
Kurt	No, honestly.
Polly	Don't you like it?
Kurt	Too much. But not when I'm working. You drink it for me, Manuel. *(Manuel accepts gratefully)*
Basil	*(raising his glass to Polly)* Well . . . cheerio.
Sybil	*(neatly confiscating his glass)* Cheerio, Basil.
Basil	Well, that smelt nice.
Kurt	*(showing Basil the sketch)* Here it is, Mr Fawlty. She's really got something, you know.
Basil	Really.
Polly	Well worth 50p anyway.
Basil	Yes. Do you win a bun if you guess what it is?
Polly	It's Manuel.
Basil	What?
Manuel	It's **me.**
Basil	. . . Where?
Kurt	Manuel is my friend. *(puts his arm round Manuel's shoulders)* We're good friends, eh?
Manuel	Oh, *si.*
Basil	*(returning the sketch)* Yes, very modern. Very socialist. *(Kurt takes the sketch and kisses it warmly)* Something to remember him by . . . you know, when he goes.
Sybil	You still here, Basil?
Basil	No, I went a couple of minutes ago, dear, but I expect I'll be back soon. *(exits)*

Sybil studies the sketch. Kurt sees Manuel performing some culinary misdeed.

Kurt	No, no, Manuel! Look, like this . . .
Sybil	*(handing Polly the sketch)* Oh, I like that. Will you do me one?
Polly	Really? . . . Of Manuel?
Sybil	Yes. It'll look nice on Basil's bedside table. *(exits)*
Polly	*(to Kurt)* Two in a day. That's as many as Van Gogh sold in a lifetime.
Kurt	Ah, but he didn't have Manuel as a model, eh?

Meanwhile Basil, watched by Sybil from the main doors, drives out of the forecourt. He goes round the corner, out of sight of Sybil, stops, gets out, takes a handful of savouries from his pocket and once again starts poking about under the bonnet.

Sunday evening; the dining room. Sybil, Basil and André are sitting at one of the tables. Some other guests are apparent, including Mr and Mrs Heath and their eleven-year-old son Ronald. The food on the Fawltys' table looks great and is.

Sybil	*(not utterly unhistrionically)* Ohh. Mmmm. This is wonderful.
André	I told you – he is one of the best.
Sybil	He's almost as good as you are, André. Oh!! It's absolutely **divine**, Basil. Go on, have a bite.
Basil	It is good, isn't it.
Sybil	Oh, listen to him. The only place I've ever really seen him eat is in your restaurant, André, and now he is stuffing it away like a hamster.
Basil	Really, Sybil.
Sybil	*(coquettishly)* We're going to have to buy him a great big wheel to run around in when he's got a moment, or he'll get like a big bad-tempered tomato.
Basil	I believe we were discussing the Gourmet Evening, dear.
Sybil	Do you know, André, he burst his zip this morning.
Basil	*(in a superior manner)* Oh dear.
Sybil	What, darling?
Basil	You're embarrassing André.
Sybil	No, dear, I'm embarrassing **you**. *(she pats Basil's stomach)* Look at that.

Basil	Well, I'd better go and have a word with the guests. Why don't you have another vat of wine, dear? *(he rises and starts to circulate, coming first to the Major's table)* Good evening, Major. Enjoying your soup?
The Major	Tasted a bit off to me, Fawlty.
Basil	Well, it's made with **fresh** mushrooms, Major.
The Major	Ah, that would explain it.

A flicker of olympian despair crosses Basil's face. He moves on to the Heaths' table.

Basil	Good evening. Is everything to your satisfaction?
Mr Heath	Yes thank—
Mrs Heath	*(interrupting)* Well . . . *(she turns expectantly to their son)*
Ronald	I don't like the chips.
Basil	Sorry?
Ronald	The chips are awful.
Basil	*(smiling balefully)* Oh dear. What's er . . . what's *wrong* with them, then?
Ronald	They're the wrong shape and they're just awful.
Mrs Heath	I'm afraid he gets everything cooked the way he likes it at home.
Basil	Ah, does he, does he?
Ronald	Yes I do, and it's better than this pig's garbage.
Mrs Heath	*(slightly amused)* Now, Ronald.
Ronald	These eggs look like you just laid them.
Mrs Heath	*(ineffectually)* Ronald . . .
Mr Heath	*(to Ronald, friendlily)* Now look here, old chap . . .
Mrs Heath	Shut up!! Leave him alone! *(to Basil)* He's very clever, rather highly strung.
Basil	Yes, yes, he should be.
Ronald	Haven't you got any **proper** chips?
Basil	Well these **are** proper French Fried Potatoes. You see, the chef is Continental.
Ronald	Couldn't you get an English one?
Mrs Heath	*(to Ronald)* Why don't you eat just one or two, dear?
Ronald	They're the wrong shape.
Basil	Oh dear – what shape do you usually have? Mickey Mouse shape? Smarties shape? Amphibious landing craft shape? Poke in the eye shape?
Ronald	. . . God, you're **dumb**.
Mrs Heath	Oh, now . . .

Basil	*(controlling himself)* Is there something we can get you instead, **Sonny?**
Ronald	I'd like some bread and salad cream.
Basil	. . . To **eat?** Well . . . *(pointing)* there's the bread, and there's the mayonnaise.
Ronald	I said **salad cream**, stupid.
Basil	We don't have any salad cream. The chef made **this** *(indicating the mayonnaise)* freshly this morning.
Ronald	What a dump!
Mr Heath	*(offering Ronald the mayonnaise)* This is very good.
Mrs Heath	*(coldly)* He likes salad cream.
Ronald	*(to Basil)* That's puke, that is.
Basil	Well, at least it's fresh puke.
Mrs Heath	*(shocked)* Oh dear!!
Basil	*(indignantly)* Well, **he** said it!
Mrs Heath	*(loftily)* May I ask why you don't have proper salad cream. I mean, most restaurants . . .
Basil	Well, the chef only buys it on special occasions, you know, gourmet nights and so on, but . . . when he's got a bottle – ah! – he's a genius with it. He can unscrew the cap like Robert Carrier. It's a treat to watch him. *(he mimes)* And then . . . **right** on the plate! None on the walls! Magic! He's a wizard with a tin-opener, too. He got a Pulitzer Prize for that. He can have the stuff in the saucepan before you can say *haute cuisine*. You name it, he'll heat it up and scrape it off the pan for you. Mind you, skill like that isn't picked up overnight. Still, I'll tell him to get some salad cream, you never know when Henry Kissinger is going to drop in, do you. *(Mrs Heath is silenced; Basil smiles charmingly, looks at his watch and in so doing neatly elbows Ronald in the head)* Sorry, sorry! *(he moves off)*
Mr Heath	Nice man.

Meanwhile, Sybil and André are deep in conversation.

André	No, no, seriously, I think it's a very good idea.
Sybil	You do, really?
André	I promise you, people round here are getting more and more keen on good food.
Basil	*(coming back and sitting down)* Well, so much for tonight's guests. Ignorant rabble.
André	Oh, there's always a few, Mr Fawlty.

Basil	Well, not on Gourmet Night there won't be. *(slightly too loudly)* None of those proles.
Sybil	Basil!
Basil	Well!
Sybil	André thinks Thursday nights would be best.
Basil	Thursdays?
André	I think so.
Basil	Right. And on the other nights we'll just have a big trough of baked beans and garnish it with a couple of dead dogs.
Sybil	Well, that's settled then.
André	Good. And I'm very pleased for Kurt too. It will be good for him to have something special to do . . . I'd like to have a word with him, do you mind?
Sybil	No, of course not.

André rises and goes towards the kitchen.

Basil	Right, well, I'll get the menus printed on Monday.
Sybil	Polly can do the menus.
Basil	No she can't.
Sybil	Yes she can.
Basil	No she can't.
Sybil	Yes she can.
Basil	No she can't.
Sybil	Yes she can . . . she **can**! You can write the advertisement in the *Echo*, only don't make it too toffee-nosed, Basil – we don't want to put people off.
Basil	I just want to keep the riff-raff away, dear.

Meanwhile in the kitchen, André and Kurt are talking; Manuel is busying himself.

André	Well, good luck, my old friend. It's good to have you down here.
Kurt	Thank you for . . . well, you know.
André	Don't mention it . . . nice to have met you, Manuel.
Kurt	*(putting an arm round Manuel)* He's my friend.
Manuel	One night I cook you both paella.

They both laugh. André turns to leave.

André	And, Kurt . . . *(waves an admonishing finger)*
Kurt	. . . You don't trust me?

André	Ciao. *(goes back into the dining room)*
Kurt	*(grandiloquently)* Manuel! Together, you and I make Fawlty Towers famous for its cooking!
Manuel	*Qué?*
Kurt	Excellent . . . tip-top . . . *famosos* . . . oh, you are so cute! *(He kisses Manuel's forehead.)*

In the dining room; it is Gourmet Night. A hand-painted Polly-style menu proclaims 'Gourmet Night at Fawlty Towers'. Basil is adjusting cutlery on one of the tables. He picks up a spoon and looks at it.

Basil	Manuel! *(Manuel takes the spoon, breathes heavily on it, wipes it on his napkin and replaces it; Basil picks it up and gives it to him again)* Get a **clean** one.
Manuel	Is clean now.
Basil	*(wiping the spoon on Manuel's hair)* Is dirty now.

Manuel runs off with it. The phone at reception is heard to ring. Basil studies the menu with disapproval.

Polly	*(coming in)* Do you like the menu, Mr Fawlty?
Basil	No I don't.
Polly	Oh good.
Basil	. . . What?
Polly	Thank you. Thank you so much.

She exits, passing Manuel who comes in with a new spoon. He goes to put it down on the table.

Basil	Give it to me, give it to me . . . thank you.

Basil puts the spoon in place. They both look at it. Basil re-adjusts it. Cautiously, Manuel reaches out towards it; Basil smacks his hand.

Sybil	*(coming in from the lobby)* Well, Basil, guess who's just called to cancel at twelve minutes past seven?
Basil	Who?
Sybil	The Coosters.
Basil	What!? All **four**?
Sybil	Marvellous, isn't it.
Basil	Aagh! What did they say?
Sybil	One of them's ill.
Basil	Well, let's hope it's nothing trivial.

Sybil	You realize there are **four people** at our grand opening dinner?
Basil	Never mind! Never mind!
Sybil	Never **mind**? There's four people, Basil. Shall we feed them in the kitchen?
Basil	But think who they **are** . . . Colonel and Mrs Hall, **both** JPs, and Lionel Twitchen, one of Torquay's leading Rotarians.
Sybil	That'll put us on the map.
Basil	He's this year's treasurer, dear.
Sybil	I should never have let you write that advert. Fancy putting 'No riff-raff'. *(exits)*
Basil	*(calling after her)* When you're presenting *haute cuisine*, you don't want the working class sticking its nose in it. *(he looks into the kitchen, where Polly is preparing some food)* Everything all right? Where's Kurt?
Polly	He and Manuel are getting the wine from the cellar.

Basil goes back into the dining room, looks round proudly and rubs his hands together.

Basil	Right . . . this is what it's all about. *(Misses Tibbs and Gatsby peer in from the lobby)* You two! You're supposed to be in your rooms.
Miss Gatsby	Oh!
Basil	You're not allowed down here tonight, remember?
Miss Gatsby	Ooh, doesn't it look pretty.
Miss Tibbs	What are you cooking?
Basil	I'll send up a menu with your bread and cheese. Now get out. *(he shoos them out)*
Sybil	*(appearing from the lobby)* They're here.
Basil	What?
Sybil	The Halls are here! *(she hurries off)*
Miss Gatsby & Miss Tibbs	The Halls!
Basil	. . . Go to your rooms!

They bustle off. Basil takes a deep breath and straightens his tie.

Manuel	*(running in from the kitchen)* Mr Fawlty . . . Mr Fawlty . . . I very upset.
Basil	Not now, Manuel. Later. *(he exits, leaving Manuel flapping)*

In the bar, the Halls are talking to Sybil. Mrs Hall is extremely small. The Colonel has a commanding manner and a head twitch.

Colonel Hall	When I went for my jog this morning, I thought it was going to be pretty warm *(he twitches)* . . . but in the event it turned out to be pretty cool really, and then it started to cloud up this afternoon, quite contrary to the weather forecast, naturally *(he twitches)* . . . and I shouldn't be a bit surprised if we got a spot of rain tonight.
Sybil	Still, it's been a lovely summer, hasn't it?
Basil	*(striding in)* Ah, Colonel! How delightful to see you again.
Colonel Hall	. . . Sorry?
Basil	How delightful to see you again. We met last year at the Golf Club dinner dance, you may remember?
Colonel Hall	No I don't.
Basil	Ah, sorry, well, we didn't talk for long, just good evening really, a blink of the eye and you'd have missed it. As indeed you did. Quite understandably. *(the Colonel twitches; Basil stares, puzzled)* Sorry?
Colonel Hall	. . . What?

Sybil nudges Basil.

Basil	Well . . . how is that lovely daughter of yours?
Sybil	*(quietly)* She's dead.
Basil	*(examining the Colonel's lapel keenly)* I like your suit. Isn't it super. The way those stripes go up and down, really super. How much did that cost, then?
Colonel Hall	*(irritated)* Who **are** you? *(Basil stares at him blankly)* . . . I mean, I don't know your name!

There is a pause.

Basil	*(to Sybil, under his breath)* What is it?
Sybil	What?
Basil	*(in a frenzied whisper)* My **name**.
Sybil	*(calmly)* This is my husband. Basil Fawlty.
Basil	That's it!!
Colonel Hall	**What?**
Basil	How do you do.
Colonel Hall	How do you do. *(Basil offers his hand; the Colonel shakes it and twitches)*

Basil	May I introduce my wife?
Colonel Hall	**She** just introduced **you**!
Basil	Oh, what a coincidence!
Colonel Hall	Yes. I don't believe you know my wife . . .

But the diminutive Mrs Hall is standing behind the Colonel and neither Basil nor Sybil can see her.

Basil	*(to Sybil)* Dead? *(Sybil nods)*
Colonel Hall	May I introduce Mrs Hall?

Basil and Sybil look round, puzzled, then spot Mrs Hall. She and they peer round the Colonel and smile at each other.

Basil	Oh, sorry! Didn't see you down there. Don't get up. *(Sybil nudges him; he takes a closer look at Mrs Hall)*

Sybil	What would you like to drink, Mrs Small? **Hall!**
Basil	Yes, a short, or . . . oh!
Sybil	A sherry . . . how about a sherry?
Mrs Hall	A sherry – lovely.
Basil	Oh good. Large, or . . . or . . . **not** quite so large?
Colonel Hall	Two, small and dry.
Basil	Oh . . . I wouldn't say that.
Colonel Hall	What?
Basil	I don't know . . .
Colonel Hall	*(irritably)* Two small, dry sherries.
Basil	Oh, I see what you mean! Sorry!

The Colonel twitches. The bell at reception sounds. Basil bows and withdraws.

In the lobby, Mr and Mrs Twitchen are waiting by reception. Basil sails up.

Basil	Ah, Mr and Mrs Twitchen, good evening . . . welcome to Fawlty Towers.
Mr Twitchen	Good evening.
Basil	*(sveltely)* How very *au fait* of you to come to our little culinary *soirée* this evening.
Mr Twitchen	Only too glad to support something new in Torquay.
Mrs Twitchen	Such an unusual idea. I do hope it works out.
Basil	Well, we have our hopes.

Polly appears from the kitchen. She looks rather agitated.

Polly	Mr Fawlty!

Basil	Ah, Polly! Would you take Mrs Twitchen's coat, please?
Polly	Yes, of course. *(she starts helping Mrs Twitchen out of her coat)*
Basil	*(with a courtly gesture towards the bar)* Thank you so much . . . would you care . . . ?
Polly	Mr Fawlty?
Basil	Yes?
Polly	Can I have a word with you?
Basil	Yes. *(to the Twitchens)* This is Polly. She will be serving you later this evening.
Polly	Er . . .
Basil	Well?
Polly	It's Kurt.
Basil	Yes?
Polly	He's potted . . . the shrimps.
Basil	What?
Polly	He's **potted** . . . the shrimps.
Basil	. . . Shrimps? We're not having shrimps tonight, Polly.

The Twitchens look at her rather oddly. Basil indicates the bar and they start to move towards it.

Polly	*(tapping Basil's arm)* He's **soused** . . . the herrings.
Basil	What are you on about?!
Polly	*(slowly)* He's **pickled** . . . the onions and he's **smashed** the eggs **in his cups** . . . **under the table**. *(she rolls her eyes strangely)*
Basil	*(to the Twitchens)* Excuse me. *(to Polly)* Have you been drinking?
Polly	No, not **me**!
Basil	*(hissing)* Well, will you behave yourself. *(to the Twitchens)* I'm sorry to have kept you waiting. Would you care . . . *(to Polly, who is still trying to detain him)* Stop that and pull yourself together!

As they move off into the bar Polly pecks at his sleeve imploringly. He turns sharply and makes as if to hit her; she gives a little yelp and jumps back. The Twitchens have seen this; he covers by pretending to flick a piece of fluff from his sleeve.

Basil	Now, may I offer you a little aperitif, while you make up your mind what you would like for dinner?

They move off towards the bar and this time Polly lets them go.

Mr Twitchen	That's very kind of you . . . Lotte?
Mrs Twitchen	Tomato juice, please.
Basil	Mr Twitchen?
Mr Twitchen	Yes, tomato juice for me, thank you.

They enter the bar. Basil hastens to make the introductions.

Basil	Ah, good . . . oh, Colonel . . . Colonel and Mrs Hall, may I introduce Mr and Mrs Tw— *(the Colonel twitches; Basil exercises tact and suppresses the name)* Have you met?
Colonel Hall	No, we haven't.
Basil	*(to Mr Twitchen)* Have you?
Mr Twitchen	No.
Basil	Oh, good. Well what would you like to drink, then?
Mrs Hall	What?
Basil	To drink?
Mrs Hall	I didn't catch the name.
Basil	Oh, you didn't catch it? What a rotten bit of luck!
Colonel Hall	Well?
Basil	Fine, thanks, and you?
Colonel Hall	No, we **still** don't know the **name**.
Basil	Fawlty. Basil Fawlty.
Colonel Hall	No, no . . . **theirs**.
Basil	Oh, **theirs**! I'm so sorry, I thought you meant mine. My, it's quite warm, isn't it. I could do with a drink too. Another sherry?
Colonel Hall	Well, aren't you going to introduce us?
Basil	Didn't I?
Colonel Hall	No!
Basil	Oh, sorry! This is Mr and Mrs . . . *(mumbles)*
Colonel Hall	What?!!!
Basil	. . . Mr and Mrs . . . *(he lets out a little cry and faints backwards; he lies still for a couple of seconds, opens his eyes and looks up)* Sorry! I fainted. *(gets up)* Ah, I feel better for that. Now, I'll get your tomato juices. *(he heads for the bar)*
Mr Twitchen	*(to the Halls)* The name's Twitchen, actually.
Colonel Hall	Hall. How do you do. Would you care to join us?

They all sit down at the Halls' table. Sybil comes up with drinks and the Gourmet Night menus.

Sybil Would you like to see the menus?

Basil is at the bar recovering and pouring out more sherries. He drinks one. Polly appears at his elbow.

Basil Yes? What is it?
Polly Please put the bottle down.
Basil What do you **want?**
Polly Please put the **bottle** down.
Basil What **is** it?
Polly Kurt is drunk.

Basil stays calm but drops the bottle. It smashes. The guests jump.

Basil *(calling)* Sorry! *(to Polly)* Drunk?!
Polly Almost unconscious.
Basil Right. *(he makes a supreme effort of self control; he fails)* Aaaagh!!! *(to guests)* Sorry!! Sorry!! *(to Polly)* How?
Polly I don't know. It happened so quickly. He had a row with Manuel.
Basil Manuel?
Polly . . . He's got a crush on him.
Basil A **what?**
Polly A crush . . . you know . . . in love.

A pause. Then, in despair, Basil hits the bar counter with his fist. Unfortunately, he catches a light metal tray, which spins in the air and lands loudly. The guests jump a lot.

Basil *(to the guests)* Sorry!! Sorry! Excuse me just one moment . . . I won't be a moment. *(he steams into the lobby, pursued by Polly)* I knew I should never have hired a Frenchman.
Polly He's Greek, Mr Fawlty.
Basil Greek?
Polly Of course.
Basil Well, that's even worse. I mean, they invented it. *(he opens the kitchen door; Kurt is standing very unsteadily against the wall with a bottle in his hand; Basil approaches him calmly but with great authority)* Right. Give that to me, Kurt. Come on, give me the bottle.

Kurt	*(mumbles and holds the bottle away from Basil)* No. Go away. Leave me alone.
Basil	*(patiently)* Come on, give it to me. *(he reaches for the bottle but Kurt resists)*
Kurt	Manuel! *(he pushes Basil, who staggers into the dining room)*
Basil	*(striding back in)* Now come on, Kurt . . .
Kurt	Manuel. He doesn't love me!
Basil	Well, you have to give these things time.
Kurt	I want Manuel!
Basil	Well, I'm sure we can arrange something. Now can I have the bottle?
Kurt	Oh, he's so sweet.
Basil	Yes, he is sweet, I know, yes.
Kurt	He's wonderful.
Basil	Yes, yes, I know. *(he grabs at the bottle; they struggle; Basil falls backwards, getting his head in a plate of salmon mousse; he pushes Kurt, who staggers back and collapses; Basil slaps his face)* Kurt! Come on, Kurt! *(to Polly)* Get me some black coffee, quick.
Polly	He can't drink it. He's out.
Basil	No he isn't, he's only drunk half a bottle. Come on, Kurt, come on . . .

Polly takes two more empties from the sink and shows him; he starts strangling Kurt. Polly tries to restrain him.

Manuel	*(from behind the dining-room doors)* Now listen to me, Kurty! I come in here but no cuddle. You hear me? *No cuddle.*
Basil	*(leaves off strangling Kurt, grabs Manuel and drags him in)* Look what you've done!
Manuel	*(recoiling)* Dead?!
Basil	To the world.
Polly	He's only drunk, Manuel.
Basil	*(to Manuel)* This is your fault.
Manuel	*Qué?*
Basil	You only had to be civil to him.
Manuel	Seville?
Basil	*Nice!*
Manuel	You no understand – is not enough. He want **kiss** me.
Basil	Oh, what's one little kiss! . . .
Polly	Mr Fawlty!! Call André – he can do the cooking!

Basil	... André?! He's **open** tonight! He's open on a Thursday, you cloth-eared bint.
Polly	But he could do it there and you can pick it up in the car!
Basil	*(pauses to take this in.)* Oh! Brilliant! *(kisses her forehead)* Brilliant! *(grabs Manuel with similar intent, then recoils)* Yech! ... Right! *(runs to the door)*
Mrs Twitchen	... I **can't** resist the lobster.
Colonel Hall	No, tournedos for me, every time.
Sybil	Would you like another drink?
Colonel Hall	No, I don't think we will – we're nearly ready to order.
Sybil	I'll be back in a moment. *(she looks round for Basil)*

In the lobby, Basil is on the phone in a high state of excitement.

Basil	You can't do lobster, no, right, **right** ... but André, the **tournedos?** ... Yes, I'm sorry, I'm **sorry** ... I'm sorry ...
Sybil	*(enters from the bar)* Basil!
Basil	Yes of course I want the duck. Yes, that's marvellous, but can you do one or two sauces? Wonderful! That's it! Thank you, thank you, André. *(puts the phone down)*
Sybil	Why are you talking to André?
Basil	What is it, what is it?!
Sybil	They're ready to order, Basil.
Basil	*(inserting a sheet of paper into the typewriter)* Well, stall them, stall them!
Sybil	What!?
Basil	Stall them!! Stall them, you stupid woman!! Tell them some lie. *(starts typing furiously with two fingers; one is off form)*
Sybil	*(firmly)* What is going on?
Basil	Ssssh!!
Sybil	Will you just tell me what you're doing?
Basil	*(wrestling with jammed keys)* We've got to change the menu.
Sybil	Why? ... Why? ... Why!!!???
Basil	*(frantically)* Listen, he's in there, he's out, flat out, so André's ...
Sybil	Who is?
Basil	... What?
Sybil	Who is out?

Basil	Kurt! Who d'you think, Henry Kissinger? *(attacks the typewriter again)*
Sybil	What do you mean, 'out'?
Basil	He's drunk.
Sybil	. . . Drunk?
Basil	Soused! Potted! I mean drunk! Got it?
Sybil	*(stunned)* . . . I don't believe it.
Basil	Neither do I. Perhaps it's a dream. *(he bangs his head hard on the desk; nothing happens)* No, it's not a dream, we're stuck with it. *(he pulls the sheet out of the typewriter)* André's doing the cooking and I'll collect it in the car.
Sybil	What's he cooking?
Basil	Duck.
Sybil	. . . Duck?
Basil	**Duck!**
Sybil	. . . **Duck!?**
Basil	You know . . . **duck??!** *(he runs around flapping his arms up and down and quacking)*

In the bar; Basil enters, still quacking, attracting some attention. He slips effortlessly into his smarmiest 'Mine Host' persona.

Basil	I'm so sorry to have kept you waiting.
Colonel Hall	Well, we'd like to order now . . .
Basil	Yes, quite . . . er . . .
Colonel Hall	My wife would like the lobster as her main . . .
Basil	Ah, yes! Er, excuse me . . .
Colonel Hall	Yes?
Basil	There is one small thing . . . I'm afraid you were given the wrong menus. This is tonight's menu.
Colonel Hall	What?
Basil	*(collecting the originals)* Er, yes, I'm afraid the chef changed his mind and forgot to tell us. He's like that, brilliant but temperamental.
Colonel Hall	What, he's changed everything?
Basil	I'm afraid so. Yes, it wasn't good enough, so he just chucked it away. He's such a perfectionist.
Mrs Twitchen	The lobster?
Basil	Lobster, tournedos, you name it, it's in the bin.
Mr Twitchen	How extraordinary.
Basil	Yes. Lucky old bin, I say! So **this** is your new menu.

Colonel Hall	Duck with orange . . . duck with cherries . . . duck surprise?
Mrs Twitchen	What's duck surprise?
Basil	Ah . . . that's duck without orange or cherries.
Colonel Hall	*(beginning to bristle)* I mean, is this all there is, **duck?**
Basil	*(peers at the menu to check)* Um . . . Ye-es . . . Done, of course, the three *extremely* different ways.
Colonel Hall	Well, what do you do if you don't like duck?
Basil	Well, if you don't like duck . . . er . . . *(humorously)* you're rather stuck. *(he laughs non-infectiously)*
Mrs Hall	Well, fortunately I love it!
Basil	Oh good! So . . . that's four ducks, is it?

In the kitchen, Sybil is kneeling by Kurt's side, looking for signs of life. Polly comes up.

Sybil	You were right. Now, he's getting this duck from André . . .
Polly	Yes, but I don't know what vegetables he's put on.
Sybil	Well, let's find out, at least we can do those.
Basil	*(running in, followed by Manuel)* Three salmon mousses, Polly. And one mullet with mustard sauce, for Mrs Hall. Right . . . where is the mullet?
Polly	There!

Polly points and starts preparing the mousse. Basil hurries to a dish containing some mullet, takes a couple out and puts them on a plate. The atmosphere is urgent but co-operative.

Sybil	What are you doing about vegetables, Basil?
Basil	Same. Same as on the other menu, dear.
Sybil	André's not doing any?
Basil	No, no, you do them, you and Polly . . . mustard sauce, mustard sauce . . . *(he pours mustard sauce onto the mullet and picks up the plate)* Right now, while I'm out in the car, you get them ready, right? Ready, Polly?
Polly	Ready.
Basil	Manuel! *(Manuel takes the mullet; Basil indicates the mousse)* Right, two of those for table nine, and one of these, and this, for table four. Come on.

In the dining room, the Halls and the Twitchens are just sitting down. Polly goes to the Twitchens' table with the mousses, and Manuel to the Halls' with the mullet and the mousse. He puts them down the wrong way round.

Basil	No, no, the other way round.
Manuel	*Qué?*
Basil	The other – way – round.
Manuel	Ah! *(to the Halls)* Please. *(he indicates that they should change places)* Please to change.
Basil	No, no, the **plates**!
Manuel	*Qué?*
Basil	The plates! **Change** the plates!
Manuel	. . . Oh, **dirty**! I change. *(he picks up the plates and heads for the kitchen)*
Basil	*(intercepting him)* No, no, come here. Look . . .

He takes the plates from Manuel and demonstrates. Manuel takes them with crossed arms, uncrosses them and puts them down exactly as before. Basil pulls Manuel away from the table and whispers to him. The Halls change their plates round themselves. Manuel returns from his briefing and changes them back.

Manuel	Sorry, sorry, is wrong.

Basil sees the plates and slaps Manuel. While he is doing this the Halls change the plates round again.

Basil	*(to the Halls)* I'm so sorry. He's from Barcelona. *(he changes the plates over with an air of finality; to Manuel)* I don't know what he sees in you!

The Halls look at each other, then, without a word, get up and change places. Both Basil and Manuel jump.

Mrs Hall	Do you think we could have a drink, dear?
Colonel Hall	May I see the wine list please, Fawlty?
Basil	Certainly, Major . . . **Colonel**! *(he hurries to the sideboard; Mr Twitchen is removing a long black hair from his mouth and peering into his mousse suspiciously)* Everything all right?
Mr Twitchen	*(doubtfully)* Er, yes . . .
Basil	*(leaning forward)* Oh good . . . Mrs Twitchen?

Mr Twitchen catches a glimpse of Basil's scalp. He stares at it.

Mrs Twitchen	Yes, yes, it's fine, thank you Mr Fawlty.

Basil	Oh good. *(he moves off)*
Mr Twitchen	*(nudging his wife)* He's got it in his hair!

Basil arrives back at the Halls' table. Mrs Hall is about to take her first mouthful. The Colonel has just done so.

Mrs Hall	How is it, dear?
Colonel Hall	Rather good, surprisingly.

Mrs Hall takes a mouthful of mullet.

Basil	There's the list, Colonel.
Colonel Hall	Thank you very much.
Mrs Hall	*(lets out a shrill cry)* Ugh! *(Basil freezes)*
Colonel Hall	What's the matter, Petal? What's the matter?
Mrs Hall	Ugggh!
Basil	*(cheerfully)* Is everything all right?
Mrs Hall	I think I'm going to be sick!
Basil	It is an unusual taste, isn't it?
Mrs Hall	It's not cooked, you ignoramus!
Colonel Hall	Look! What are you trying to do to us? *(to Mrs Hall)* Do you mean that's **raw**?
Basil	Would you prefer a **cooked** one?
Colonel Hall	Of course she'd prefer it cooked!
Basil	Certainly. *(he whisks the plate away)* I'll get you a cooked one, then – it'll be even nicer.
Mrs Hall	No! No!

In the kitchen, Sybil is working at the vegetables with Polly. Manuel is with Kurt who is propped up against the wall. Basil rushes in.

Basil	It's raw. This mullet is raw! I mean, what do we do to it? *(they look blankly at him; he runs over to Kurt)* Kurt! Kurt, listen . . . **what do we do to this**? *(Kurt groans quietly)* Do we grill it? . . . *(Kurt opens his eyes, stares at the mullet and groans)* If we grill it, just go 'uh-huh'. *(Kurt shakes his head slightly)* All right! Do we **fry** it? Just go 'uh-huh'. *(Kurt rolls his eyes and throws up over the plate; Basil addresses the others)* . . . Going well, isn't it.
Sybil	Basil, will you just get out. I will deal with the fish. Just go and get the duck. *(she ushers him out)*
Basil	*(not unwillingly)* Right. Right. Oh! **Wine**!
Sybil	What?
Basil	The Colonel wants some wine. I'll just . . . *(takes a pace*

towards the dining room then checks himself) No, **you** go,
Polly. He won't hit a woman. *(dashes for the front door)*

*In the dining room. Polly enters and approaches the Colonel,
who is peering closely at his mousse.*

Polly	*(tentatively)* Have you . . . have you chosen yet, Major . . . **Colonel?**
Colonel Hall	Mmm?
Polly	Have you chosen your wine?
Colonel Hall	Oh yes, Chablis, please.
Polly	*(picking up the wine list)* Thank you.
Colonel Hall	Waitress!
Polly	. . . Yes?
Colonel Hall	*(heavily)* There's a **hair** in my mousse.
Polly	. . . Well, don't talk too loud or everybody will want one.
Colonel Hall	**What!!!!**
Polly	Sorry. *(she snatches the mousse and hurries away with it; the Colonel twitches)*

*Basil meanwhile is driving furiously, muttering at other
motorists.*

Basil	. . . Oh, get out of the way . . . get out!

*Back in the dining room, Polly hastens in with some more
mousse. She puts it down in front of the Colonel.*

Polly	*(charmingly)* I'm sorry about that. *(to Mrs Hall)* The mullet's on its way.

*Basil meanwhile draws up outside André's restaurant and
races into the kitchen. André has the duck ready on a serving
dish.*

André	Ah, Mr Fawlty . . . there you are . . . a beautiful duck for you . . . it will be – mmm – delicious. There you are, don't forget the sauces.
Basil	Oh, marvellous . . .
André	I hope all goes very well for you . . . good luck.

*He puts a cover over the duck and hands it to Basil, together
with the sauces. Basil runs out to the car, jumps in and tries to
start it. It won't.*

Basil	Come on!

Back in the dining room. Manuel is standing attentively as the Colonel tastes his wine. The Colonel nods and twitches.

Manuel   What, no good?
Colonel Hall No, no, it's very good.

Manuel puts some more wine in the Colonel's glass. The Colonel sips from it. Manuel tops it up again immediately; the Colonel jumps, spilling some. Manuel tops it up again.

In the forecourt, Basil drives up. Polly, waiting at the main door, sees the car and runs inside. Basil leaps out of the car with the duck and runs into the hotel.

Basil   *(running into the kitchen)* Here it is, Polly.

Sybil starts dealing with the sauces. Basil peers at the duck. It looks fine.

Basil   Right, I'll carve it on the trolley. **Well done** everybody! Manuel, get the trolley ready. Right, let's go . . .

Manuel runs through the swing doors to the dining room.

Sybil   *(waving a sauce dish at Basil)* Basil!

He stops and turns. The door swings back and knocks the duck out of his hands.

Basil   Oh my God! Look what you've done, you stupid great tart!
Polly   Wait a minute . . . I think it'll be all right.
Basil   . . . What? *(he kneels and peers at the duck; it is intact!)* Yes! You're right!

Joyfully he reaches for it. The swing door opens and catches him a fearful blow on the head. Manuel enters, treads in the duck and walks several paces with it on his foot. Basil howls, springs at Manuel and tries to get the shoe out of the duck. The duck comes off; but the poor thing is terribly injured.

Basil   Look! Look at it! I mean, look at that!
Sybil   Can I help?
Basil   Yes! Go and kill yourself! No!!! Call André first! Tell him we need another one. *(he throws the duck at the unconscious Kurt; to Polly)* Go and talk to them!

Polly	What?
Basil	Entertain them or something!

In the lobby, Sybil is on the phone.

Sybil Oh, André, it's Sybil Fawlty . . . Well, I'm afraid it got trodden on . . .

In the forecourt, Basil jumps into the car and drives off. In the dining room Manuel is twanging the guitar and emitting strange Spanish sounds to the puzzled guests. Basil meanwhile rockets up to André's restaurant. He bursts into the kitchen; André puts a fresh duck onto a serving tray and covers it. Basil is about to pick it up when André distracts him by offering him some fresh sauces. As he is looking away, a waiter comes in, puts down a similar serving dish with cover, and takes Basil's duck away. Basil declines the sauces, turns and picks up the serving dish. He hurries out, vaults into the car and presses the starter. It whinges.

Basil Come on. Come **on!**

In the dining room Manuel has finished his song. Polly applauds enthusiastically; the guests applaud without enthusiasm. There is a pause, then Polly launches into her act.

Polly *(singing)* I'm just a girl who can't say 'No' . . . I'm in a terrible fix . . .

Basil meanwhile has turned into a narrow road. It is blocked by a parked van. He curses, sounds his horn, waits, gives up, reverses back and stalls. He tries to start the car again. This time it refuses completely. He becomes more frantic.

Basil Come on, start, will you!? Start, you vicious bastard!! Come on! Oh my God! I'm warning you – if you don't start . . . *(screams with rage)* I'll count to three. *(he presses the starter, without success)* One . . . two . . . three . . . !! Right! That's it! *(he jumps out of the car and addresses it)* You've tried it on just once too often! Right! Well, don't say I haven't warned you! I've laid it on the line to you time and time again! Right! Well . . . this is it! I'm going to give you a damn good thrashing! *(he rushes*

*off and comes back with a large branch; he beats the car
without mercy)*

Back in the dining room, Polly is ending her performance.

Polly   . . . I can't be prissy and quaint . . . How can I be what I
                  ain't . . . I can't . . . say . . . 'No'! *(Manuel applauds loudly)*
Colonel Hall *(loudly)* Any sign of the duck?
Polly   Er . . . it's just coming.

*Basil meanwhile is running up the forecourt. Back in the
dining room, Sybil is the next on.*

Sybil   So Uncle Ted comes in with this crate of brown ale, ha
                  ha ha . . . and Mother says, 'Oh Ted, look who's here'
                  . . . and he says, ha ha ha . . .

*Basil comes flying into the kitchen, slides to a halt, and sees
Polly, who has the vegetables ready.*

Basil   OK, Polly?!
Polly   OK!
Basil   Got the sauces?
Polly   Got them!
Basil   Right.

*He enters the dining room in triumph. He places the serving
dish on the trolley and wheels it ceremoniously forward.*

Basil   Ladies and gentlemen!! So sorry to have kept you
                  waiting.

*He sharpens his knife with panache. Then he lifts the cover
and beams at the guests. Looking down, he sees, not a duck,
but a large ornate pink trifle. He regards it approvingly, then
does a double-take and slams the cover down. He lifts it a
little and peers disbelievingly beneath. He takes the cover off
and looks round the room for the escaped duck. He fails to see
it. Clutching at straws, he looks on the lower shelf of the
trolley. Finally he plunges both hands into the trifle and
ransacks it. Unfortunately it does not conceal a duck. He turns
to his guests and smiles brightly.*

Basil   Well, er . . . who's for trifle?
Colonel Hall What?

Basil   Trifle for you, Mrs Hall?
Colonel Hall   *(dangerously)* What about the duck, Fawlty?
Basil   . . . Duck's off. Sorry.

The Germans

Sixth of first series, first broadcast on 24 October 1975, BBC2.

Basil Fawlty   John Cleese
Sybil Fawlty   Prunella Scales
Sister   Brenda Collins
Doctor   Louis Mahoney
Major Gowen   Ballard Berkeley
Polly   Connie Booth
Manuel   Andrew Sachs
Mr Sharp   John Lawrence
Mrs Sharp   Iris Fry
Miss Tibbs   Gilly Flower
Miss Gatsby   Renée Roberts
Large woman   Claire Davenport
German guests   Nick Lane
　　　　　　　　　Lisa Bergmayr
　　　　　　　　　Willy Bowman
　　　　　　　　　Dan Gillan

A private room in a hospital. Sybil is sitting up in bed, eating chocolates. Basil is visiting.

Basil	So you're sure you'll be all right?
Sybil	What, Basil?
Basil	I said, you're sure you'll be all right?
Sybil	Will you get my bed jacket?
Basil	Er . . . bed jacket *(he gets up and fumbles in the drawer beside the bed)*
Sybil	In the drawer, the blue one, in the **drawer**.

Basil crosses the room to the chest of drawers, sighing a little.

Sybil	Now, you won't forget the fire drill tomorrow, will you?
Basil	No, I won't, dear, no, I **can** cope, you know . . . This one? *(holding up a pink bed jacket)*
Sybil	That's not blue.
Basil	Well . . . it's got blue things on it.
Sybil	They're flowers, and I didn't ask you for the one with the flowers, did I?
Basil	No, you didn't, quite right. I only picked that one up to annoy you, actually. I mean, what have you got all this stuff **for**?
Sybil	What?
Basil	I mean, you're only here for three days. Are you going to play charades every night? *(holding up a bright blue bed jacket)* This one?
Sybil	Is it blue?
Basil	It's blue-ish, I suppose.
Sybil	Now, you will remember to collect the stuff from Thomas's, won't you.
Basil	Yes, I will.
Sybil	Oh, and I forgot to scrape the mould off the cheddar this morning, so remind Chef.
Basil	Right.
Sybil	And **do** try and find time to put the moose's head up. *(Basil sighs)* It's been sitting there for **two weeks**, Basil.
Basil	Yes, yes, yes.
Sybil	I don't know why you bought it.
Basil	It will lend the lobby a certain ambience, Sybil. It has a touch of style about it.
Sybil	It's got a touch of **mange** about it.
Basil	That is not so.

Sybil	It's got things **living** in it, Basil – it's nasty.
Basil	It is not nasty, it is superb.
Sybil	I'm not going to argue with you, Basil, just get it up out of the way, I don't want to snag any more cardies on it. And will you get me my telephone book, please?
Basil	*(gets up and prowls about looking for the book)* I mean, it's not as though I don't have enough to do. I mean, I'm on my own, the Germans are arriving tomorrow . . .
Sybil	Not till lunchtime. You could do it in the morning.
Basil	I've got the **fire drill** in the morning!
Sybil	Well, that only takes ten minutes. . . . In the **bag**.
Basil	*(peering around for a bag)* I thought slavery had been abolished.
Sybil	Don't you ever think about **anyone** but yourself?
Basil	Oh . . .
Sybil	In the **bag**. *(she points it out to him – it is on the bed)*
Basil	Oh yes, in the bag. You let me do it. You just lie there with your feet up and I'll go and carry you up another hundredweight of lime creams . . . *(he hands her the book)*
Sybil	I'm actually about to undergo an operation, Basil.
Basil	Oh yes, how **is** the old toe-nail? Still growing in, hmmmm? Still burrowing its way down into the bone? Still macheting its way through the nerve, eh? Nasty old nail.
Sybil	It's still hurting, if that's what you mean, Basil.
Basil	Well, it'll be out in the morning, poor little devil. I wonder if they'd mount it for me, just for old time's sake?
Sybil	I'm sure it's worth asking. You could hang it on the wall next to the moose. They'd go rather well together.
Basil	Ha, ha, ha.

Sister enters briskly.

Sister	*(to Sybil)* Ah, there you are. *(to Basil)* Come along, out you go.
Basil	*(pointedly peering under the bed)* Oh, were you talking to me? I'm sorry, I thought there was a dog in here.
Sister	Oh no, no dogs in here.
Basil	*(looking at her closely)* I wouldn't bet on it.
Sister	Oh no, not allowed. Now come along, you're in the way.

Basil	Fawlty's the name, **Mr** Fawlty.
Sister	*(to Sybil)* Let's sit you up a bit.
Sybil	*(very sweetly)* Thank you, Sister.
Sister	*(putting a thermometer in Sybil's mouth)* Now, just pop that under your tongue. *(she sees Basil)* You still here?
Basil	Apparently.
Sister	The doctor's coming.
Basil	*(jumps up as if startled)* My God! A doctor – I mean, here, in the hospital? Whatever can we do?
Sister	You can leave!
Basil	Why **do** they call you 'Sister'? Is it a term of endearment?

Sybil makes a warning noise – the thermometer prevents her speaking.

Sister	Now look, Mr Fawlty, I'm not going to ask you again.
Basil	Presumably you wouldn't mind if I said goodbye to my wife? She is under the knife tomorrow.
Sister	It's an ingrowing toe-nail!
Basil	Oh, you know, do you? Well, that'll help. *(to Sybil)* Well, take care now, and if you can think of any more things for me to do, don't hesitate to call.

Another warning noise from Sybil.

Sister	Finished?
Basil	Just. Thank you so much.
Sister	Not at all.
Basil	Charmed, I'm sure . . . Ingrowing toe-nail. Right foot. You'll find it on the end of the leg. *(he sweeps out into the corridor, almost colliding with the doctor who is just about to go into the room)*
Doctor	Mr Fawlty?
Basil	Yes?
Doctor	Doctor Fin.
Basil	Oh, how do you do, doctor.
Doctor	You've just seen your wife?
Basil	Yes. Just said goodbye . . . well, *au revoir.*
Doctor	Yes. Well, it's a very simple operation. But it will be quite painful afterwards.
Basil	Will it, will it, oh dear.
Doctor	Just for a time, but please don't worry.
Basil	No, well, I'll try not to. . . . Quite painful?

Doctor	Yes.

The doctor goes into Sybil's room. Basil rubs his hands in satisfaction.

The hotel reception. Major Gowen is in the lobby as Basil struts in and goes behind the desk.

Basil	*(breezily)* Evening, Major.
The Major	Evening, Fawlty. Hampshire won.
Basil	Did it? Oh isn't that good, how splendid!
The Major	Oh, Fawlty, how's . . . um . . . um . . .
Basil	. . . My wife?
The Major	That's it, that's it.
Basil	Fine, absolutely fine. They're taking it out tomorrow morning.
The Major	Is she? Good.
Basil	Not her, the nail. They won't have operated until tomorrow.
The Major	What?
Basil	The nail. They're taking it out tomorrow.
The Major	How did she get a nail in her?
Basil	I thought I told you, Major, she's having her toe-nail out.
The Major	What, just one of them?
Basil	Well, it's an ingrowing one, Major.
The Major	Ah well . . . if it's causing you pain . . . you have it out.
Basil	Exactly. So . . . I'm on my own now, start running this place properly.
The Major	. . . So you're on your own now, are you?
Basil	Apparently.
The Major	Well, she won't be gone for long, will she?
Basil	No, no, no, not unless there's a serious mistake.
The Major	Still . . . you've always got Elsie to help you.
Basil	. . . Who?
The Major	Elsie.
Basil	Well, she . . . er . . . she left a couple of years ago, Major.
The Major	Funny – I thought I saw her yesterday.
Basil	No, I don't think so – she's in Canada.
The Major	. . . Strange creatures, women.
Basil	Well, can't stand around all day . . .

The Major	I knew one once . . . striking-looking girl . . . tall, you know . . . father was a banker.
Basil	Really.
The Major	Don't remember the name of the bank.
Basil	Never mind.
The Major	. . . I must have been rather keen on her, because I took her to see . . . India!
Basil	**India?**
The Major	At the Oval . . . fine match, marvellous finish . . . now, Surrey had to get thirty-three in about half an hour . . . she went off to powder her . . . powder her hands or something . . . women . . . er . . . never came back.
Basil	What a shame.
The Major	And the strange thing was . . . throughout the morning she kept referring to the Indians as niggers. 'No no no,' I said, 'the niggers are the **West** Indians. These people are wogs.' 'No, no,' she said. '**All** cricketers are niggers.'
Basil	They do get awfully confused, don't they? They're not thinkers. I see it with Sybil every day.
The Major	. . . I do wish I could remember her name. She's still got my wallet.
Basil	As I was saying, no capacity for logical thought.
The Major	Who?
Basil	Women.
The Major	Oh yes, yes . . . I thought you meant Indians.
Basil	No, no, no, no . . . wasn't it Oscar Wilde who said. 'They have minds like Swiss cheese?'
The Major	What do you mean – hard?
Basil	No, no – full of holes.
The Major	Really? . . . Indians?
Basil	No, **women!**
The Major	Oh.

Polly comes in and bends down behind Basil looking for something.

Basil	Yes, can we help you?
Polly	Hello.
Basil	You see. Three years at college and she doesn't know the time of day.
The Major	It's . . . er . . . about two minutes to six.
Basil	*(to Polly)* What are you looking for?

Polly	My German book.
Basil	*(to the Major)* We've got some Germans arriving tomorrow morning, Major, so Polly's brushing up another one of her languages.
The Major	Germans! Coming here?
Basil	Just for a couple of days, Major.
The Major	. . . I don't much care for Germans . . .
Basil	I know what you mean, but . . .
The Major	Bunch of Krauts, that's what they are, all of 'em. Bad eggs!
Basil	Yes, well, forgive and forget, Major . . . God knows how, the bastards. Still, I'd better put the moose up.
The Major	You've got to love 'em, though, I suppose, haven't you?
Basil	. . . Germans?
The Major	No, no – **women!** Hate **Germans** . . . love women.
Polly	*(rising from behind the desk)* What about German women?
The Major	Good card players . . . but mind, I wouldn't give them the time of day . . . *(he wanders off, mumbling)*
Polly	*(showing Basil her phrase book)* Found it.
Basil	I don't know what you're bothering with that for.
Polly	Well, they said some of them don't speak English.
Basil	Well, that's their problem, isn't it. *(Polly exits)* I don't know why she's got to complicate everything. *(he goes into the office and picks the moose up; affectionately)* Got her cardy, did you? Hmmmmm . . .

He comes back into the lobby and climbs with the moose onto a chair by the wall where he intends it to hang. The Major emerges from the bar looking at his watch.

The Major	By jove, it's nearly six o'clock, Fawlty!
Basil	Is it?
The Major	Yes, well, when you're ready I might have a . . . er . . . fruit juice or something.
Basil	I'll open up the moment I've done this, Major.
The Major	No immediate hurry . . . *(potters back into bar)*
Basil	Drunken old sod. *(holds the moose head against the wall and is trying to make a pencil mark when the phone rings)* Polly! . . . Polly!! . . . Manuel!!! *(sighs heavily and gets down, carrying the moose head with him; he puts it on the desk and answers the phone)* Yes, Fawlty Towers, yes, hello? . . . *(it is evidently Sybil)* I was just doing it, you

stupid woman! I just put it down to come here to be reminded by you to do what I'm already doing! I mean, what's the point of reminding me to do what I'm already doing . . . I mean, **what is the bloody point??!** I'm **doing** it, aren't I?! . . . Yes, I picked it up, yes. No, I haven't had a chance yet, I've been at it solidly ever since I got back . . . Yes, I will, yes. No, I haven't yet but I will, yes. I know it is, yes. I'll try and get it cleared up. Anything else? I mean, would you like the hotel moved a bit to the left, or . . . yes, well, enjoy the operation, dear. Let's hope nothing goes wrong. *(puts the phone down)* I wish it was an ingrowing tongue.

Manuel comes in beaming from the kitchen.

Manuel	Yes?
Basil	Oh, it's the Admirable Crichton. Well?
Manuel	You called, sir.
Basil	Last week, but not to worry.
Manuel	*Qué?*
Basil	Oh, Buddah . . . Look, go and get me a hammer.
Manuel	Er . . . *cómo?*
Basil	Hammer.

A pause while Manuel thinks this out.

Manuel	Oh, hammer sandwich.
Basil	Oh, do I have to go through this every time? Look, a **hammer!**
Manuel	My hamster?
Basil	No, not your hamster! How can I knock a nail in with your hamster? Well, I could try – no, it doesn't matter, I'll get it, you come here and tidy, you know, tidy.
Manuel	Tidy, *si*.
Basil	*(striding towards kitchen)* I get hhhammmmmer and hhhit you on the hhhead with it. Hhhard . . .

He vanishes. Manuel stands behind the desk and practises his English.

Manuel	Hhhhammer. How are you, sir? You see, I speak English well, I learn it from a book. Hhhello. I am English. Hhhello. *(he leans down behind the desk; the Major comes in from the bar – he can hear Manuel but can only see the moose)* How are you, sir. I can speak

	English. *(Manuel stands up momentarily just as the Major turns away)* Hello, Major. How are you today?
The Major	*(turns, but Manuel has disappeared again)* Er . . . er . . . er . . . I'm fine, thank you.
Manuel's voice	Is a beautiful day today.
The Major	*(peering closely at the moose)* Er . . . is it? Yes, yes, I suppose it is . . .
Manuel's voice	I can speak English. I learn it from a book.
The Major	Did you? Did you really? *(Basil comes back with a hammer)* Ah! There you are, Fawlty.
Basil	Yes, I'm just going to open up, Major. *(he picks up the moose and places it on the chair)*
The Major	Oh, fine . . . I say, that's a remarkable animal, Fawlty . . . where did you get it?
Basil	Samsons, in the town.
The Major	Really? Was . . . was it expensive?
Basil	Er, twelve pounds, I think. *(starts hammering the nail)*
The Major	Good Lord! . . . Japanese, was it?
Basil	. . . Canadian, I think, Major.
The Major	*(goes off towards bar, shaking his head)* I didn't know the Canadians were as clever as that.
Basil	*(staring after the Major)* He's started early. *(he gets down from the chair as Polly comes in and places a vase of flowers on the desk)* Polly? What's that smell?
Polly	Flowers. I've just got them from the garden.
Basil	Well, what are you stinking the place out with those for? What's happened to the plastic ones?
Polly	. . . Being ironed.

Basil picks up the moose and is about to re-mount the chair when the telephone rings.

Basil	Oh, will you answer that please? I'm trying to put this up.
Polly	Fawlty Towers . . . Oh, hello, Mrs Fawlty.
Basil	I'm **doing** it! I'm doing it now! Tell her! **I'm doing it now!**
Polly	He says he's doing it now. How's the nail?
Basil	I wish it was this one! *(he hangs the moose on the nail)* There, tell the Tyrant Queen that her cardies are safe for ever. Mr Moose is up. It's done, done, done.
Polly	It's up. *(the moose falls off the wall on to Basil's head)* It's down again. *(to Basil)* Did you use a wall plug?

Basil	Give it to me, give it to me.

He rushes for the phone, falling over Manuel who is still messing about out of sight behind the desk.

Polly	*(to phone)* No, he just fell over Manuel . . . and he seems to have got himself jammed under the swivel chair . . . and the flowers have just fallen on him . . . no, everything else is fine.

Next morning; in reception. Basil is replacing the moose. Manuel is in attendance.

Manuel	Is up. Good. Up. Very good.
Basil	Right, good. *(one antler sags)* Well, what is it? . . . Right! Well go on, get back to work! *(to himself)* Twelve pounds . . .

Manuel goes into the kitchen. Mr and Mrs Sharp come in through the main doors.

Basil	Good morning.
Mr Sharp	Good morning.
Basil	You know there's a fire drill in a few minutes, do you?
Mr Sharp	No, we didn't.
Basil	You hadn't read the notice.
Mr Sharp	. . . No.
Basil	Right, well, when you hear the bell, if you'd be so kind as to get out for a few moments, we have to clear the building. Thank you so much.
Mr Sharp	Oh.

As the Sharps exit Polly comes out from the dining room.

Polly	Mr Fawlty, you know it's nearly twelve?
Basil	Yes?
Polly	Well, the fire drill . . .
Basil	Yes, I haven't forgotten, you know, I've just told somebody – I can cope. I mean, you know what you're doing, do you?
Polly	Help get the people out of the bedrooms upstairs.
Basil	While learning two oriental languages, yes.
Polly	Mr Fawlty?
Basil	Yes?
Polly	Who else is doing the upstairs?
Basil	Only you. It doesn't take a moment.

Polly	Yes, but I'm only here at mealtimes.
Basil	So?
Polly	Well, what happens if there's a fire when I'm not here, who does the upstairs then?
Basil	. . . We'll worry about that when we come to it, shall we? What's the panic? There's always got to be an **argument** about everything. *(the phone rings; he picks it up)* Hallo, Fawlty Towers . . . Oh, what is it **now**, can't you leave me in peace? Yes, we're just going to have it, I hadn't forgotten! Yes, I know, I **know** I need the key, it's on top of the . . . *(but it isn't)* Well, **where** is it? . . . Well, what d'you put it in there for, nobody's going to steal it, are they? . . . Yes, I know that **you** know, but **I** don't, do I . . . Yes, I do now, thank you so much . . . *(puts the receiver down and goes into the office)* . . . Why has she got to complicate everything – I put something down, I know where it is, so she has to come along and move the damned thing so that I can't find it . . . *(he opens the safe and the burglar alarm goes off)* Well, what's she put **that** on for? Oh, I might have guessed . . . *(he goes into the lobby; the Major has come in)* Sorry, sorry, Major, only the burglar alarm. *(he turns off the bell)*
The Major	What?
Basil	*(to Miss Tibbs, who has come in with Miss Gatsby)* Sorry, Miss Tibbs!
Miss Tibbs	What?
Basil	That was the burglar alarm, the fire drill's not for a couple of minutes. *(to a large woman who has come into the lobby)* Sorry – excuse me!
The Major	Burglars, Fawlty?
Basil	No, no burglars. My wife left the . . . er . . . *(to the large woman)* Excuse me!
Large woman	Yes?
Basil	That wasn't the fire bell, sorry, that was just the . . . er . . .
Large woman	I thought there was a drill?
Basil	Yes, there is. At twelve o'clock, but not yet.
Large woman	But it is twelve o'clock.
Basil	Not quite, thank you. *(to the Sharps who are just going out)* Excuse me!
Mrs Sharp	Yes?
Large woman	Well, I make it twelve o'clock.

Basil	I'm afraid that wasn't . . .
Large woman	*(to the Major)* What time do you make it?
Basil	Look!
The Major	Burglars about, I think.
Basil	It doesn't **matter** what time he makes it – it hasn't started yet.
Mrs Sharp	What?
Basil	It hasn't started yet!
Mrs Sharp	But that was the bell, wasn't it?
Basil	No!
Large woman	*(to Mrs Sharp)* He means the **drill** hasn't started yet.
Mr Sharp	What drill? We didn't hear a drill.
Basil	No, no, look, that was the burglar alarm.
The Major	See!
Large woman	The burglar alarm?
Basil	Yes.
Large woman	Are there burglars?
The Major	Evidently.
Basil	Look! What's the matter with you all? It's perfectly simple. We have the fire drill when I ring the fire bell. **That wasn't the fire bell.** Right?
Mr Sharp	Well, how are we supposed to know it wasn't the fire bell?
Basil	Because it doesn't **sound** like the fire bell!
All	It did.
Basil	It didn't!
All	It did.
Basil	No it didn't! The fire bell is different . . . it's a semitone higher.
Large woman	A **semitone?**
Basil	At least. Anyway the fire drill doesn't start till twelve o'clock.
Mr Sharp	It **is** twelve o'clock.
Basil	. . . Well, it is now, but that's because we've been standing round arguing about it!
Large woman	Look, how on earth can you expect us to tell which bell is which? We haven't heard them, have we?
Basil	You want to hear them? Right! Suits me. Here's the burglar alarm. *(switches it on)*
The Major	Oughtn't we to catch them first?
Basil	There **aren't** any.
The Major	Well, why does the alarm keep going?

Basil	All right! Got that? Right! *(he turns it off)*
Large woman	What's happening now?
Basil	Now here's the fire bell, right? It's a completely different sound. Listen!

The fire bell rings; it is indeed a semitone higher. The guests start to leave.

Basil	Well, where are you going?
Large woman	Well, there is a fire drill, isn't there?
Basil	No, no, no! This is just so that you can hear the bell so you know what it's like when I do ring it in a moment! **What are you doing**! Will you come **back**!
Miss Tibbs	We're going outside!
Basil	Not yet! Just listen to it, you old fool!
Miss Tibbs	*(affronted)* What?
Basil	Listen, just listen to it!!
Manuel	*(comes running out of the kitchen)* Fire! Fire! Everybody out, please. Fire!
Basil	No, no!
Manuel	Please now out! Out!
Basil	Shut up!
Manuel	Is fire!
Basil	Is not fire! Is only bell!

Polly runs out from the kitchen and starts to go upstairs.

Basil	*(to Polly)* Where are you going?
Polly	Upstairs to tell the . . .
Basil	There isn't a drill yet! I'm just showing them what the bell sounds like!! Now will you go in there, go help Chef.
Manuel	Chef not here.
Basil	Go and . . . start the chips.
Manuel	Chips.
Basil	Yes. When bell go again . . . stay!
Manuel	What?
Basil	No fire, only practice . . . tell him, Polly. *(Manuel is despatched back to the kitchen)* Thank you, thank you so much, ladies and gentlemen, thank you.
The Major	Perhaps they're upstairs, Fawlty.
Large woman	What is happening now?
Basil	*(switching off the fire bell)* Now . . . *(the phone rings; he grabs it)* We're having it!!! *(slams the phone down)* Now,

	are we all agreed on what the fire bell sounds like? Splendid. Well, now that's settled we'll have the fire drill which will commence in exactly thirty seconds from now. Thank you so much. *(nobody moves)* Well, what are you doing? . . . I mean, are you just going to stand there?
Mr Sharp	What do you suggest?
Basil	Well, couldn't one or two of you go in the bar, and a few in the dining room . . . I mean, use your imagination?
Large woman	Why?
Basil	Well, this is supposed to be a fire drill!
Mr Sharp	But there's only a few seconds.
Basil	Right, right!! Just stay where you are, because obviously if there was a fire you'd all be standing down here like this in the lobby, wouldn't you? . . . I don't know why we bother, we should let you all burn . . .

Meanwhile in the kitchen, Manuel sets the chip pan alight. In trying to beat it out he sets fire to his oven gloves, and then spreads the fire around the kitchen.

Manuel	Oh, no . . . no . . . please . . . Mr Fawlty! . . . *fuego, fuego, fuego!* . . .

Back in the lobby, the fire bell goes off again; the guests are leaving in an orderly fashion.

Basil	No, there **weren't** any, Major, it went off by accident.
Miss Tibbs	Come on, Angina.
Miss Gatsby	Thank you, thank you so much.
Manuel	*(erupting from the kitchen)* Fire! Fire! Fire! Fire!
Basil	No! No!
Manuel	*Si! Si!*
Basil	Look, will you get back in there! *(throws Manuel into the kitchen and slams the door; Manuel screams and rushes out again)* Shut up – just get on with your work!
Manuel	Mr Fawlty! Is fire!
Basil	Did you hear what I said?
Manuel	No, no, but is fire!
Basil	*(shouting)* Is no fire! Is only bell!
Manuel	Is fire, is fire, is fire!!

Basil pushes him back in the kitchen. Polly comes running down the stairs.

Basil	Will you get back in there and stop that!
Manuel	*(screaming)* Is fire! Aaaaaaaaaagh!
Basil	*(locking the kitchen door)* He thinks there's a fire.
Polly	Everybody's out upstairs.

Manuel is still howling.

Polly	*(calling through door)* Manuel! Listen. Listen! *De nada, de nada,* **there is no fire!!** *(goes behind reception desk)*
Manuel's voice	Is fire! Is fire!
Basil	*(switching off the alarm)* Well, that'll keep the fire department happy for another six months. Why do we bother . . . *(to Manuel)* Will you shut up! *(he goes outside and speaks to the guests)* Thank you, ladies and gentlemen, you can come back in now.

He comes back into the lobby. Polly is on the telephone; the noise from Manuel is terrific.

Polly	Yes, yes, yes . . . yes, we've just had it.
Basil	Oh, shut up!
Polly	Yes, I will, all right. Goodbye. *(replaces receiver; to Basil)* Have you told Chef about the cheddar?
Large woman	Mr Fawlty, Mr Fawlty.
Basil	Yes?
Large woman	There's an awful row in there!
Basil	Yes, I know, it's only . . . right, right, I'll deal with it, thank you so much for poking your nose in . . . *(he unlocks the kitchen door; Manuel staggers out clutching a frying-pan)* Now look! I've had enough of this. If you go on I'm . . . *(he sees the fire)* Excuse me, ladies and gentlemen – could I have everyone in the lobby?

The guests all return complaining and grumbling.

Basil	Sorry . . . sorry . . . sorry to disturb you all like this, but . . . there is something I think I ought to mention. I'm . . . I'm not quite sure how this happened . . . this has not happened at this hotel before, and I'm not quite sure how it's started now . . . er . . .
Large woman	What is it?
Basil	Well . . . the point is . . . er . . . can I put it this way . . . fire!
Large woman	What?
Basil	F-f-f-f-f-f-f-fire!

Mrs Sharp	Fire?
Mr Sharp	Where?
Basil	Fire! . . . Fire!!! Fire!!! Fire!!!

The guests move yet again towards the main doors. Polly has appeared.

Basil	What do we do, what do we do? *(he rushes to the phone, to call Sybil)*
Polly	Ring the alarm! *(she rushes out after the guests)*
Basil	Ring the alarm . . . right! Right! . . . Where's the key? Where is the key? Would you believe it – I mean, would you believe it – the first time we've ever had a fire in this hotel and somebody's lost the key, I mean, isn't that typical of this place . . . *(shaking his fist at the ceiling)* Oh thank you, God, thank you so bloody much!
Polly	*(racing back in)* Smash the glass!
Basil	What?
Polly	Smash the glass!

Basil hits the alarm with his fist and injures himself. He throws the typewriter at the glass – it misses. The phone rings; he snatches the receiver.

Basil	Hello! *(uses the receiver to smash the glass and start the bell; to phone)* Thank you, thank you! *(drops phone and gets the fire extinguisher; he starts reading the instructions)* Quick! Manuel . . . pull it, man . . . pull it, man, pull it . . . open the door . . .

He sets the extinguisher off – it squirts in his face. Blinded, he drops it and doubles over. Polly rescues it and drags it into the kitchen. Basil stands up and bangs his head on Manuel's frying pan. He staggers, grabs Manuel and tries to throw a punch at him, but reels backwards and passes out on the floor.

In the hospital. Basil is lying in bed, a white turban-like bandage round his head. He regains consciousness with a series of strange expressions. He turns his head and sees Sybil sitting in a wheel-chair.

Sybil	Well, thank you for coming to see me.
Basil	*(very slurred)* Oh not at all, I was just . . . er . . .
Sybil	How are you feeling?

Basil	. . . The fire!
Sybil	It's all . . .
Basil	The fire!!
Sybil	It's out. There's not much damage . . .
Basil	Oh my God, where is it, what have they . . . *(gets out of bed)*
Sybil	Basil, what are you doing?
Basil	Got to get back, got to get back . . .
Sybil	Basil! Will you get back into bed!
Basil	Tch! Caw! What is it now?
Sybil	I'm going to call someone if you don't get back into bed. Come on!
Basil	Listen, Sybil, please! I'll handle this if you don't mind. Now . . . what sort of a room do you want?
Sybil	Basil!
Basil	Oh, there you are . . . look, I can't stand round chattering all day, I've got to get back . . .
Sybil	Basil, you are not well. The doctor says you've got concussion. You must rest.
Basil	I'll rest when I get to the hotel.
Sybil	I've just spoken to Polly, they are managing perfectly well.
Basil	. . . I mean, do you know what that fire extinguisher did? It exploded in my face! I mean, what is the **point** of a fire extinguisher? It sits there for months, and when you actually have a fire, when you actually **need** the bloody thing . . . it blows your head off!! I mean, what is happening to this country?! It's **Bloody Wilson!!!**

Sister enters briskly.

Sister	. . . My my, what a lot of noise. Now, what are you doing out of your bed?
Basil	Going home, thank you so much.
Sister	Yes, well, we'll let the doctor decide that now, shall we? *(she guides the protesting Basil back to bed)*
Basil	No, let's not.
Sister	Now, come along, back into bed. *(she pushes his legs under the bedclothes)*
Basil	Don't touch me, I don't know where you've been.
Sister	Yes, we must have our little jokes, mustn't we?

Basil	Yes, we must, mustn't we . . . *(stares at her)* My God, you're ugly, aren't you.
Sybil	Basil!
Sister	I'll get the doctor. *(she hurries out)*
Basil	*(calling after her)* You need a plastic surgeon, dear, not a doctor!
Sybil	How dare you talk to Sister like that! . . . Get back into bed!
Basil	*(getting out of bed again)* You do not seem to realize that I am needed at the hotel.
Sybil	No you're **not**. It's running beautifully without you.
Basil	Polly cannot cope!
Sybil	Well, she can't fall over waiters, or get herself jammed under desks, or start burglar alarms, or lock people in burning rooms, or fire fire extinguishers straight in her own face. But I should think the hotel can do without that sort of coping for a couple of days, what do you think, Basil . . . hmmm?

The doctor comes in.

Doctor	What?
Basil	Oh, hello, doctor.
Doctor	Out of bed, Mr Fawlty?
Basil	Sort of . . . *(points vaguely at his slippers on the floor)* Ah! There they are, good! Well, better get back into bed . . . feel a little bit woozy.
Doctor	You will for a time, Mr Fawlty, you will.
Basil	Yes, quite, quite . . .
Doctor	*(gently manipulating Basil's head to make him sleepy)* You should get as much rest as you can . . . as much rest as you can . . . as much rest as you can . . .
Basil	Yes . . . absolutely . . . I, er . . . I . . .

His eyes close. Sybil and the doctor leave the room and close the door gently. A pause; then Basil opens one eye and looks around furtively . . .

The hotel reception. Polly is finishing a phone call. As she puts the receiver down, a guest approaches the desk, clicks his heels, and bows.

1st German	*Gnädiges Fräulein, können sie mir sagen, wann das Mittagessen serviert wird, bitte?*

Polly	*Um ein Uhr, fünf Minuten.*
1st German	*Vielen dank.*
Polly	*Bitte schön.*

Polly goes into the kitchen. The German retires upstairs. Misses Tibbs and Gatsby come down the stairs as Basil enters through the main doors, dressed but still bandaged.

Basil	*(masterfully)* Manuel!
Miss Tibbs	Oh, Mr Fawlty!
Basil	Ah, good evening.
Miss Tibbs	Are you all right now?
Basil	Perfectly, thank you. *(handing Manuel, who has just come in, his case)* Take this to the room please, dear.

Manuel takes it, somewhat taken aback.

Miss Gatsby	Are you sure you're all right?
Basil	Perfectly, thank you. Right as rain.

He makes his way a little unsteadily towards the desk, but misses. He reappears, and takes up his position behind the desk.

Manuel	You OK?
Basil	Fine, thank you, dear. You go and have a lie down.
Manuel	*Qué?*
Basil	Ah, there you are. Would you take my case . . . how did you get that?
Manuel	What?
Basil	Oh never mind . . . take it . . . take it upstairs!
Manuel	*Qué?*
Basil	Take it . . . take it . . .
Manuel	I go get Polly.
Basil	I've already had one. Take it, take it now . . . *(Manuel hurries off)* Tch! The people I have to deal with . . .

He looks up to see a couple approaching the desk. He beams at them.

Elderly German	*Sprechen Sie Deutsch?*
Basil	. . . Beg your pardon?
Elderly German	*Entschuldigen Sie, bitte, können Sie Deutsch sprechen?*
Basil	. . . I'm sorry, could you say that again?

German lady	You speak German?
Basil	Oh, **German**! I'm sorry, I thought there was something wrong with you. Of course, the Germans!
German lady	You speak German?
Basil	Well . . . er . . . a little . . . I get by.
German lady	*Ein bisschen.*
Elderly German	*Ah – wir wollen ein Auto mieten.*
Basil	*(nodding helpfully)* Well, why not?
Elderly German	*Bitte.*
Basil	Yes, a little bit tricky. . . . Would you mind saying it again?
German lady	Please?
Basil	Could you repeat . . . amplify . . . you know, reiterate? Yes? Yes?
Elderly German	*Wir* . . .
Basil	*Wir?* . . . Yes, well we'll come back to that.
Elderly German	*. . . Wollen* . . .
Basil	*(to himself)* Vollen . . . Voluntary?
Elderly German	*Ein Auto mieten.*
Basil	Owtoe . . . out to . . . Oh, I see! You're volunteering to go out to get some meat. Not necessary! **We have meat here!** *(pause; the couple are puzzled)* We haf meat hier . . . in ze buildink!! *(he mimes a cow's horns)* Moo! *(Polly comes in)* Ah, Polly, just explaining about the meat.
Polly	Oh! We weren't expecting you.
Basil	Oh, weren't you? *(hissing through his teeth)* They're Germans. Don't mention the war.
Polly	I see. Well, Mrs Fawlty said you were going to have a rest for a couple of days, you know, in the hospital.
Basil	*(firmly)* Idle hands get in the way of the devil's work, Fawlty. Now . . .
Polly	Right, well why don't you have a lie-down, and I can deal with this.
Basil	Yes, yes, good idea, good idea, Elsie. Yes. Bit of a headache, actually . . .
Miss Tibbs	We don't think you're well, Mr Fawlty.
Basil	Well, perhaps not, but I'll live longer than you.
Miss Gatsby	You must have hurt yourself.
Basil	My dear woman, a blow on the head like that . . . is worth two in the bush.
Miss Tibbs	Oh, we know . . . but it was a nasty knock.

Basil	Mmmmmmmmm . . . would you like one? *(hits the reception bell impressively)* Next, please.

Two men and two women come down the stairs.

Basil	*(a hoarse whisper)* Polly! Polly! Are these Germans too?
Polly	Oh yes, but I can deal . . .
Basil	Right, right, here's the plan. I'll stand there and ask them if they want something to drink before the war . . . before their lunch . . . **don't mention the war!** *(he moves in front of the guests, bows, and mimes eating and drinking)*
2nd German	Can we help you?
Basil	*(gives a startled jump)* Ah . . . you speak English.
2nd German	Of course.
Basil	Ah, wonderful. *Wounderbar!* Ah – please allow me to introduce myself – I am the owner of Fawlty Towers, and may I welcome your war, your wall, you wall, **you all** . . . and hope that your stay will be a happy one. Now would you like to eat first, or would you like a drink before the war. . .ning that, er, trespassers will be – er, er – tied up with piano wire. . . . Sorry! Sorry! *(clutches his thigh)* Bit of trouble with the old leg . . . got a touch of shrapnel in the war . . . **Korean**, Korean war, sorry, Korean.
2nd German	Thank you, we will eat now.

Basil bows gracefully and ushers them into the dining room.

Basil	Oh good, please do allow me. May I say how pleased we are to have some Europeans here now that we are on the Continent . . .

They all go into the dining room. Polly meanwhile is on the phone.

Polly	Can I speak to Doctor Fin please?

In the dining room, Basil is taking the orders.

Basil	I didn't vote for it myself, quite honestly, but now that we're in I'm determined to make it work, so I'd like to welcome you all to Britain. The plaice is grilled, but that doesn't matter, there's life in the old thing yet. . . . No, wait a minute, I got a bit confused there. Oh yes, the plaice is grilled . . . in fact the whole room's a bit

	warm, isn't it . . . I'll open a window, have a look. . . . And the veal chop is done with rosemary . . . that's funny, I thought she'd gone to Canada . . . and is delicious and nutritious . . . in fact it's **veally** good . . . **veally** good?
2nd German	The veal is good?
Basil	Yes, doesn't matter, doesn't matter, never mind.
1st German	May we have two eggs mayonnaise, please?
Basil	Certainly, why not, why not indeed? We are all friends now, eh?
2nd German	*(heavily)* A prawn cocktail . . .
Basil	. . . All in the Market together, old differences forgotten, and no need at all to mention the war . . . Sorry! . . . Sorry, what was that again?
2nd German	A prawn cocktail.
Basil	Oh, prawn, that was it. When you said **prawn** I thought you said **war**. Oh, the war! Oh yes, completely slipped my mind, yes, I'd forgotten all about it. Hitler, Himmler, and all that lot, oh yes, completely forgotten it, just like that. *(snaps his fingers)* . . . Sorry, what was it again?
2nd German	*(with some menace)* A prawn cocktail . . .
Basil	Oh yes, Eva Prawn . . . and Goebbels too, he's another one I can hardly remember at all.
1st German	And *ein* pickled herring!
Basil	Hermann Goering, yes, yes . . . and von Ribbentrop, that was another one.
1st German	And four cold meat salads, please.
Basil	Certainly, well, I'll just get your *hors d'oeuvres* . . . *hors d'oeuvres* vich must be obeyed at all times without question . . . Sorry! Sorry!
Polly	Mr Fawlty, will you please call your wife immediately?
Basil	Sybil!! . . . Sybil!! . . . she's in the hospital, you silly girl!
Polly	Yes, call her there!
Basil	I can't, I've got too much to do. Listen . . . *(he whispers through his teeth)* Don't mention the war . . . I mentioned it once, but I think I got away with it all right . . . *(he returns to his guests)* So it's all forgotten now and let's hear no more about it. So that's two eggs mayonnaise, a prawn Goebbels, a Hermann Goering and four Colditz salads . . . no, wait a moment, I got a

bit confused there, sorry . . . *(one of the German ladies has begun to sob)* I got a bit confused because everyone keeps mentioning the war, so could you . . .

The second German, who is comforting the lady, looks up angrily.

Basil	What's the matter?
2nd German	It's all right.
Basil	Is there something wrong?
2nd German	Will you stop talking about the war?
Basil	Me? You started it!
2nd German	We did not start it.
Basil	Yes you did, you invaded Poland . . . here, this'll cheer you up, you'll like this one, there's this woman, she's completely stupid, she can never remember anything, and her husband's in a bomber over Berlin . . . *(the lady howls)* Sorry! Sorry! Here, she'll love this one . . .
2nd German	Will you leave her alone?
Basil	No, this is a scream, I've never seen anyone not laugh at this!
1st German	Go away!
Basil	Look, she'll love it – she's German! *(places a finger under his nose preparatory to doing his Hitler impression)*
Polly	No, Mr Fawlty!! . . . do Jimmy Cagney instead!
Basil	What?
Polly	**Jimmy Cagney!**
Basil	Jimmy Cagney?
Polly	You know . . . 'You dirty rat . . .'
Basil	I can't do Jimmy Cagney!
Polly	Please try . . . 'I'm going to get you . . .'
Basil	Shut up! Here, watch – who's this, then?

He places his finger across his upper lip and does his Führer party piece. His audience is stunned.

Basil	I'll do the funny walk . . .

He performs an exaggerated goose-step out into the lobby, does an about-turn and marches back into the dining room. Both German women are by now in tears, and both men on their feet.

Both Germans	Stop it!!
Basil	I'm trying to cheer her up, you stupid Kraut!

2nd German	It's not funny for her.
Basil	**Not funny?** You're joking!
2nd German	Not funny for her, not for us, not for any German people.
Basil	You have absolutely no sense of humour, do you!
1st German	*(shouting)* **This is not funny!**
Basil	**Who won the bloody war, anyway?**

The doctor comes in with a hypodermic needle ready.

Doctor	Mr Fawlty, you'll be all right – come with me.
Basil	Fine.

Suddenly Basil dashes off through the kitchen, out across into the lobby and into the office. He spots the doctor in pursuit and leaves by the other door into reception. He meets Manuel under the moose's head and thumps him firmly on the head. Manuel sinks to his knees. The moose's head falls off the wall; Basil is knocked cold. The moose's head lands on Manuel. The Major, entering from the bar, is intrigued.

Manuel	*(speaking through the moose's nose)* Ooooooh, he hit me on the head . . .
The Major	*(slapping the moose's nose)* No, you hit **him** on the head. You **naughty** moose!
2nd German	*(sadly)* However did they win?

Communication Problems

First of second series, first broadcast on 19 February 1979, BBC2.

Basil Fawlty   John Cleese
Sybil Fawlty   Prunella Scales
Polly   Connie Booth
Manuel   Andrew Sachs
Mr Yardley   Mervyn Pascoe
Mr Thurston   Robert Lankesheer
Mrs Richards   Joan Sanderson
Mr Firkins   Johnny Shannon
Major Gowen   Ballard Berkeley
Miss Tibbs   Gilly Flower
Miss Gatsby   Renée Roberts
Terry   Brian Hall
Mr Mackintosh   Bill Bradley
Mr Kerr   George Lee

The hotel lobby. Things are busy; Sybil and Polly are dealing with guests; Basil is finishing a phone call. He goes into the office. Mr Mackintosh comes to the reception desk.

Mackintosh	*(to Polly)* Number seventeen, please.
Sybil	*(to her guest)* Goodbye. Thank you so much. *(he moves off; the phone rings and Sybil answers it)* Hallo, Fawlty Towers . . . Oh, hallo, Mr Hawkins . . .
Polly	*(giving Mackintosh his key)* I've arranged your car for two this afternoon, then . . .
Mackintosh	Thank you. *(he moves off)*
Sybil	*(to phone)* Well, you did say today, Mr Hawkins.
Polly	*(to Mr Yardley, who has approached the desk)* Sorry to keep you.
Yardley	That's all right. You do accept cheques?
Polly	With a banker's card, yes.
Sybil	*(to phone)* Well we'll have to cancel the order, then . . . yes. No, no, five o'clock will be fine. *(she rings off)* Oh, Polly . . . Brenda can't start till Monday so would you mind doing the rooms till then?
Polly	Oh, no, I could do with the money.
Sybil	Oh, good. *(she goes into the office)*
Polly	*(checking Yardley's cheque)* There you are . . . thank you, Mr Yardley.

Yardley moves off. Mr Thurston approaches Polly. Mrs Richards comes in through the main door, followed by a taxi driver carrying her case.

Polly	*(to Thurston)* Oh, hello . . . can I help you?
Mrs Richards	Girl! Would you give me change for this, please.
Polly	In one moment – I'm just dealing with this gentleman. Yes, Mr Thurston?
Mrs Richards	What?
Thurston	Thank you. I was wondering if you could . . .
Mrs Richards	I need change for this.
Polly	In a moment – I'm dealing with this gentleman.
Mrs Richards	But I have a taxi driver waiting. Surely this gentleman wouldn't mind if you just gave me change.
Polly	*(to Thurston)* Do you?
Thurston	No, no, go ahead.
Polly	*(giving Mrs Richards her change)* There you are.
Thurston	Can you tell me how to get to Glendower Street . . .

Mrs Richards has paid the driver, who exits. She turns back to Polly.

Mrs Richards	Now, I've booked a room and bath with a sea view for three nights . . .
Polly	*(to Thurston)* Glendower Street? *(gets a map)*
Thurston	Yes.
Mrs Richards	You haven't finished with me.
Polly	Mrs? . . .
Mrs Richards	Mrs Richards. Mrs Alice Richards.
Polly	Mrs Richards, Mr Thurston. Mr Thurston, Mrs Richards. *(Mrs Richards, slightly thrown, looks at Mr Thurston)* Mr Thurston is the gentleman I'm attending to at the moment.
Mrs Richards	What?
Polly	*(loudly)* Mr Thurston is the gentleman I'm attending to . . .
Mrs Richards	Don't shout, I'm not deaf.
Polly	Mr Thurston was here before **you**, Mrs Richards.
Mrs Richards	But you were serving **me**.
Polly	I gave you change, but I hadn't finished dealing with him. *(to Thurston)* Glendower Street is this one here, just off Chester Street.
Mrs Richards	Isn't there anyone else in attendance here? Really, this is the most appalling service I've ever . . .
Polly	*(spotting Manuel)* Good idea! Manuel! Could you lend Mrs Richards your assistance in connection with her reservation. *(to Thurston)* Now . . . *(she continues to give Thurston directions)*
Mrs Richards	*(to Manuel)* Now, I've reserved a very quiet room, with a bath and a sea view. I specifically asked for a sea view in my written confirmation, so please be sure I have it.
Manuel	*Qué?*
Mrs Richards	. . . What?
Manuel	. . . *Qué?*
Mrs Richards	K?
Manuel	*Si.*
Mrs Richards	C? *(Manuel nods)* KC? *(Manuel looks puzzled)* KC? What are you trying to say?
Manuel	No, no – *Qué* – what?
Mrs Richards	K – what?
Manuel	*Si! Qué* – what?

Mrs Richards	C. K. Watt?
Manuel	. . . Yes.
Mrs Richards	Who is C. K. Watt?
Manuel	*Qué?*
Mrs Richards	Is it the manager, Mr Watt?
Manuel	Oh, manager!
Mrs Richards	He is.
Manuel	Ah . . . Mr Fawlty.
Mrs Richards	What?
Manuel	Fawlty.
Mrs Richards	What are you talking about, you silly little man. *(turns to Polly, Mr Thurston having gone)* What is going on here? I ask him for my room, and he tells me the manager's a Mr Watt and he's aged forty.
Manuel	No. No. Fawlty.
Mrs Richards	Faulty? What's wrong with him?
Polly	It's all right, Mrs Richards. He's from Barcelona.
Mrs Richards	The manager's from Barcelona?
Manuel	No, no. He's from Swanage.
Polly	And you're in twenty-two.
Mrs Richards	What?
Polly	*(leaning over the desk to get close)* You're in room twenty-two. Manuel, take these cases up to twenty-two, will you.
Manuel	*Si.*

He goes upstairs with the cases; Mrs Richards follows. Mr Firkins arrives at the desk as Basil emerges from the office.

Firkins	Very nice stay, Mr Fawlty.
Basil	Ah, glad you enjoyed it. Polly, would you get Mr Firkins' bill, please. Well, when will we be seeing you again?
Firkins	Not for a few weeks.
Basil	Oh.
Firkins	You . . . you're not by any chance a betting man, Mr Fawlty?
Basil	Er . . . *(looks towards the office; then, more quietly)* Well, I used to be.
Firkins	Only there's a nice little filly running at Exeter this afternoon.
Basil	Really?
Firkins	Dragonfly. *(Polly gives him his bill)* Ah.

Basil	Dragonfly?
Firkins	Yes, it's well worth a flutter . . . but pay the tax on it before . . .
Basil	*(seeing Sybil coming out)* Ssssshhhh! . . . Well, I'm delighted you enjoyed your stay.
Firkins	Very nice.
Basil	Hope to see you again before long.
Firkins	*(paying his bill)* There you are.
Basil	Thank you.
Firkins	'Bye, Mr Fawlty.
Sybil	Goodbye, Mr Firkins.
Basil	*(to Sybil)* A satisfied customer. We should have him stuffed.
Firkins	*(from the main door)* Oh, Mr Fawlty. Three o'clock Exeter. Dragonfly. Right? *(he leaves)*
Basil	. . . Yes. Good luck. Jolly good luck with it. *(he busies himself; Sybil stares at him; the Major wanders up)* Morning, Major.
The Major	Morning, Fawlty.
Basil	*(catching Sybil's eye)* Yes, dear?
Sybil	What was that about the three o'clock at Exeter, Basil?
Basil	Oh, some horse he's going to bet on I expect, dear. *(to the Major)* You're looking very spruce today, Major.
The Major	St George's Day, old boy.
Basil	Really?
The Major	Got a horse, have you? What's its name?
Basil	Um . . . *(to Sybil)* Did you catch it, dear?
Sybil	Dragonfly, Major.
The Major	Going to have a flutter, Fawlty?
Basil	No-o, no, no . . .
Sybil	No, Basil doesn't bet any more, Major, do you, dear?
Basil	No dear, I don't. No, that particular avenue of pleasure has been closed off.
Sybil	*(quietish)* And we don't want it opened up again, do we, Basil? *(she goes into the office)*
Basil	No, you don't dear, no. The Great Warning-Off of May the 8th. Yes. Good old St George, eh, Major?
The Major	Hmmm.
Basil	He killed a hideous fire-breathing old dragon, didn't he, Polly?
Polly	Ran it through with a lance, I believe.
Manuel	*(running in)* Mr Fawlty, Mr Fawlty. Is Mrs . . . er,

	room, no like . . . she want speak to you, is problem.
Basil	*(moving off)* Ever see my wife making toast, Polly? *(he mimes breathing on both sides of a slice of bread)*
The Major	Why did he kill it, anyway, Fawlty?
Basil	I don't know, Major. Better than marrying it. *(he follows Manuel upstairs)*
The Major	Marrying it? But he didn't have to kill it though, did he? I mean, he could have just not turned up at the church.

Upstairs, Basil follows Manuel at a good pace towards Mrs Richards' room. They go in.

Basil	Good morning, madam – can I help you?
Mrs Richards	Are you the manager?
Basil	I am the **owner**, madam.
Mrs Richards	What?
Basil	I am the owner.
Mrs Richards	I want to speak to the manager.
Basil	I am the manager too.
Mrs Richards	What?
Basil	I am the manager as well.
Manuel	Manaher! Him manaher!
Basil	Shut up!
Mrs Richards	Oh . . . you're Watt.
Basil	. . . I'm the **manager**.
Mrs Richards	Watt?
Basil	I'm . . . the . . . manager.
Mrs Richards	Yes, I know, you've just told me, what's the matter with you? Now listen to me. I've booked a room with a **bath**. When I book a room with a bath I expect to **get** a bath.
Basil	You've **got** a bath.
Mrs Richards	I'm not paying seven pounds twenty pence per night plus VAT for a room without a bath.
Basil	*(opening the bathroom door)* **There** is your bath.
Mrs Richards	You call **that** a bath? It's not big enough to drown a mouse. It's disgraceful. *(she moves away to the window)*
Basil	*(muttering)* I wish you were a mouse, I'd show you.
Mrs Richards	*(at the window, which has a nice view)* And another thing – I asked for a room with a view.
Basil	*(to himself)* Deaf, mad and blind. *(goes to window)* This is the view as far as I can remember, madam. Yes, this is it.

Mrs Richards	When I pay for a view I expect something more interesting than that.
Basil	That is Torquay, madam.
Mrs Richards	Well, it's not good enough.
Basil	Well . . . may I ask what you were hoping to see out of a Torquay hotel bedroom window? Sydney Opera House perhaps? The Hanging Gardens of Babylon? Herds of wildebeeste sweeping majestically . . .
Mrs Richards	Don't be silly. I expect to be able to see the sea.
Basil	You **can** see the sea. It's over there between the land and the sky.
Mrs Richards	I'd need a telescope to see that.
Basil	Well, may I suggest you consider moving to a hotel closer to the sea. Or preferably **in** it.
Mrs Richards	Now listen to me; I'm not satisfied, but I have decided to stay here. However, I shall expect a reduction.
Basil	Why, because Krakatoa's not erupting at the moment?
Mrs Richards	Because the room is cold, the bath is too small, the view is invisible and the radio doesn't work.
Basil	No, the radio works. You don't.
Mrs Richards	What?
Basil	I'll see if I can fix it, you scabby old bat. *(he turns the radio on loudly. Manuel puts his fingers in his ears; Basil turns the radio off)* I think we got something then.
Mrs Richards	What?
Basil	I think we got something then.
Mrs Richards	*(to Manuel, who still has his fingers in his ears)* What are you doing?
Manuel	*(loudly) Qué?*
Basil	Madam . . . don't think me rude, but may I ask . . . do you by any chance have a hearing aid?
Mrs Richards	A what?
Basil	A hearing aid!!!
Mrs Richards	Yes, I do have a hearing aid.
Basil	Would you like me to get it mended?
Mrs Richards	Mended? It's working perfectly all right.
Basil	No, it isn't.
Mrs Richards	I haven't got it turned on at the moment.
Basil	Why not?
Mrs Richards	The battery runs down. Now what sort of a reduction are you going to give me on this room?
Basil	*(whispering)* Sixty per cent if you turn that on.

Mrs Richards	What?
Basil	*(loudly)* My wife handles all such matters, I'm sure she will be delighted to discuss it with you.
Mrs Richards	I shall speak to her after lunch.
Basil	You heard that all right, didn't you.
Mrs Richards	What?
Basil	Thank you so much. Lunch will be served at half past twelve.

He sweeps out of the room with Manuel just ahead of him. In the corridor he catches Manuel up.

Basil	Manuel! Manuel!
Manuel	*Si.*
Basil	Are you going to the betting shop today?
Manuel	What?
Basil	Oh, don't you start. You go betting shop. Today?
Manuel	Oh, vetting shop. *Si, si.*
Basil	Yes. Now put this *(gives Manuel a fiver)* on this little horse – Dragonfly *(writes it on the back of Manuel's hand)* . . . but big secret. Sybil no know . . .

The lobby, about 6 p.m. that evening. Sybil is on the phone at the reception desk; she is discussing a wig on a plastic display head.

Sybil	No, no, it's lovely, it's just a bit buttery with my skin. I think I need something more topazy, for my colouring, you know, more tonal . . . Have you got *Cosmopolitan* there? . . . well on page 42 . . . you see Burt Reynolds . . . well there's a girl standing behind him looking at James Caan . . . that sort of colour . . . mmm . . . lovely, all right. *(she rings off and looks into the office where Polly is adding up bills)* Polly, I've got to check the laundry, could you keep an eye on reception for me?
Polly	Sure.

Sybil goes off. Manuel comes furtively through the main doors. He dodges Sybil and peeps into the office.

Manuel	*(whispering)* Polly . . . Polly . . . where Mr Fawlty?
Polly	I don't know. What's the matter?
Manuel	*(very agitated)* I have money for him. He win on horse. But Big Secret. Sh! Mrs Fawlty . . . Sh!

Polly	Well give it to me, I'll give it to him.

Manuel gives Polly the money. He sees Sybil coming back and dashes fearfully off. Sybil looks into the office and sees Polly who, rather impressed, is counting the money. Sybil, unseen by Polly, looks at this and then goes into the lobby. Misses Tibbs and Gatsby are coming in through the main doors.

Sybil	Good afternoon, Miss Gatsby. Good afternoon, Miss Tibbs.
Miss Tibbs	Good afternoon.
Miss Gatsby	Good afternoon.

They turn towards the stairs, down which comes Mrs Richards in a huff.

Misses Tibbs & Gatsby	Good afternoon.
Mrs Richards	First they give me a room without a bath, then there's no lavatory paper.
Miss Tibbs	Oh.
Miss Gatsby	Would you like some of ours?

Mrs Richards bangs the reception bell.

Miss Tibbs	We keep an extra supply.
Miss Gatsby	Would you like some of ours?

Mrs Richards continues to bang the bell. Misses Tibbs and Gatsby go upstairs.

Mrs Richards	Hallo! *(Polly emerges)* Girl. There's no paper in my room. Why don't you check these things? That's what you're being paid for, isn't it?
Polly	Well, we don't put it in the rooms.
Mrs Richards	What?
Polly	We keep it in the lounge.
Mrs Richards	In the **lounge**?!!
Polly	*(really trying to help)* I'll get you some. Do you want plain or ones with our address on it?
Mrs Richards	**Address** on it?!!
Polly	How many sheets? *(Mrs Richards looks appalled)* How many are you going to use?
Mrs Richards	*(hitting the bell)* Manager!!
Polly	Just enough for **one**? Tell me.
Mrs Richards	Manager!! Manager!!!

Basil	*(apearing from kitchen)* Yes? Testing, testing . . .
Mrs Richards	There you are! I've never met such insolence in all my life. I come down here to get some lavatory paper and she starts asking me the most insulting . . . personal . . . **things** I ever heard in my life.
Polly	*(to Basil)* I thought she wanted **writing** paper.
Mrs Richards	I'm talking to you, Watt.
Basil	. . . Watt?
Mrs Richards	Are you deaf? I said I'm talking to you. I've never met such insolence in my life. She said people use it in the lounge.
Basil	Yes, yes, she thought you . . .
Mrs Richards	. . . Then she starts asking me the **most** . . .
Basil	No, no, please listen.
Mrs Richards	. . . **appalling** questions . . .
Basil	. . . Please. I can explain! . . .
Mrs Richards	. . . about . . . about . . .
Basil	*(actually managing to shout her down)* No, no, look, you see . . . she thought you wanted to **write.**
Mrs Richards	Wanted a **fight?** I'll give her a fight all right.
Basil	No, no, no, no, wanted to **write.** *(he mimes writing)*
Mrs Richards	. . . What?
Basil	Wanted to **write.** On the paper.
Mrs Richards	. . . Why should I want to **write** on it?
Basil	*(giving up)* Oh! I'll have some sent up to your room immediately. Manuel! *(rings the bell)*
Mrs Richards	**That** doesn't work either. What were you saying just then?
Basil	Oh . . . turn it **on!**
Mrs Richards	What?
Basil	Turn it . . . *(furious, he writes on a piece of paper)* Turn . . . it . . . on. *(shows it to her)*
Mrs Richards	I can't read that. I need my glasses! Where are they? *(they are in fact propped up on her forehead)*
Polly	They're on your head, Mrs Richards.
Mrs Richards	I've lost them. They're the only pair I've got. I can't read a thing without them.
Basil	Excuse me . . .
Mrs Richards	Now, I had them this morning when I was buying the vase. I put them on to look at it. And I had them at tea-time . . .
Basil	. . . Mrs Richards . . .

Polly	. . . Mrs Richards . . .
Basil	. . . Mrs Richards . . . *(she looks up; they both point at her glasses)* Your glasses are there.
Mrs Richards	*(looks round and sees the dining room)* There?! Well, who put them in there? *(she goes towards the dining room)*
Polly	. . . No!
Basil	No, no, no, on your head . . . *(Mrs Richards does not hear him)* On your . . . look . . . on . . . **on your head!!!**
Mrs Richards	*(stopping and turning)* What?

Basil starts to write again, realizes, throws the paper at her and disappears into the office. Mrs Richards goes on into the dining room. Polly follows Basil into the office.

Polly	I'm sorry about that, Mr Fawlty . . . Manuel asked me to give this to you. *(hands him the money)*
Basil	Oh!! Thank you, Polly. Er . . . Polly . . . not a word to the dragon, eh?

Polly goes out to the lobby; Manuel is there.

Polly	Manuel, get some loo paper, *muchos*, for twenty-two.

Manuel runs off towards the bar. Mrs Richards emerges from the dining room.

Mrs Richards	Are you blind? They were on my head all the time. Didn't you see?
Polly	Yes.
Mrs Richards	Didn't God give you eyes?
Polly	Yes, but I don't use them 'cos it wears the batteries out.
Mrs Richards	Send my paper up immediately.

Manuel enters from bar carrying a huge stack of loo paper.

Polly	Manuel, that's too much.
Manuel	You say twenty-two.

Mrs Richards goes upstairs, followed by Manuel. Basil bustles into the kitchen merrily rubbing his hands together. Terry is there, vaguely preparing for the evening's cooking.

Basil	Evening, Terry. *(sings a quick bit of* Cav*)* Do you like *Cavallero Rusticana*, Terry?
Terry	I never had it, Mr Fawlty.
Basil	Never mind. *(he sings another bit, while getting himself a snack)*

Terry	You're in a good mood, Mr Fawlty.
Basil	Had a little bit of luck on the gee-gees, Terry. Er . . . not a word to the trouble and strife, eh? *(prepares his snack)* De Camptown ladies sing dis song, doo dah, doo dah, the Camptown race track five miles long, doo dah doo dah day. Going to run all night . . . *(Sybil enters)* Going to run all day . . . I'll bet my money on the bob-tail nag . . . *(sees Sybil)* . . . I did it my-y way. Can't stand Frank Sinatra. 'You make me feel so young' . . . rubbish.
Sybil	*(suspiciously)* You seem very jolly, Basil.
Basil	Hmmm?
Sybil	You seem very jolly.
Basil	Jolly?
Sybil	Yes, jolly. Sort of . . . happy.
Basil	Oh, 'happy'. Yes, I remember that. No, not that I noticed, dear. I'll report it if it happens, though.
Sybil	*(accusingly)* Well, you look happy to me, Basil.
Basil	No I'm not, dear.
Sybil	All that dancing about, singing and rubbing your hands.
Basil	No, just my way of getting through the day, dear. The Samaritans were engaged.
Sybil	I thought maybe you were in love. *(laughs)*
Basil	Only with you, light of my life.
Sybil	Or had a bit of luck or something . . . *(Basil reacts guiltily; then catches her eye and stares uncomprehendingly; Sybil turns to Terry)* Did Mr Hawkins deliver those tonics, Terry?
Terry	Yes he did, Mrs Fawlty.

Sybil goes out into the lobby. Basil dashes into the dining room where Manuel is laying tables.

Basil	Manuel, Manuel.
Manuel	Your horse, it win, it win!
Basil	Ssh!! . . . Manuel . . . *(putting his head close to Manuel)* You know nothing. *(Manuel is puzzled)* You know **nothing**.
Manuel	You always say, Mr Fawlty. But I learn.
Basil	What?
Manuel	I learn, I learn.
Basil	No, no, no, no . . .

Manuel	I get better.
Basil	No, you don't understand.
Manuel	I do.
Basil	No, you don't.
Manuel	I do understand that.
Basil	Shh . . . you know nothing about the **horse**.
Manuel	*(doubtfully)* I know nothing about the horse.
Basil	Yes.
Manuel	Ah . . . which horse?
Basil	What?
Manuel	Which horse I know nothing?
Basil	**My** horse, nitwit.
Manuel	**Your** horse, 'Nitwit'.
Basil	No, no, **Dragonfly**.
Manuel	It **won**!
Basil	Yes, I **know**.
Manuel	I know it won, too.
Basil	What?
Manuel	I put money on for you. You give me money. I go to vetting-shop, I put money on . . .
Basil	I know, I know, I know.
Manuel	Why you say I know nothing?
Basil	Oh. Look . . . look . . . look . . . you know the horse?
Manuel	Witnit? Or Dragonfly?
Basil	Dragonfly. There isn't a horse called Nitwit. **You're** the nitwit.
Manuel	What is witnit?
Basil	*(puts his hand round Manuel's throat)* It doesn't matter . . . look . . . it doesn't matter . . . Oh . . . I could spend the rest of my life having this conversation. Please try to understand before one of us **dies**.
Manuel	I try.
Basil	You're going to forget everything you know about nitwit.
Manuel	No, Dragonfly.
Basil	Dragonfly! Yes!
Manuel	*Si, si, si* . . . eventually.
Basil	What?
Manuel	. . . Eventually. At the end.
Basil	. . . No, no, no, forget it **now**!
Manuel	Now?
Basil	Well, pretend you forget.

Manuel	Pretend?
Basil	**Don't say anything to anyone about the horse!!!**
Manuel	Oh, I **know** that, you tell me this morning. Tch! Choh!

Basil stares. Sybil puts her head round the door.

Sybil	Basil.
Basil	*(to Manuel)* So don't do it again. *(to Sybil)* Yes, dear?
Sybil	It's Mrs Richards.
Basil	A fatal accident?
Sybil	She's had some money stolen.

Sybil leaves. Basil moves after her emitting a moan. Manuel grabs his arm.

Manuel	Ah, Mr Fawlty, I tell Polly.
Basil	What? Oh, that's all right. But don't tell anyone else. Not even me. You know nothing.
Sybil	*(from lobby)* Basil!
Basil	Yes, dear? *(he catches her up in the lobby)*
Sybil	Basil, you've got to help me handle this. She's in a frightful state, I can't get a word in edgeways. She's had eighty-five pounds taken from her room, I've said we'll search everywhere but she insists we call the police. What do you do with someone like that, she just keeps on.

They go into the office; Mrs Richards is there.

Basil	*(loudly)* Mrs Richards, how very nice to see you. Are you enjoying your stay?
Mrs Richards	There's no need to shout. I have my hearing aid on.
Basil	. . . Oh!
Sybil	Mrs Richards, I've explained to my husb—
Mrs Richards	I've just been up to my room. Eighty-five pounds has been taken from my bag which I had hidden under the mattress.
Basil	Oh, yes? . . .
Mrs Richards	It's a disgrace, I haven't been here a day. What sort of staff do you employ here?
Sybil	Mrs Richards . . .
Mrs Richards	If you knew anything at all about running a hotel, this sort of thing wouldn't happen! Well . . . what have you got to say for yourself?

Basil launches into a long, but entirely mimed, speech.

Mrs Richards　What?

Basil continues to mime. Sybil nudges him.

Sybil　*(very quietly)* Basil.
Basil　*(mimes 'Yes, dear?')*
Sybil　*(very quietly)* Don't.
Mrs Richards　Wait. Wait. Wait, wait, I haven't turned it up enough. *(she fiddles with the control and looks at Basil; he rubs his hands)*
Sybil　*(whispers warningly)* Basil!

Mrs Richards turns the control full up.

Basil　*(fortissimissimo)* I said I suggest . . .

Mrs Richards reels back holding her head in her hands and bangs her head on the shelf on the wall behind her.

Mrs Richards　My head!
Basil　Has it come away?
Sybil　*(pushing past Basil)* Get away. *(to Mrs Richards)* Did you bang your head?
Mrs Richards　Yes, yes.
Sybil　Oh dear, let me have a look.
Basil　You'd better go and lie down before something else happens.
Sybil　*(elbowing him)* Shut up, Basil.
Mrs Richards　Why don't you call the police?
Sybil　We will the moment we've searched the rooms.
Mrs Richards　My money's been taken.
Sybil　Yes, yes, I know, try not to speak.
Basil　*(offering something he has found on the floor)* Is this a piece of your brain?

Sybil kicks his shin. He sits down clutching it.

Mrs Richards　Eighty-five pounds.
Sybil　Take my arm.
Mrs Richards　I don't need your arm, thank you. I can get down the stairs perfectly well by myself.
Basil　**Down** the stairs? Oh well, don't stop when you get to the basement. Keep straight on. Give my regards to the earth's core.

Mrs Richards has left the office. Sybil is looking after her.

Sybil	Are you sure you can manage?
Basil	And if you give us any more trouble I shall visit you in the small hours and put a bat up your nightdress. *(still rubbing his shin)* Well, that was fun, wasn't it, dear. The odd moment like that, it's almost worth staying alive for, isn't it. *(Sybil is poker-faced)* It's nice to share a moment like that, isn't it, dear. It's what marriage is all about. I know, it said so on the back of a matchbox.
Sybil	Basil, sometimes . . .
Basil	*(putting a hand on her waist)* Seriously, Sybil, do you remember, when we were first . . . manacled together, we used to laugh quite a lot.
Sybil	*(pushing him away)* Yes, but not at the same time, Basil.
Basil	That's true. That was a warning, wasn't it. Should have spotted that. Zoom! – what was that? That was your life, mate. That was quick, do I get another? Sorry mate, that's your lot.
Sybil	Basil.
Basil	Back to the world of dreams. Yes dear?
Sybil	*(irritated)* What are we going to do?
Basil	Give it another fifteen years?
Sybil	About the **money**. Do you think we should . . .
Basil	Oh, she's left it in her room, or she's dropped it or eaten it or something. We'll get Manuel to go through the room. Polly can check the lounge . . .
Sybil	Wait a moment. I saw Polly with some money just now.
Basil	Well, there you are.
Sybil	It was quite a bit, too. She was counting it in here.
Basil	*(gripped by sudden fear)* Well, it's probably hers.
Sybil	No . . . she's been very short lately, Basil. I'll ask her.
Basil	Well, you can't. You can't just ask her like that, Sybil!
Sybil	Why not?
Basil	Well . . . it's terribly rude asking someone if money is theirs or not. It'd be so embarrassing. *(the reception phone rings)*
Sybil	Rubbish, Basil.

Basil moves into the lobby and answers the phone.

Basil	Hallo, Fawlty Towers. *(he cuts off the call by putting his finger on the cradle, but continues to talk as if still connected)*

Sybil	Polly Shearman? Certainly. I'll get her straight away. *(he puts the phone down and hurries towards the kitchen)* *(calling)* Polly . . .

Basil rushes into the kitchen.

Basil	Terry, where's Polly?
Terry	*(indicating the dining room)* In there.

Basil goes into the dining room; Polly is putting flowers on the tables.

Basil	Polly! . . . Polly, she saw you with the money.
Polly	What?
Basil	Sybil. She saw you counting the horse money. She's coming to ask you . . . *(Sybil enters)* Hallo dear. Here she is. Found her in here. As I was just saying, Polly, my wife would like to have a word with you about a slightly delicate matter.
Sybil	It's not delicate, Basil, don't be silly. *(to Polly)* He thinks it's embarrassing for me to ask you about that money I saw you with earlier on in the office. I was wondering if someone had handed it in. Mrs Richards has lost some.
Polly	The money . . . in the office . . .
Sybil	You were counting it, weren't you. Did someone hand it in?
Polly	Oh, no. No, it's mine.
Sybil	Yours?
Polly	I won it.
Sybil	You **won** it?
Polly	On the horse Mr Fawlty got a tip on. *(to Basil)* I hope you don't mind, I just . . .
Basil	No, no, not at all.
Sybil	I didn't know you bet on the horses, Polly?
Polly	Oh, I don't . . . I was in the town, passing the betting shop, and I thought . . . well, why not?
Basil	Why not indeed. *(to Sybil)* Jolly good question, eh, dear? Pity you didn't let me put something on, really. Do you realize how much we would have won? Seventy-five pounds for a five-pound stake. Still, you know best.
Sybil	Those were the odds, were they, Basil?

Basil	Yes, that's right, dear. Fourteen to one. I listened in on the wireless just to make sure it had triumphed. *(to Polly)* Enjoy your winnings, Polly. *(he goes into the lobby)*
Polly	Thank you.
Sybil	*(quietly)* Polly?
Polly	Yes, Mrs Fawlty?
Sybil	What was the name of the horse?
Polly	Er . . . the **name** . . . I've gone blank . . .

Basil dashes to the dining-room door, behind Sybil. He mouths 'Dragonfly'. Polly stares. He points to Sybil and flaps his hands.

Polly	Bird Brain.
Sybil	Bird Brain?
Polly	No, no, that came in third. *(Basil makes flying movements, then points at Sybil)* Fishwife.
Sybil	What?
Polly	No, no, not fishwife. *(Basil points at Sybil, then at his fly)* Small . . . fly! Flying . . . Flying Tart . . . no, no . . . *(Basil repeats his Sybil-making-toast mime)* No, it got off to a flying **start**, and its name was *(with relief)* Dragonfly.
Sybil	Thank you, Polly. *(she goes into the lobby and turns on Basil)* If I find out the money on that horse was yours, you know what I'll do, Basil. *(she exits upstairs)*
Basil	*(calling after her)* You'll have to sew 'em back on first. *(the Major appears, heading for the bar; Basil has an inspiration)* Major!
The Major	*(without checking his stride)* Six o'clock, old boy.

He goes into the bar. Basil follows him.

Basil	Oh, so it is, Major. Can I offer you . . .
The Major	Oh, that's very decent of you. Just a quick one, going to a memorial service.
Basil	Tie's a bit bright, isn't it, Major?
The Major	What?
Basil	For a memorial service?
The Major	Oh, I didn't **like** the chap. One of those. Know what I mean. Cheers!
Basil	Major . . . could you do me a favour?
The Major	Well, I'm a bit short myself, old boy.

Basil	No, no, no, could you look after some money for me. *(he takes it out)* I won it on that horse, only Sybil's a bit suspicious you see, and she goes through my pockets some nights . . .
The Major	Oh, absolutely. Which horse?
Basil	. . . Dragonfly. *(gives the Major the money)*
The Major	When's it running?
Basil	No, no. It ran today. I won that on it.
The Major	Oh! *(starts to give the money back)* Well done, old boy.
Basil	No, no, could you keep it.
The Major	Oh, no, no, I couldn't do that. No, it's very decent of you.
Basil	No, no, could you keep it just for tonight. It's Sybil, you see. Secret?
The Major	Ah. Present.
Basil	Sort of, yes. Don't mention it.
The Major	Mum's the word.
Basil	I'll get it from you in the morning and bank it.
The Major	Understood, old boy. Cheers.

The Major makes off out of the bar. Basil pours himself a whisky and cheerfully bounces an ice cube off his forearm into the drink.

The lobby. Basil is at reception making out Mr Mackintosh's bill.

Basil	There you are, Mr Mackintosh. *(gives him the bill)*

The Misses Tibbs and Gatsby appear at the foot of the stairs.

Misses Tibbs & Gatsby	Good morning, Mr Fawlty.
Basil	Good morning, ladies. *(the phone rings and he answers it)* Hallo. Fawlty Towers.
Mrs Richards	*(off, loudly)* Watt!
Basil	*(seeing Mrs Richards bearing down on him)* . . . I didn't say anything. *(to phone)* Yes?
Mrs Richards	Have you called the police yet?
Basil	Er, excuse me, I'm just trying to take a telephone call.
Mrs Richards	Have you called them yet?
Basil	*(about to say no, but changes his mind)* . . . Yes. Yes, we have.
Mrs Richards	Well, when are they going to be here?
Basil	As soon as possible. They're very busy today.

Mrs Richards	Busy. Tch. *(she moves off)*
Basil	There was a lot of bloodshed at the Nell Gwynn tea-rooms last night. *(to phone)* Hello . . . yes, certainly, yes . . . *(calling after Mrs Richards)* Mrs Richards! **Mrs Richards!!!** *(Mr Mackintosh jumps)* Sorry, sorry . . . *(to Mrs Richards as she returns)* Telephone for you. Here. *(she takes the phone; Mackintosh points at his bill)* Yes?
Mackintosh	What's this for?
Basil	Er . . . telephone calls?
Mackintosh	But I haven't made any.
Basil	Oh. Er . . . cigarettes?
Mackintosh	I don't smoke.
Mrs Richards	*(to phone)* Hallo!! *(to Basil)* There's nobody there.
Basil	*(taking the phone)* Hallo . . . yes, yes, I know she is. Yes . . . *(to Mrs Richards)* It's your sister. *(Mrs Richards grabs the phone)*
Mackintosh	Well, what is it for?
Basil	Drinks?
Mackintosh	Drinks – me?
Mrs Richards	*(to phone)* Hallo. Hallo. We've been cut off.
Basil	*(grabbing the phone)* Hallo . . . look, you tell **me**, and I'll tell **her** . . .
Mrs Richards	*(to Mackintosh)* Even the phones don't work.
Basil	Your sister says you've had an offer of eighty-seven thousand pounds for your house in Brighton.
Mrs Richards	Eighty-seven? Give it to me. *(grabbing the phone back)* Don't be a fool, Stephanie. Nine two seven fifty I said and I'm not taking a penny less, you tell him that. *(slams the phone down)* Why don't people listen? *(heads off towards dining room)*
Mackintosh	Well?
Basil	Well, let's scrub that 32p then, shall we? Let's enjoy ourselves. There.
Mackintosh	Oh, thank you very much.

Mackintosh writes out the cheque. The Major appears from the dining room.

Basil	Ah! Major! *(hurries from behind the desk and catches the Major)* Major . . . can I have it now?
The Major	What, old boy?
Basil	The money . . . the money I gave you last night.
The Major	What is all this, Fawlty?

Basil	You remember . . . I gave you some money last night. Just before you went to that remembrance service.
The Major	Remembrance service?
Basil	Yes.
The Major	I don't remember **that**, old boy.
Basil	It was for . . . a chap you didn't like. Um . . . you know . . . he was one of those.
The Major	One of those what?
Basil	Well . . .
The Major	Pansy?
Basil	Yes.
The Major	*(indicating the dining room)* Which one?
Basil	No, no. Look, you were in your best suit.
The Major	Was I? Oh yes, of course – I went to the theatre, of course.
Basil	No, no.
The Major	Yes, with Winnie Atwell.
Basil	Winnie Atwell?
The Major	Well, **Marjorie** Atwell, Marjorie . . . I always call her Winnie 'cos she looks like Winnie.
Basil	. . . She's not black.
The Major	Black? Churchill wasn't black.
Basil	Look, look, I gave you seventy-five pounds – you put it in there . . . *(indicates the Major's pocket)*

The dining-room door flies open and Mrs Richards strides out and up to Basil. The Major wanders off upstairs.

Mrs Richards	What do you mean by telling me you called the police?
Basil	I . . .
Mrs Richards	You've done no such thing. Your wife's just told me you're still searching the rooms.
Basil	Well, I thought **she'd** called them.
Mrs Richards	You lying hound!
Sybil	*(coming in)* Mrs Richards . . .
Mrs Richards	*(to Basil)* Go and call them now. Immediately.
Basil	Yes, but look . . .
Sybil	Mrs Richards, we will, the moment we've searched the . . .
Mrs Richards	Right. I shall call them myself, then. *(she makes for the reception desk, followed by Sybil)*
Sybil	Couldn't we just wait until . . .
Mrs Richards	I've never **seen** such a place. *(picks up the phone)*

Sybil	*(intercepting her)* All right, Mrs Richards. Would you like to use the office phone?
Mrs Richards	What?
Sybil	In **here**. Thank you. *(shows her into the office, and calls back to Basil)* Basil. Get the key and check her room. *(goes into the office)*
Basil	Right. *(gets the key)*
The Major	*(appearing at the foot of the stairs holding a wad of notes)* I've found it, Fawlty!
Basil	What?
The Major	It was in my pocket.
Basil	Ah! *(glances furtively towards the office)*
The Major	Yes, in my new suit. In there. *(puts the notes into his inside pocket)* See?
Basil	*(trying to regain the money)* That's marvellous, Major.
The Major	Stuffed right down.
Basil	Yes, can I . . .
The Major	I don't know how it got there.
Basil	No, can I . . .
The Major	I always make a point of keeping my money in my hip pocket.
Basil	Please! Please!
The Major	What, old boy?
Basil	Can I have it.
The Major	Oh! Yes, yes, the money . . . yes, of course . . . *(reaches into his back pocket)* Oh! *(pokes about inside the pocket)* Good God, it's gone.
Basil	No, no – you put it in there.
Sybil	*(appearing at the office door)* Basil!
The Major	*(finding it)* Here it is! *(produces the money and holds it out)*
Sybil	What's that?
The Major	I found it, Mrs Fawlty. The money.
Sybil	Oh, that's marvellous. Mrs Richards!!
Basil	What?
Sybil	We've found your money.

Mrs Richards emerges from the office.

Basil	*(frozen with horror)* Er . . . no!
Sybil	The Major's found your money.
Basil	No dear.
Sybil	What? *(takes the money)* Thank you, Major. *(gives it to Mrs Richards)* You see, I knew it'd turn up.

Mrs Richards looks at it suspiciously and starts to count it.

Basil   *(whimpering unintelligibly)* Er . . . er . . .

Sybil   What is it, Basil?

*But he can't think of anything to say. Mrs Richards
continues to count.*

The Major   Bit of luck, eh, Fawlty?

Mrs Richards   It's ten pounds short.

Sybil   Oh dear.

Basil   *(dramatically)* It's not!! Ten pounds! Oh my **God**!!
                   Don't worry, we'll have a whip-round! *(grabs the blind
                   box and shakes it frantically, upside down)*

Sybil   Basil!! Stop it!!

Mrs Richards   What's he doing **now**?

*Basil is still shaking the box. Sybil stares at him for a
moment and then throws a cup of coffee in his face. He
freezes.*

Sybil   What on earth do you think you're doing? *(to Mrs
                   Richards)* I'll look for the other ten immediately, Mrs
                   Richards. *(to the Major)* Where exactly did you find it,
                   Major?

The Major   In my pocket.

Sybil   In your **pocket**?

The Major   Yes, yes, not this suit – the new one.

Sybil   Would you mind if I just popped up and had a look?

The Major   Oh, not at all, not at all.

Sybil   *(to Mrs Richards)* I'll see if I can find it. Won't be a
                   moment.

The Major   It's in with the . . . er . . . *(he can't remember)*

Sybil disappears up the stairs.

Basil   *(to Mrs Richards)* Excuse me . . .

Mrs Richards   *(to the Major)* Did you say it was in your pocket?

The Major   Yes.

Basil   Mrs Richards, can I . . .

Mrs Richards   What was it doing in your pocket?

Basil   Can I explain . . .

Mrs Richards   You're not explaining anything. You're completely
                   loopy. Mad as a March hare.

Basil   Yes. Yes, I am. Yes, I am completely loopy. That's why
                   I gave **him** the money to look after.

Mrs Richards	What?
Basil	You see, there's been a mistake. The money there is in fact mine.
Mrs Richards	Yours?
Basil	Yes. As the Major will confirm. I've been saving it up for a present for my wife, right, and that's why I couldn't say anything just now but I gave it to the Major last night.
Mrs Richards	What rubbish. This is my money.
Basil	No, no, well the Major will verify what I've said.
The Major	Hmmmm?
Basil	Could you verify that, Major?
The Major	What, old boy?
Basil	The money I gave you last night, you know, for my wife's present . . . You remember I gave it to you just before you went to the theatre.
The Major	Theatre!?
Basil	Yes. You remember. *(whispering)* That money I won on the horse.
The Major	A horse.
Mrs Richards	Why are you whispering? What are you saying?
The Major	He says he won it on a horse.
Mrs Richards	*(loudly)* Won it on a horse!
Basil	Ssssh. Doesn't matter. *(to the Major)* Do you remember me **giving** it to you? *(the Major thinks)* Think. Please think.
	Pause.
The Major	. . . What was the question again?
Basil	The money! The money!! Do you remember? . . . *(sees Manuel emerging from the dining room)* Manuel. Manuel. Come here. Manuel . . . you remember I had some money yesterday. *(Manuel look suspicious; Basil whispers)* The money I won on the horse.
Manuel	Ah! *Si* . . .
Basil	Tell Mrs Richards. Tell her I had the money yesterday.
Manuel	*(with pride)* Ahem. I know nothing.
Basil	What?
Manuel	I know nothing.
Basil	No, no.
Manuel	**Nothing.**

Basil	No, no, forget that.
Manuel	I forget **everything**. I know nothing.
Basil	No, you can tell her. You can tell her.
Manuel	No I cannot.
Basil	Yes, yes, tell her, tell her, please, please, tell her, tell her . . . I'll kill you if you don't.
Manuel	*(runs his finger along his throat and winks at Basil)* No, I know nothing. *(to Mrs Richards)* I am from Barcelona. *(he leaves)*
Mrs Richards	I'm not listening to any more of this rubbish. I'm going to finish my breakfast. When I come back I want the rest of the money. *(she steams off into the dining room)*
Sybil	*(coming down the stairs)* Give it to her, Basil.
Basil	What?
Sybil	I can't find it. Give her ten from the till.
Basil	. . . Right. *(he opens the till by banging it with his head and takes ten pounds out)* Ten pounds. *(he slaps it down on the counter and starts taking his shirt off)*
Sybil	What are you doing?
Basil	I'm going to give her the shirt off my back too.
Manuel	*(poking his head out of the kitchen)* You see, I know nothing.
Basil	I'm going to sell you to a vivisectionist. *(Manuel disappears; the Major wanders off; Basil finishes folding his shirt)* There. Now . . .
	He stands for a moment, then starts to wail. Mr Kerr comes in through the main door, carrying a large ornate vase.
Kerr	Good afternoon, Mr Fawlty.
Basil	*(in between sobs)* Good afternoon.
Kerr	You got a Mrs Richards staying with you?
Basil	*(falls out of sight behind the desk; he reappears)* Yes.
Kerr	Ah. Only she bought this yesterday, asked us to deliver it. The thing is . . . *(takes a glove out of his pocket)* she left some money behind. Keeps it in this, ninety-five quid . . . look. *(Basil looks)* The cleaner found it this morning, almost threw it in the bin, lucky, eh? *(Basil is transfixed)* . . . Is she around?
Basil	. . . Nope. I'll give it to her.
Kerr	*(giving it to him)* Oh, thanks, Mr Fawlty. Goodbye.
	He goes out, leaving the vase on the desk. Polly enters. Basil looks at the money and blows a kiss to God.

Basil	We found her money!
Polly	Where?
Basil	. . . She left it . . . it doesn't matter . . . I'm ten pounds **up** on the deal.
Polly	Ten pounds **up?**
Basil	Yes – even if I give her ten – I'm still up . . . Polly . . . for the first time in my life I'm ahead! I'm winning! Ah ha! *(sees Mrs Richards approaching; gleefully)* Hallo, Mrs Richards. How lovely to see you. Your beautiful vase that you bought yesterday has just arrived. Now, remind me, that money you had, was it yours or mine?
Mrs Richards	I told you, it's mine.
Basil	You're absolutely sure?
Mrs Richards	Yes, I am.
Basil	But you're still ten pounds short. *(pulls out the wad of notes he has received and peels one off)* Polly, give Mrs Richards this, would you?
Mrs Richards	*(sensing something)* What's that?
Basil	This is **mine**. *(he flourishes it)*

Mrs Richards stares undecided. Basil beams. Sybil appears behind him and looks at the wad.

Sybil	What's that, Basil?

Basil jumps but cannot think of an answer.

Polly	It's mine.
Sybil	What?
Polly	It's the money I won on the horse.
Basil	That's right, dear. Polly asked me to put it in the safe for her. So . . . that's all sorted out . . . and this is your money, Polly . . . this is your beautiful vase, Mrs Richards.

Still holding the money in his right hand, he picks up the vase carefully with his left and holds it out to her. The Major sails into view, quite excited.

The Major	Fawlty . . . you **did** give me that money! You won it on that horse!

Basil is horrified. Sybil grabs the money; he clutches at it with his left hand, dropping the vase. It shatters. He screams.

Mrs Richards	That cost seventy-five pounds.
Sybil	Oh, I **am** sorry, Mrs Richards. We **must** pay you back for it.

She counts out the money for Mrs Richards. Basil despairs.

The Psychiatrist

Second of second series, first broadcast on 26 February 1979, BBC2.

Basil Fawlty   John Cleese
Sybil Fawlty   Prunella Scales
Polly   Connie Booth
Mr Johnson   Nicky Henson
Dr Abbott   Basil Henson
Mrs Abbott   Elspet Gray
Raylene Miles   Luan Peters
Manuel   Andrew Sachs
Terry   Brian Hall
Miss Tibbs   Gilly Flower
Miss Gatsby   Renée Roberts
Major Gowen   Ballard Berkeley
Mrs Johnson   Aimée Delamain
Girlfriend   Imogen Bickford-Smith

	The hotel lobby. Polly is checking a couple in. Sybil is on the phone. Basil is on the other phone . . . he is waiting.
Sybil	Oh dear . . . oh dear . . .
Basil	Hallo?
Sybil	What a shame.
Polly	Oh Manuel . . .
Basil	Hallo, operator. What is going on?
Sybil	Oh, I know . . .
Polly	Number ten.
Basil	. . . I've been trying to get through to the speaking clock.
Sybil	Oh dear . . .
	Manuel leads the guests off.
Basil	. . . Well, it's engaged.
Sybil	Oh, how awful . . .
Basil	. . . Well, it's been engaged for ten minutes. How is this possible, my wife isn't talking to it.
Sybil	Well, hold your head right back, that usually stops it.
Basil	Right. *(he rings off and re-dials)* The speaking clock has obviously taken the phone off the hook. Either that or there's been a light shower within twenty miles.
Sybil	Well, you'd better not go on if it's getting on the bedspread.
Basil	Unobtainable. *(he puts the phone down)* The clock's been cut off. Obviously it didn't pay its bill. *(goes into the office)*
Sybil	Well, call me back when you've staunched it. *(she puts the phone down)* I don't know why she stays with him. *(looks at a magazine)* Oh, that's pretty.
	Mr Johnson walks in through the main doors; he is casually dressed and has his shirt open to the waist.
Polly	Oh, hallo. You got the guide? *(he shows it to her)*
Sybil	Good evening, Mr Johnson.
Mr Johnson	Evening. Any messages?
Polly	Three, I think. *(she gets his messages)*
Sybil	Three . . . everybody wants you, don't they.
Mr Johnson	Oh, I wouldn't say that.
Sybil	Oh, well . . . you're only single once.
Basil's voice	*(from the office)* Twice can be arranged.
Sybil	What, Basil?
Basil	Nothing, my dear. *(he comes in and stares at Johnson who is*

on the simian side) Have we got enough bananas this week, dear?

Sybil gives him a look; he goes back into the office, where he sits down. He hears Sybil's grating laugh; it irritates him. She laughs again and he walks mock-casually back into reception and sits at the typewriter. Johnson is telling Sybil a story.

Mr Johnson So Harry says, 'You don't like me any more. Why not?' And he says, 'Because you've got so terribly pretentious.' And Harry says, 'Pretentious? *Moi?*' *(Sybil laughs; Basil remains straight-faced)* I'll just try that number. *(he goes into the bar)*

Sybil Oh, that's awfully good, isn't it. *'Moi'* . . . did you hear it, Basil?

Basil What, dear?

Sybil The joke.

Basil Oh, a joke. No, I heard you laugh, I thought perhaps he was having a tea party.

Sybil Tea party? Oh, now I understand the banana reference. You mean you think he looks like a monkey.

Basil Only from some angles.

Sybil Well, from this angle he's very attractive.

Basil Attractive?

Sybil You know, easy and amusing and charming.

Basil Charming, eh – well he's certainly covered in charms. I've never seen so many medals round one neck in my life. He must be the bravest orang-utang in Britain. What is the point of decorating yourself like that?

Sybil They're not just there for decoration – they have symbolic meaning.

Basil Sybil, that type would wear a dog turd round its neck if it was made of gold.

Sybil Basil, you're so ignorant sometimes. One of them **happens** to be a rhino's tooth, one's an ancient Egyptian fertility symbol . . .

Basil Well, that must come in handy.

Sybil It's not supposed to be handy, Basil. It goes back to the dawn of civilization.

Basil Well, by the look of his forehead, so does he.

Sybil Tell me, Basil, what is it about the . . . the Mediterranean type that antagonises you so? Is it because women find them attractive?

Basil	Sybil . . .
Sybil	You seem to think that we girls should be aroused by people like Gladstone and Earl Haig and Baden-Powell . . . don't you.
Basil	Well, at least they had a certain dignity. It's hard to imagine Earl Haig wandering round with his shirt open to the waist covered with identity bracelets.
Sybil	Well, he didn't mind the medals, did he. The military decorations.
Basil	That's not the point.
Sybil	I suppose the reason you confuse them with monkeys is that monkeys have fun – they know how to enjoy themselves. That's what makes them sexy, I suppose. *(Dr and Mrs Abbott enter through the main doors)* I'd never thought of that. *(to the Abbotts)* Good evening.
Dr Abbott	Good evening. I telephoned earlier, the name is Abbott.
Sybil	Oh yes. There **hasn't** been a cancellation, I'm afraid, so it is **still** a room without bath.
Dr Abbott	That's fine.
Sybil	Good. Would you just fill that in for me please. Yes, we're terribly busy at the moment.

At his end of the desk Basil does a subdued monkey impression. Mrs Abbott looks at him. He sees her.

Basil	Just enjoying myself. Good evening.
Mrs Abbott	Good evening.
Basil	*(to Dr Abbott)* Good evening.
Dr Abbott	Good evening.
Basil	*(beats his chest a few times, Tarzan style)* Ah . . . that felt better.
Sybil	Thank you, Mr Abbott. *(she takes another look at the card)* Oh, **Doctor** Abbott, I'm sorry.
Basil	*(freezes for a split second)* Doctor?
Dr Abbott	. . . Yes.
Basil	I'm terribly sorry, we hadn't been told. *(Dr Abbott looks at him questioningly)* We hadn't been told you were a doctor.
Dr Abbott	Oh.
Basil	How do you do, doctor. *(he offers his hand; Dr Abbott shakes it briefly)* Very nice to have you with us, doctor.
Dr Abbott	Thank you.
Sybil	You're in room five, doctor.
Basil	And Mrs Abbott, how do you do. *(he shakes hands with her)*

Dr Abbott	Dr Abbott, actually.
Basil	. . . I'm sorry?
Dr Abbott	**Doctor** Abbott.
Mrs Abbott	Two doctors.
Basil	*(to Dr Abbott)* You're **two** doctors?
Mrs Abbott	Yes.
Basil	Well, how did you become two doctors? That's most unusual . . . I mean, did you take the exams twice, or . . . ?
Dr Abbott	No, my wife's a doctor . . .
Mrs Abbott	. . . **I'm** a doctor.
Basil	You're a doctor too! So you're **three** doctors.
Dr Abbott	No, I'm just one doctor. My wife is another doctor.
Sybil	*(ringing the bell pointedly)* Manuel! *(Basil is silenced; to the Abbotts)* Your room is at the top of the stairs along to the left.
Basil	Oh I see! You see, I thought, when you said you were two doctors . . . *(Manuel comes running in from the kitchen)* Manuel, would you take the doctors' cases up to number five, please. *(he shows the way, then follows them up the stairs. Manuel comes behind with the cases)* Yes, this way please, doctors . . . Yes, when you said you were two doctors I thought perhaps you were a doctor of **medicine**, perhaps a doctor of archaeology . . .

They have gone. Mr Johnson comes up to the desk.

Sybil	Did you get through all right?
Mr Johnson	One was busy, I'll try again in a moment. Look, I forgot to ask, any news on that room for my mother?
Sybil	Oh yes, number sixteen **has** decided to stay, I'm afraid . . . I tried a couple of other places for you but everywhere's full at the moment.
Mr Johnson	Oh well, no hassle . . . she won't mind sharing with me.
Sybil	Lucky mum, ha ha ha.
Mr Johnson	I'll just go and try that number again.
Sybil	Oh, here, use this one.
Mr Johnson	Oh, thank you. *(he starts to dial; Sybil looks at the adornments round his neck)*
Sybil	May I ask . . . the sign on the chain, **by** the Egyptian fertility symbol . . . what is that . . . ?
Mr Johnson	It's a Greek astrological sign.
Sybil	Oh, it's beautiful. Where did you get it?
Mr Johnson	Er, Colchester, I think.

Sybil	Colchester!
Mr Johnson	*(to phone)* Oh, hello, can I speak to John Lawson please . . . oh all right, I'll hold on . . .
Sybil	So your mother will be arriving tomorrow?
Mr Johnson	Yes, first thing. She's getting the overnight train down from Newcastle.
Sybil	Newcastle.
Mr Johnson	Yes, visiting grandchildren. She's seventy-seven . . .
Sybil	Seventy-seven! Isn't that amazing . . . old people are wonderful when they have so much life, aren't they? Gives us all hope, doesn't it.
Mr Johnson	Mmmm . . .
Sybil	My mother . . . on the other hand . . . is a little bit of a trial really . . . you know, it's all right when they have the life force, but mother, well, she's got more of the death force really . . . she's a worrier . . .
Mr Johnson	*(to phone)* No, it's all right, I'll hold.
Sybil	She has these, well, morbid fears they are, really . . . vans is one . . . rats, doorknobs, birds, heights, open spaces . . . confined spaces, it's very difficult getting the space right for her really, you know . . .
Mr Johnson	*(nodding, not much interested)* Mmmm . . .
Sybil	Footballs, bicycles, cows . . . and she's always on about men following her . . . I don't know what she thinks they're going to do to her . . . vomit on her, Basil says . . .
Mr Johnson	*(to phone)* Can I leave my number, he can call me back . . .
Sybil	And death.
Mr Johnson	Oh, I see, right.
Sybil	She's frightened of death. On about it the whole time. I told her there's nothing she can do about it, I mean, nature can only take its course . . . the only thing you can hope is that it won't be long drawn out and painful, but she can't accept that . . .
Mr Johnson	Excuse me . . . *(to phone)* Hallo, John. How are you . . . fine . . . no, just down for the weekend . . .

Basil appears down the stairs and walks across the lobby towards the desk, seeing Johnson and registering displeasure. Sybil ignores this. He joins her behind the desk.

Basil	Charming people.
Sybil	Hmmm.
Basil	The Abbotts . . . charming couple.

Sybil	Yes. All three of them.
Mr Johnson	. . . No, I'm all right for tonight . . .
Basil	You know, dear, that outfit that Mrs Abbott is wearing, you should get yourself something like that.
Sybil	What, for the gardening, you mean?
Mr Johnson	. . . No, no, I can't tomorrow night, but how about lunch?
Basil	Attractive woman. How old would you say she was, Sybil?
Sybil	Forty-eight, fifty.
Basil	Oh, no, Sybil.
Sybil	I really don't know, Basil. Perhaps she's twelve.
Mr Johnson	. . . No, favourite . . . magic . . .
Basil	Yes, nice to have that kind of person staying, isn't it. Professional class. Educated, civilized . . . *(he looks at Johnson)* We've got both ends of the evolutionary scale this week, haven't we.

Moving behind Johnson's field of vision he comes out from behind the desk and does a monkey walk. The Abbotts appear at the foot of the stairs. He checks himself, but just a little late.

Basil	Good evening.
Dr Abbott	We're just going out for a stroll. What time do you serve dinner?
Basil	Seven-thirty till nine.
Mr Johnson	. . . See you tomorrow, then. *Ciao. (rings off)*
Mrs Abbott	Do you have a guide to Torquay?
Basil	A guide . . . um . . . oh dear, I think we're out of them again.
Mr Johnson	*(to Mrs Abbott)* Do you want to look at this one? I got it in the town.
Mrs Abbott	Oh, thanks . . . *What's on in Torquay.*
Mr Johnson	Yes, it's one of the world's shortest books. *(they laugh)*
Basil	What?
Mr Johnson	One of the world's shortest books . . . like 'The Wit of Margaret Thatcher' or 'Great English Lovers'.

They all laugh except you know who.

Sybil	*(amused)* Oh, very funny, isn't it, Basil. *(goes into the office)*
Mrs Abbott	*(to Johnson)* Thank you.

The Abbotts go out.

Basil	*(to Johnson)* Are you taking dinner here tonight?

Mr Johnson	Sorry?
Basil	Are you dining here tonight? Here in this unfashionable dump.
Mr Johnson	. . . Well, I wasn't planning to.
Basil	Not really your scene, is it.
Mr Johnson	I thought I'd try somewhere in town. Anywhere you'd recommend?
Basil	Well, what sort of food were you thinking of – fruit? Or . . .
Mr Johnson	Is there anywhere they do French food?

Sybil comes back from the office.

Basil	Yes, France, I believe. They seem to like it there. And the swim would certainly sharpen your appetite. You'd better hurry, the tide leaves in six minutes.
Sybil	Excuse my husband's sledge-hammer wit, Mr Johnson. There is a very nice place – La Pomme d'Amour.
Mr Johnson	La Pomme d'Amour? The apple of love.
Sybil	Yes, in Orchard Street.
Basil	*(thoughtfully)* Or that Ancient Egyptian place . . . The Golden Dog . . . something . . .
Sybil	*(to Johnson)* Do enjoy yourself . . . we'll see you later.
Mr Johnson	Thank you. *(he goes out)*
Sybil	*(turns and speaks quietly to Basil)* I've had it up to here with you.
Basil	What, dear?
Sybil	You never get it right, do you. You're either crawling all over them licking their boots, or spitting poison at them like some benzedrine puff-adder. *(she goes into the office)*
Basil	*(to himself)* Just trying to enjoy myself.

The dining room, towards the end of dinner. The Abbotts are just finishing their main course. Basil approaches them.

Basil	Ah . . . did you enjoy your beef?
Mrs Abbott	Oh, yes, thank you.
Basil	Oh good. Would you care for a dessert?
Mrs Abbott	No, just coffee, thank you.
Dr Abbott	Just coffee for me.
Basil	Two coffees, Sybil! Two coffees here, please, dear . . . would you care for a little something with us . . . *(the Abbotts look puzzled)* . . . Um . . . a little aperitif, cognac,

	brandy . . . on us, with us . . . which we'll pay for, on the house – as it were.
Mrs Abbott	Well, thank you. Yes, I'd like a cognac if I may . . .
Basil	Dr Abbott?
Dr Abbott	A port, thank you.
Basil	*Mon plaisir.*

He moves off to the sideboard to get the drinks. Sybil slides up.

Sybil	Coffee for you, doctor?
Mrs Abbott	Thank you.
Sybil	And for you, doctor.
Dr Abbott	Thank you.
Sybil	Have you been to Torquay before?
Mrs Abbott	Well, not for a few years, no – we had a free weekend and we suddenly thought we'd like to get out of London.
Sybil	Lovely . . . white or black?
Mrs Abbott	Black, thank you.
Sybil	*(to Dr Abbott)* Black for you, doctor?
Dr Abbott	Thank you.
Basil	*(arriving with the drinks)* A cognac for you, doctor. It's rather fascinating your both being doctors – port for you, doctor – because at one point I was contemplating becoming a surgeon.
Sybil	A tree surgeon. *(laughs)*
Basil	Thank you, Sybil.
Sybil	He had to give it up. Couldn't stand the sight of sap. *(laughs)*
Basil	That's a bit old, isn't it, dear. My great-grandfather on my mother's side was a doctor, and so it was always felt that I might . . .
Sybil	Run a hotel. Are you both in general practice?
Mrs Abbott	No, I'm a paediatrician.
Basil	Feet?
Mrs Abbott	Children.
Sybil	Oh, Basil.
Basil	Well, children have feet, don't they? That's how they move around, my dear. You must take a look next time, it's most interesting. *(to Dr Abbott)* And you, doctor? Are you a . . .
Dr Abbott	I'm a psychiatrist.
Basil	Very nice too. Well cheers. *(he sips Dr Abbott's port, then*

	realizes) I'll get you another one. *(he hurries off to the sideboard)*
Sybil	A psychiatrist, how fascinating. We've never had a psychiatrist staying here before. We had a faith healer the first month we were open.
Dr Abbott	Really.
Sybil	It's a relatively new profession, psychiatry, isn't it?
Mrs Abbott	Well, Freud started about 1880.
Sybil	Yes, but it's only now we're seeing them on the television.
Basil	*(returning with the port)* There we are. I must just . . . er . . . excuse me . . . *(he retires to the kitchen)*
Dr Abbott	*(changing the subject)* How long have you had this hotel?
Sybil	Well, my husband and I bought it in 1966 . . .

In the kitchen, Basil is standing by the door peeping back into the dining room.

Basil	Keep back, keep back.
Polly	. . . What is it?
Basil	. . . Abbott . . .
Polly	What's the matter with him?
Basil	. . . Psychiatrist . . . look at him . . . look . . . look at the way he's listening . . . see . . . ? He's taking it all in. She doesn't realize. Look! Look at the way she's talking! They've got photographic memories. *(looks to Polly but she's gone calls)* Sybil! Sybil! *(he moves back into the dining room)*
Sybil	Yes, Basil?
Basil	Could I bother you, dear?
Sybil	What is it?
Basil	Just a little problem. *(Dr Abbott turns towards Basil)* Nothing personal. Nothing of a private nature or anything. Just to do with . . .
Sybil	Excuse me, would you?

Basil and Sybil move into the kitchen.

Sybil	What is it, Basil?
Basil	Just . . . just . . . take it easy . . . OK?
Sybil	What?
Basil	Just keep your distance. I mean, remember who you are, all right?
Sybil	. . . Remember who I . . .
Basil	Well, just don't tell him about yourself.

Sybil	Basil, I'm perfectly capable . . .
Basil	All right, all right . . . what have you told him?
Sybil	Nothing. We were talking about Scotland.
Basil	Scotland? What does he want to know about Scotland? *(Sybil touches him to calm him; he jumps)*
Sybil	Oh Basil . . . why are you so nervous?
Basil	I'm not nervous. I'm just saying 'take it easy'. All right? All of us. Just take it easy, right?
Sybil	What's got into you?
Basil	Nothing's got into me. I just said 'take it easy'. Can't I say 'take it easy' without starting a panic? *(with increasing mania)* I mean, what is going on here?
Sybil	Now, Basil, look . . .
Terry	Look, Mr Fawlty, take it easy.
Basil	Now look – get one thing clear. All right? You don't tell me to take it easy. I don't pay you to tell me to take it easy. I pay **you** to take it easy. No – I pay you to **tell** you to take it easy. So take it easy. All right? *(Sybil puts a hand on his arm; he jumps)*
Sybil	*(taking his arm anyway and leading him aside)* Listen – why are you getting so upset?
Basil	I'm **not** . . .
Sybil	You liked him when he arrived . . .
Basil	Look . . .
Sybil	. . . and then just because you find out he's a psychiatrist you get all . . .
Basil	I'm not bothered by that. I'm not . . . I'm not bothered by that. If he wants to be a psychiatrist that's his own funeral. They're all as mad as bloody March hares anyway but that's not the point. Look. Look! How does he earn his money? . . . He gets paid for sticking his nose . . .
Sybil	Oh, Basil . . .
Basil	No, I'm going to have my say . . . into people's private . . . um . . . details. Well, just speaking for myself, I don't want a total stranger nosing around in my private parts. Details. That's all I'm saying.
Sybil	They're down here on holiday. They're just here to enjoy themselves . . .
Basil	He can't.
Sybil	Can't what?
Basil	He can't tell me anything about myself that I don't know already. All this psychiatry, it's a load of tommy-rot. *(Sybil*

gives him the Abbotts' bill; he takes it and goes muttering
towards the dining room) You know what they're all
obsessed with, don't you.

Sybil	What?
Basil	You know what they say it's all about, don't you . . . mmm? Sex. Everything's connected with sex. Choh! What a load of cobblers . . . *(he goes into the dining room)*

In the dining room. Basil approaches the Abbotts' table.

Mrs Abbott	Yes, but you see, if they want to do that they'd have to close the hotel, wouldn't they.
Basil	*(putting the bill down next to Dr Abbott)* Yes . . . if you would just sign that. Thank you so much. *(he moves away and* *clears the Major's table, then goes into the kitchen)*
Dr Abbott	Yes. *(studying the bill)* We were just speculating how people in your profession arrange their holidays. How often can you get away? *(but Basil has not heard this; he* *arrives back at the table just before Dr Abbot glances up and* *asks)* How often do you manage it?
Basil	I beg your pardon?
Dr Abbott	How often can you and your wife manage it? *(a fairly long* *pause as various thoughts go through Basil's head)* . . . You don't mind my asking?
Basil	Not at all, not at all . . . about average, since you ask.
Mrs Abbott	Average?
Basil	Uh huh.
Dr Abbott	What would be average?
Basil	Well, you tell me, ha ha ha.
Mrs Abbott	Well . . . a couple of times a year?
Basil	. . . What?!
Dr Abbott	Once a year?

Basil looks astonished.

Dr Abbott	Well, we knew it must be difficult . . . my wife didn't see how you could manage it at all . . . you know . . .
Basil	Well, as you've asked . . . two or three times a week, actually. *(the Abbotts stare)*
Dr Abbott	A week . . .
Basil	Yes. Pretty normal, isn't it? We're quite normal down here in Torquay, you know.

He turns and heads for the kitchen, leaving them puzzled. He enters the kitchen briskly but as soon as the doors have shut behind him reverts to a dazed state. Sybil and Polly are chatting.

Sybil . . . and he says, 'Pretentious? *Moi?*' I always like a man who can make me laugh.

Polly *(noticing Basil's fixed stare)* Are you all right, Mr Fawlty?

Basil Mmmm? Yes, yes . . . thanks . . .

Sybil What's the matter, Basil?

Basil Nothing, dear, just talking to . . . Dr Abbott . . .

Sybil Oh, now, if I had the money to go to a psychiatrist he's just the sort I'd choose, I can't think of anything nicer than having a good old heart-to-heart, I'm sure they understand women . . .

Basil Sybil . . .

Sybil What, darling?

Basil Do you know . . . do you know what he asked me just now . . . out there?

Sybil What?

Basil He asked me . . . *(whispers in her ear)*

Sybil Oh, don't be ridiculous, Basil.

Basil I'm telling you the truth, honestly, as God is my witness.

Sybil What's got into you today?

Basil He turned round and asked me. Just like that.

Sybil Well, what did he say?

Basil He said . . . *(whispers)* . . . Then his wife said . . .

Sybil They're talking about holidays, Basil . . . I was just saying to them about how difficult it is to get any . . .

Basil Twice a year!! Oh my God. . . . What did I say?

Sybil It doesn't matter.

Basil Well, how was I to know?

He exits rapidly into the dining room, but the Abbotts have left. He sprints into the lobby, catching the Abbotts up at the main door.

Basil Hallo! You know, we were at cross purposes just now, there you were talking about sex and I thought you were talking about walks. Not sex!! Holidays. Holidays. Sex! Ha ha ha. No, my wife and I have one about twice a year – I mean holiday, a holiday, whereas so far as a good walk goes, well, we have a jolly good walk about two or three times a week, average . . .

Dr Abbott	Well, we're just taking ours now.
Basil	Thank you . . . well, enjoy it . . . The walk! The **walk!**

The Abbotts go out. Basil turns to the reception desk, where Raylene Miles, a very attractive Australian girl, is waiting.

Basil	I'm so sorry . . .
Raylene	My name is Raylene Miles. I have a reservation.
Basil	Ah yes, that's right. Would you be so good as to fill this in . . . *(she takes the card and bends over the desk to write on it; she is wearing a rather low-cut dress and Basil's eyes stray downwards; she glances up at this very moment; he turns away embarrassed and then looks back)* Very nice.
Raylene	. . . Oh. Thank you.
Basil	Your thing. I mean, your charms! Charm! *(indicating her pendant)* In the middle . . .
Raylene	Yes, I know.
Basil	May I ask what it is?
Raylene	*(writing)* It's a Saint Christopher's medal.
Basil	Saint . . . ?
Raylene	Saint Christopher. *(she holds it up so that Basil can look at it; he affects great interest, and at this moment Sybil approaches)* Patron saint of travellers.
Basil	Oh, hallo dear. St Christopher's medal. *(Sybil gives him a look and moves behind him at the desk)* Protects travellers. *(to Raylene)* Very pretty.
Sybil	Yes, isn't she . . . where did you put the order forms, Basil?
Basil	Er . . . down there, dear.
Sybil	Where?
Basil	Down here, dear . . .

They both crouch down to look for them, and thus fail to see Johnson come in very cautiously through the main door. A pretty girl is with him, keeping out of sight. When he sees that both Basil and Sybil are occupied he signals to the girl, and she nips upstairs. He approaches the desk looking nonchalant.

Mr Johnson	Hallo. Could I have the key to number six, please.
Sybil	Oh, you're back early this evening, Mr Johnson.
Mr Johnson	Yes, well I've got to be up early for mother.

Sybil gives him the key, with much smiling. He goes upstairs.

Basil	*(to Raylene)* Thank you. We've put you in number seven.
Sybil	*(ringing the bell)* Manuel . . .
Basil	*(moving round the desk to take Raylene's cases)* It's all right, dear, I'll take them up. *(to Raylene)* We have a Spanish porter – we're training him at the moment . . . be quicker to train an *(loudly, after Johnson)* **ape**!!

He leads off up the stairs, followed by Raylene. Sybil looks after them beadily. Manuel comes out of the bar.

Sybil	Never mind, Manuel. *(she spots a small carrier bag Raylene has left)* Oh! *(she picks it up and moves off; Manuel looks perplexed)*

The upstairs corridor. Johnson runs along it, opens the door to his room, letting the girl in. He closes the door behind them just as Basil and Raylene appear. They pass the Abbotts' and Johnson's rooms before coming to Raylene's – all three rooms are on the same side.

Basil	I was just wondering – are you in fact Australian, at all, by any chance, may I ask?
Raylene	Oh dear, is my accent that strong?
Basil	Oh, no, no, no, it's just that you're quite tall, so I thought . . . *(they go into Raylene's room; Basil puts the cases down)* Here we are, this is your room. I hope it's to your liking, view of the English Riviera down there behind the trees. *(she admires the view; he admires her)* This is your bathroom . . . here we are . . . *(he turns the bathroom light switch, which is just outside the door, on and goes in; then comes out again)* Oh . . . light's not working. *(he goes into the bathroom)* I'll just fix it . . . have you had a tiring journey?
Raylene	Seven hours in the coach. *(she starts doing some yoga-type relaxing exercises, rotating her head)* Is the dining room still open?
Basil	*(from the bathroom)* Well, the chef leaves at nine I'm afraid. We could always do you sandwiches.
Raylene	*(moving to the wall by the bathroom door)* I'd like a hot meal, really. Is there a restaurant near here? *(she stands against the wall and does a knees-bend)*
Basil	Yes, there's an awfully good little Welsh place, Leek House, about five minutes walk – you'd have to go straight away.
Raylene	Oh, that'll do fine. *(she stretches her arms up)*

Basil	Just turn left out of the gate and straight on and it's on your right.

Without looking, he reaches out of the bathroom for the switch. His hand engages Raylene's left boob. He tries to switch it on, senses something is wrong, and feels it. Raylene looks down in disbelief just as Sybil enters the room. Basil leans out of the bathroom, sees where his hand is, looks at Raylene and then turns and sees Sybil. He snatches his hand away. There is an embarrassed pause.

Sybil	*(to Raylene)* You left this downstairs.

She turns and leaves. Basil stares after her, then turns to Raylene.

Basil	I'm sorry . . . I was trying the switch . . . I'm sorry . . . *(he rushes out after Sybil)*

The corridor. Sybil turns as Basil comes out of the room, her hands on her hips.

Basil	Sybil, Sybil, Sybil, I'm sorry, I didn't know she was there, I was trying the switch . . .
Sybil	It's **pathetic**, Basil.
Basil	No, no look, Sybil, I was reaching for the switch . . .
Sybil	Don't bother . . .
Basil	Look, the lights weren't working in the bathroom, right, OK? So I went in, checked the fitting, which was loose . . .
Sybil	I've read about it, Basil. The male menopause it's called. Oh . . . and one word of advice. If you're going to grope a girl, have the gallantry to stay **in** the room with her while you're doing it, mmm?

She turns and leaves. Basil starts after her but gives up. He goes back to Raylene's room.

Basil	I'm sorry, I do apologize for . . . I was feeling for the switch.
Raylene	Oh, I realize, that's perfectly all right. I hope your wife didn't . . .
Basil	Oh, my wife, no, no, she's been on about that switch.
Raylene	Where was that restaurant again?
Basil	Out of the gate, turn left, five minutes, on your right. Leek House.

Raylene	Thank you.
Basil	Not at all.

He leaves. As he walks down the corridor he passes Johnson's door.

Mr Johnson's voice . . . 'Pretentious? *Moi?*'

Basil stops. He hears a female laugh. He listens at the door for a moment, then moves back just before the door opens and Johnson comes out.

Basil	Yes? Can I help you?
Mr Johnson	Um . . . I was wondering if I could get . . . um . . . a drink now.
Basil	A drink.
Mr Johnson	*(closing the door behind him)* Well . . . a bottle of champagne.
Basil	Champagne?
Mr Johnson	Yes.
Basil	I see . . . you are aware of our rule about visitors, are you?
Mr Johnson	*(innocently)* Mmm?
Basil	No visitors in guests' rooms after ten o'clock.
Mr Johnson	. . . Oh.
Basil	. . . Of the opposite . . . um . . . sex.
Mr Johnson	No, I wasn't.
Basil	Ah.
Mr Johnson	But I am now. So you'll send up the champagne, will you?
Basil	*(surprised)* What?
Mr Johnson	. . . The champagne.
Basil	You're drinking it on your own, are you?
Mr Johnson	I guess I'll have to.
Basil	Very well. One bottle of champagne for one.
Mr Johnson	Thank you.
Basil	And one glass.
Mr Johnson	That's all I need . . . unless you care to join me.
Basil	No thank you. Not when I'm on the job.
Mr Johnson	Oh, that's when I enjoy it the most.

He goes inside the room. Basil hurries down the stairs and calls.

Basil	Manuel! *(Manuel appears)* A bottle of champagne and one glass. Quick!

Basil darts off upstairs again and stands by Johnson's door listening hard. Miss Tibbs and Miss Gatsby come up behind him.

Miss Tibbs	Mr Fawlty.
Basil	*(jumping slightly)* Mm?
Miss Tibbs	Did you know there's a psychiatrist staying?
Basil	. . . Yes, yes I did.
Miss Gatsby	Has he come for the Major?
Basil	What?
Miss Tibbs	Has he come for the Major?
Basil	No.
Miss Gatsby	Oh good!
Miss Tibbs	We were rather worried. *(they start to move away)*
Miss Gatsby	*(to Miss Tibbs)* I'm sure they have them in Birmingham too.

They go off up the corridor. Basil moves to listen at the door again and as he does so it opens and Johnson is standing there.

Basil   Good night, ladies. *(to Johnson)* It's just coming. *(he stands there; Johnson stands looking at him; he has to move off)* Won't be a moment.

He moves away and Johnson closes his door. Basil pauses by the next door, looks around, unlocks it, and slips in. It is the Abbotts' room. In the dark he closes the door behind him and goes over to the wall contiguous with Johnson's room. Putting his ear to the wall he listens intently. The Abbotts walk in and switch the light on. He sees them and starts, reacting a second time when he realizes that the man is the dreaded psychiatrist person. He goes smoothly into a wall-checking routine, tapping it in the manner of a doctor sounding someone's chest.

Basil   This wall . . . er, we had some complaints from downstairs . . . I'm just giving it a check, OK? . . . yes, I think that's fine . . . Hang on . . . *(pauses dramatically)* No! No, we're all right. Fine, well, sorry to disturb you. Good night. Good night. *(he slips out of the door)*

The Abbotts *(bemused)* Good night.

In the corridor, Basil sees the coast is clear and puts his ear to Johnson's door. Mrs Abbott comes out of her room. Basil sees her and sounds the door a couple of times, just as he did in the Abbotts' room.

Basil	Ah . . . *(turns to Mrs Abbott)* Can I help you?
Mrs Abbott	The bathroom?
Basil	Yes. Second on the left.

She moves off. The door opens and Johnson is standing there behind Basil.

Mr Johnson	Yes?
Basil	It's just coming.

Johnson gives him a very meaningful look and closes the door. In his room, he indicates to the girl, who is sitting on his bed, that someone is hovering about in the corridor. He bolts the door. In the corridor, Manuel runs up with a tray with a champagne bottle in an ice bucket and a glass on it. Basil takes it, puts his other hand on the doorknob. Takes a deep breath and turns the knob and hits the door with his shoulder. As it's bolted he bounces back dropping the tray. Manuel neatly catches the ice bucket with the bottle in it; the tray and glass drop noisily. Johnson's door opens. Basil sees Johnson and slaps Manuel on the head. Manuel drops the ice bucket.

Basil	*(to Manuel) Stupidissimo!* You continental cretin! *(to Johnson)* I'm sorry. I'll get another. *(to Manuel) Un altero. Pronto! Pronto! Pronto! (he waves Manuel away)*
Dr Abbott	*(looking out of his room)* Everything all right?
Basil	Yes, fine, thank you. I'm afraid that Spanish ape . . . sorry . . . person . . . bungled it again. Dago bird brain! God knows how they ever got an Armada together. Still, I'll clear this up . . . right, well, if you'd like to go back to your rooms, thank you.

The good Dr Abbott disappears and Johnson also closes his door. Basil steps back for a moment and the Major hurries up to him.

The Major	Fawlty!
Basil	Yes?
The Major	Here, here . . . I thought you ought to know . . .
Basil	What?
The Major	There's a psychiatrist in the hotel.
Basil	Yes, I know.
The Major	You **know**?
Basil	Yes.
The Major	Oh! Well apparently he's dressed up as a guest.

Basil	Well, he **is** a guest, Major. *(the Major wanders off; to himself)* Perhaps he **has** come to get you.

Manuel hurries up with another tray with champagne and a glass on it. Basil takes the tray and knocks on Johnson's door. In Johnson's room, the girl is sitting on the bed. She nips into the bathroom and he lies nonchalantly back on the bed reading a newspaper.

Mr Johnson	Come! *(Basil enters; everything looks normal)* Thank you. On the table, please. Thank you.

Basil puts the tray down, having a good look round. He spots an ashtray.

Basil	Ah! *(he empties its contents into his hand, glances round once more and goes to the door)* Thank you. *(he goes out; there is a pause, then he suddenly re-opens the door)* Yes?

Failing to catch Johnson doing anything he closes the door. In the corridor, he opens his palm and peers at the ashes. He holds a cigarette butt up close to his eye. Dr Abbott comes out of his room behind Basil. Basil sees him after a moment, puts his hand behind his back suspiciously and then produces it again and opens it to show he is not behaving suspiciously.

Basil	Filthy habit. *(dusts the ash off his hands)*
Dr Abbott	The bathroom.
Basil	Oh, second on the left.

Dr Abbott moves off. Basil creeps up to Raylene's room, opens the door and slips in. It is dark. He makes for the wall. But Raylene is asleep on the bed, and just as he gets there she wakes and screams.

Raylene	Aaaaaah! Who is it?!
Basil	It's all right. It's all right. It's only me! Please, please, it's only me!
Raylene	What are you doing? What do you want?

Dr Abbott comes in and switches on the light.

Dr Abbott	What's going on?
Basil	Nothing! I didn't know she was in here. Just came in to check the wall. *(to Raylene)* Do you mind? . . . Sorry . . . I thought you'd gone down to the restaurant. *(he sounds the wall)*

Raylene	*(puzzled)* I was just so tired.
Basil	No, that's fine. Well, sorry to disturb you. *(to Dr Abbott)* Bloody walls. *(he leaves)*
Dr Abbott	*(to Raylene)* Are you all right now?

The corridor. Basil comes out. Sybil is hurrying up.

Sybil	What was that?
Basil	What? Er . . . nothing, dear . . .
Sybil	Why was she screaming? What were you doing?
Mr Johnson	*(looking out of his room)* What's going on?
Basil	Nothing. She thought there was someone in her room.
Mr Johnson	Someone in her room?!
Basil	Yes, someone in her room!
Mr Johnson	Oh . . . you'll have to charge her double then.

He goes back inside. Dr Abbott comes out of Raylene's room.

Sybil	*(to Basil)* What were you **doing** in there?
Basil	*(to Dr Abbott)* Is she all right?
Dr Abbott	She's all right now. *(he goes into his room)*
Sybil	*(taking Basil's arm)* What were you **doing** in there?

Raylene comes out of her room.

Raylene	Oh, I'm sorry, Mr Fawlty. I didn't realize it was you.
Basil	That's all right. That's all right. *(to Sybil)* I'll tell you . . . I'll tell you later. *(he hurries off; Sybil is looking distinctly thoughtful)*
Raylene	Silly of me, sorry, I didn't know it was him. He came in to check the walls.
Sybil	To check the **walls**?

The lobby. Manuel is standing eating an ice-cream. Basil hurtles down the stairs.

Basil	Manuel! Manuel! Quick! Come on!

He flies out through the main door. Manuel puts his ice-cream down and follows. They run outside. Basil picks up a ladder lying on the ground and they position it beneath a lighted window. In Johnson's room, Johnson is pouring champagne into a plastic mug for the girl. Outside, Basil starts to climb the ladder. Manuel follows, until Basil motions him back. He slides down. In Johnson's room he and the girl are drinking their champagne. Outside, Basil reaches the top of the ladder.

He peers in through the window. However, it is the Abbotts' room he is looking into. Mrs Abbott, in her nightdress, is brushing her hair. Dr Abbott is undressing. Just as Basil realizes his mistake they see him. They stare. He smiles wanly and starts sounding the window. He reaches too high and overbalances out of sight. The ladder falls back. Basil lands on his back with the ladder on top of him. He groans.

Manuel	Help! Help! *(he rushes back into the hotel)*

In the lobby, Sybil is just coming down the stairs.

Sybil	Basil! Basil! *(she goes into the dining room)*
Manuel	*(running in)* Mrs Fawlty! Oh, Mrs Fawlty . . . **Mr** Fawlty!
Sybil	What?
Manuel	He hurt. He fall off ladder.
Sybil	Off a **ladder**?
Manuel	*Si*. Please come, come, come.

They move into the lobby.

Sybil	What was he doing up a ladder?
Manuel	He try to see girl.
Sybil	**What!**
Manuel	He try to see in room to see girl. Come! Come!
Sybil	*(setting her mouth)* I see.
Manuel	I tell him careful but he got to see girl.
Sybil	Right!

They go out of the main doors at a good pace. Basil is on his feet, groggily setting the ladder up again. Sybil comes round the corner at a good speed.

Basil	Hallo, dear. I was just going to . . .

He receives the mother of a smackeroo and falls flat on his back. Sybil turns on her heel and strides off. He staggers up to his feet.

Basil	What the . . .

He starts after her, furious. Manuel gets out of the way quickly. Basil runs in through the main doors and up the stairs. Sybil has opened the door of her room by the time Basil catches her up.

Basil	What in God's name do you think you're doing??! What did you hit me for?

Sybil	. . . How dare you!! *(she hits him again)* How **dare** you!
Basil	Have you gone mad, what's got into you?
Sybil	You really don't know?
Basil	No, I don't.
Sybil	What were you doing up that ladder? Come on . . .
Basil	I was trying to see the girl. Is that so strange? *(Sybil hits him)* Will you stop hitting me!
Sybil	Get away from this door. And don't you dare try and come in here tonight.

She slams the door. Basil stares uncomprehendingly. Manuel has come into view. Basil sees him.

Basil	Mad. She's gone completely mad.
Manuel	Crazy. She go crazy.
Basil	I mean, **what** in . . . ?
Manuel	Crazy! I say to her, 'You try to see in girl's room' and . . . *(shrugs)* she go crazy.
Basil	. . . What?
Manuel	I tell her! You got to see girl . . . in bedroom. You crazy about this girl. OK? OK. So you go up to look at her . . . Mrs Fawlty . . . *(shrug)* She go crazy.

Basil imitates the shrug, then advances on Manuel, picks him up, turns him upside down and shakes him furiously.

Basil	I am punishing you for being alive. And as long as you go on being alive, I shall go on . . . *(then he notices Mrs Abbott, returning from the bathroom, who is standing watching him; he drops Manuel and pretends to lecture him)* Now that's how an Englishman would do it, you see. Now, a German . . . a German would go . . . *(demonstrates a kick without actually connecting)* No, that's enough for tonight . . . all right, we'll go on with your training in the morning. *(to Mrs Abbott)* We're just training him in the art of hotel management. It's rather interesting, actually . . . *(he puts a casual arm out to rest against the Abbotts' door)* He's from Barcelona . . . *(but Dr Abbott opens the door and Basil falls right into the room, landing heavily; he gets up)* Sorry. I missed the door.
Dr Abbott	. . . Oh . . .
Basil	Everything all right? Everything er . . . **normal?**
Dr Abbott	Yes, thank you.

Mrs Abbott goes into the room past Basil.

Basil	Fine. Well . . . I'll leave you to it, then. I mean . . . to go to bed, to sleep . . . perchance to dream. Hah! Have a good night. Good night's sleep. Sleep well.
Mrs Abbott	Good night. And you.
Basil	Thank you! I will. *(he closes the door and stands in the corridor)* God knows **where** . . . (he looks around, looks at the broom cupboard, opens it, then looks at Johnson's door opposite) I'll get you, you Piltdown ponce.

The upstairs corridor. Early next morning. Basil, unshaven, is sitting at the top of the stairs. Polly appears carrying two tea-trays. She sees Basil and stares.

Polly	Are you all right?
Basil	Mmmm?
Polly	Are you all right?
Basil	Yes. Let me have one of those. *(takes one of the trays)* For Sybil. Yes, go on, go on! *(he hurries to Sybil's room and knocks on the door)* Sybil . . . dear . . . ?
Sybil's voice	What do you want?
Basil	Got your tea for you, dear.
Sybil's voice	Just leave it outside the room.
Basil	*(putting the tray down)* Yes, all right, dear . . . er, Sybil . . . ?
Sybil's voice	I'm not **speaking** to you, Basil.
Basil	Could I just have my electric razor, dear . . . just for the guests . . . *(the door opens and Sybil gives it to him; he puts his foot in the door)* Thank you dear . . . look . . .
Sybil	*(trying to close the door)* Basil, will you . . .
Basil	I just want to explain something, dear.
Sybil	Get your foot out of the door.
Basil	Let me explain.
Sybil	I'm not interested.
Basil	Look . . . when I said I wanted to look at that girl last night I wasn't talking about that . . . Raylene . . . something . . . that Australian girl . . . I was talking about the girl in the room next to her . . . in **Johnson**'s room.
Sybil	. . . Basil.
Basil	Johnson smuggled a girl into his room last night . . . that

was the one I was trying to get a look at, not that . . . Australian hayseed.

Sybil   Basil, you've had eight hours to think of something . . . is that really the best you can come up with?

Basil   You don't believe me.

Sybil   Oh, go away.

Basil   Right! I'll get her. I'm going to get her and show her to you.

Sybil   Yes, you do that . . .

Basil   Right, I will. *(she slams the door)* Right! All right . . . *(he runs off)*

In Johnson's room he and the girl are fully dressed. She is sitting on the bed putting on make-up. There is a knock at the door; she dodges into the bathroom.

Mr Johnson   Come in.

Mrs Abbott looks in.

Mrs Abbott   Oh, Mr Johnson. Do you want your guide back?

Mr Johnson   Oh, thank you, yes . . .

She comes in; the door swings to behind her. In the corridor Basil steams into view. As he approaches Johnson's door he hears female laughter. Basil slips into the broom cupboard, leaving the door ajar. Mrs Abbott comes out of Johnson's room.

Mr Johnson's voice   I'll see you later then. Thank you.

Mrs Abbott   *(calling towards her room)* OK, darling.

Dr Abbott comes out. Basil leaps out of the cupboard brandishing a broom.

Basil   Right! The game's up. *(he sees who he has confronted, then looks at a point high up on the wall)* Up there. Bit of game pie, got stuck up there. *(he jabs at the wall with the broom; the Abbotts stare for a moment)* There we are. Right. Everything back to normal. Enjoy your walk. *(he starts sweeping the floor; the Abbotts move off downstairs)*

Dr Abbott   *(quietly, as they reach the foot of the stairs)* There's enough material there for an entire conference.

Upstairs, Basil puts the broom back into the cupboard but in doing so knocks something over. He bends down to sort it out, and picks up a bottle. He realizes that he has got dark sticky stuff all over his hand. In the corridor, Johnson looks out of his room.

Mr Johnson   OK, all clear.

The girl starts to come out but hears something and goes back in. Raylene comes out of her room. As she passes the cupboard Basil leaps out.

Basil   Right! That's it!

He grabs her from behind. Unbeknown to him his messy hand clasps Raylene's right boob. She squeals.

Raylene   What are you doing?! Jesus, what's going on?
Basil   *(releasing her)* Shh! I'm sorry, I thought you were somebody else.

Raylene   You scared the hell out of me . . .
Basil   Yes, I'm awfully sorry, you see there's a girl in there, the bloke smuggled her in last night . . . *(Sybil appears)* . . . I was just explaining to Miss Miles about . . . our little problem . . . *(Raylene turns towards Sybil, the black handprint on her boob deafeningly apparent; Basil has not noticed it; Sybil has)* . . . with the extra guest . . . Mr Johnson's friend . . . in six . . . last night . . .
Sybil   What's that on your hand, Basil?
Basil   What? . . . Oh, that's some stuff in the cupboard, dear. Something I knocked over . . . *(he follows Sybil's eye-line and sees Raylene's hand-printed right boob)* Agh! *(instinctively reaches out to hide it, touches Raylene again, then pulls back sharply)* Sorry!! I got confused.
Raylene   What?
Basil   Sorry . . . I got confused.

Sybil has gone. Basil rushes after her. He catches her at the kitchen door.

Basil   Sybil! Sybil! Sybil!!! Look. I'll tell her to go. I'm going to get the other girl just to prove it to you but I'll tell Miss Miles to . . . to leave . . . Out! Out! Right! Out! Out!

He rushes back up to Raylene's room. The door is ajar. He enters the room very cautiously. It is empty.

Basil   Um . . . excuse me . . . I do want to apologize but I'm afraid I shall have to ask you to . . .

Raylene comes in from the bathroom, dressed in white trousers and a sexy push-up bra. She doesn't see Basil, who drops out of sight behind the bed. She returns to the bathroom; he is about to get out when there is a knock at the door. He leaps away. Raylene, in the bathroom, hears the knock and turns.

Raylene   Come in.

She goes back into the bedroom. Sybil comes in. There is no sign of Basil.

Sybil   I'm sorry to bother you, I thought I'd better apologize for my husband's behaviour . . .

Raylene   No, please, really Mrs Fawlty . . .

Sybil   He's going through rather a disturbed time at the moment . . .

Raylene   No please, look really, I don't quite understand, he **does** seem a bit worked up about something but I'm sure there's some quite innocent explanation . . .

But Sybil has noticed Basil's finger sticking out of the wardrobe, holding the door shut.

Sybil   Basil.

There is no response. She bangs on the door. The finger disappears rapidly. Basil comes out.

Basil   Oh, hallo dear . . . just checking the doors . . .

Sybil looks at Raylene, whose jaw sags.

Sybil   *(to Raylene)* All right, what's going on?

Raylene   . . . I was in the bathroom!

Basil   Yes she was, dear, so I just popped in to have a look at these hinges and . . .

Sybil   Do you **really** imagine, even in your **wildest dreams**, that a girl like this could possibly be interested in an ageing brilliantined stick insect like you?

Basil   . . . A girl like who, dear?

Sybil   **This** one, Basil. The one you've been chasing ever since she arrived.

Basil   My dear woman, have you gone out of your mind?

Sybil   What are you doing in here?

Basil   Look, you know the trouble we've been having with these hinges . . . All right, all right, if you really want to know, I came to apologize for the incident just now when I thought she was the girl in Johnson's room . . . you know, when I put my hand on . . .

Sybil walks out into the corridor. Basil comes running after her.

Basil	Sybil, Sybil, Sybil, look . . .
Sybil	If you think I've got time to listen to any more of your hopeless lily-livered jellyfish lies . . .
Basil	They are not lies, I am trying . . .
Sybil	Why can't you be a man? If you want to grope the guests, why can't you at least be **honest** about it, without making up some pathetic song and dance . . .
Basil	*(finally losing his temper)* Shut up!
Sybil	. . . Oh, you've done it now.
Basil	No I haven't. I'm just going to. I'm fed up with you, you . . . rancorous coiffeured old sow. Why don't you syringe the doughnuts out of your ears and get some sense into that dormant organ you keep hidden in that rat's maze of yours? There is a woman in that room that Johnson smuggled in last night, right? That's the woman I've been trying to get hold of. *(Sybil is clearly unimpressed)* Right! Right! *(he pulls her towards Johnson's room)* Stand there! Stand there! . . . and watch. *(he is so forceful that Sybil is momentarily stunned into submission; he knocks on Johnson's door; Johnson opens it)* Champagne?
Mr Johnson	. . . What?
Basil	Another bottle of champagne, perhaps? I thought you said you rather enjoyed it when you were on the job.
Mr Johnson	Have you got a screw loose?
Basil	A screw? No, it's just that I thought that I'd rather formed the impression that there was someone in the room with you. A female person, perhaps, a lady, you know – an opposite person of the contradictory gender.
Mr Johnson	Mrs Johnson is in here, yes.
Basil	*(with heavy irony)* Oh, of course, I should have guessed. Oh yes, of course . . . the little woman, eh. The only thing is . . . I thought you told my wife that you were single.
Mr Johnson	I am.
Basil	I see. So who's this Mrs Johnson then, eh? The late President's wife? Or . . .
Mr Johnson	She's my mother.

Basil   . . . Your mother. Oh, I see. This little bit of crumpet's your old mummy, is she? Oh this is rich. Mrs Johnson popped up for a quickie, did she?

Mr Johnson   Certainly. *(he goes into the room)*

The Misses Tibbs and Gatsby and the Major have appeared in the background. Basil rubs his hands in sarcastic glee.

Basil   Mother Johnson. Mother Johnson. Come out, come out, wherever you are. *(a very nice and very elderly lady appears at the door; Basil switches to charm)* How do you do, are you enjoying yourself? . . .

Mrs Johnson Yes, thank you.

Basil   Well, I'll get the champagne, this calls for a celebration.

Mrs Johnson goes back inside. The door shuts. Sybil, Misses Tibbs and Gatsby and the Major move off. Basil buries his face in his hands, then, pulling his jacket right over his head he squats down and hops about in agony. The Abbotts come up the stairs in time to see this performance. Mrs Abbott looks to her husband for professional advice.

Dr Abbott   I'm on holiday.

They go into their room. Basil rolls onto his side and assumes the foetal position.

Waldorf Salad

Third of second series, first broadcast on 5 March 1979, BBC2.

Sybil Fawlty   Prunella Scales
Mr Libson   Anthony Dawes
Basil Fawlty   John Cleese
Mrs Johnstone   June Ellis
Mr Johnstone   Terence Conoley
Miss Hare   Dorothy Frere
Miss Gurke   Beatrice Shaw
Mr Arrad   Norman Bird
Mrs Arrad   Stella Tanner
Manuel   Andrew Sachs
Polly   Connie Booth
Mrs Hamilton   Claire Nielson
Mr Hamilton   Bruce Boa
Major Gowen   Ballard Berkeley
Miss Tibbs   Gilly Flower
Miss Gatsby   Renée Roberts

*The hotel dining room. It is towards the end of dinner-time.
The room is very full and Basil, Polly and Manuel are
bustling about frantically. Sybil, however, is standing by a
central table, ignoring the confusion. She is talking to Mr
Libson, who is sitting by himself at the table. He looks
extremely bored.*

Sybil	Oh, it's a lovely part of the world, isn't it? All those beautiful trees and fields and a variety of birds.
Mr Libson	Yes, that's true.
Sybil	And you can just go there and get away from it all, away from the helter-skelter of modern life. Because we all do **need** our solitude, don't we.
Mr Libson	*(feelingly)* Yes, we do.
Sybil	I mean, nowadays it's **not** easy to find the time to . . . I don't know, **enjoy** life because there's always things to do, it's all so hectic, isn't it. All of us just running around letting things get on top of us, and quite honestly what's the point?

*Basil rushes by on his way to a table where Mr and Mrs
Johnstone sit. Mrs Johnstone has a half-finished prawn
cocktail in front of her. Mr Johnstone has a finished melon.*

Basil	Have you finished?
Mrs Johnstone	Er, yes . . .
Basil	*(starting to collect the plates)* Thank you.
Mr Johnstone	Er, my wife . . .
Basil	Yes?
Mrs Johnstone	I think those prawns might be a bit off.
Basil	Oh, I don't think so.
Mrs Johnstone	Well, they do taste rather funny.
Basil	Well, no one else has complained.
Mrs Johnstone	Well, I really do think they're off.
Basil	But you've eaten half of them.
Mrs Johnstone	Well, I didn't notice it at the start.
Basil	You didn't notice at the start?
Mrs Johnstone	Well, it was the sauce, you see. I wasn't sure.
Basil	So you ate half to **make** sure?
Mr Johnstone	Look, my wife thinks they're off.
Basil	Well, what am I supposed to do about it . . . do you want another first course?
Mrs Johnstone	No thank you.

Mr Johnstone	You're sure?
Mrs Johnstone	No, really, I'll just have the main.
Mr Johnstone	*(to Basil)* Well, we'll just cancel it.
Basil	Cancel it? Oh, deduct it from the bill, is that what you mean?
Mr Johnstone	Well, as it's inedible . . .
Basil	Well, only **half** of it's inedible apparently.
Mr Johnstone	Well, deduct half now, and if my wife brings the other half up during the night, we'll claim the balance in the morning. And now we'd like our lambs, please.

Basil makes off towards the kitchen. Sybil is still boring Mr Libson.

Sybil	Well, three we know have passed on this year, all in their early sixties. So I've cut out butter . . .

Manuel comes in with a jug of water. He can't remember who it is for and looks round. Mr Arrad, sitting with his wife, tries to attract Manuel's attention, but Manuel puts the jug down at a table occupied by two middle-aged women, Miss Gurke and Miss Hare.

Miss Hare	No, really it's all right.
Miss Gurke	But it's all gristle.
Miss Hare	No, honestly, there's a nice bit, see?
Miss Gurke	Oh, Doris, it's awful.
Miss Hare	Oh, no, dear, it's not as bad as that. I've had worse.
Miss Gurke	I don't know how they get away with it.
Basil	*(checking as he passes, pro forma)* Everything all right?
Miss Gurke	Yes, thank you.
Miss Hare	Very good, thank you very much . . .

Basil moves away. Miss Gurke looks disapprovingly after him. Sybil finally leaves Mr Libson and goes into the kitchen. Basil comes up to Mr and Mrs Arrad's table.

Basil	Everything to your satisfaction?
Mr Arrad	Yes, thank you.
Basil	Thank you. *(he moves on)*
Mrs Arrad	*(to her husband)* Why don't you **say** something?
Mr Arrad	There's no point, is there. We just won't come here again.
Mrs Arrad	Then I'll say something.
Mr Arrad	Look, it won't do any good, we're leaving tomorrow.

Mrs Arrad	Well, I'm going to. We've been sitting here waiting for nearly half an hour . . .

But Manuel has at last arrived with their meals – plaice for Mrs Arrad and lamb for Mr Arrad.

Mr Arrad	What's this?
Manuel	*Si.*
Mr Arrad	Look, I ordered the cold meat salad. I've been waiting about half an hour for it.
Manuel	Salad?
Mr Arrad	Yes.
Manuel	You want change?
Mr Arrad	. . . No! I don't want to change . . .
Manuel	OK. *(starts to leave)*
Mr Arrad	Wha . . . where are you **going?** I don't **want** this!
Manuel	You say you no want change.
Mr Arrad	I want the salad.

Manuel moves off mystified. Basil is in the vicinity.

Mrs Arrad	*(nudging her husband)* Go on . . .
Mr Arrad	*(to Basil)* Excuse me.
Basil	Yes.
Mr Arrad	Look, we've been waiting here for about half an hour now, I mean we gave the waiter our order . . .
Basil	Oh, him. He's hopeless, isn't he.
Mr Arrad	Yes, well, I don't wish to complain, but when he finally does bring something, he's got it wrong.
Basil	You think I don't know? I mean, you only have to eat here. We have to live with it. I had to pay his fare all the way from Barcelona. But we can't get the staff, you see. It's a nightmare. *(he moves off feeling better)*
Mrs Arrad	*(to her husband)* You were supposed to be complaining to **him.**

Manuel comes running up with a plate of meat salad. He puts it in front of Mr Arrad. Then he looks at it and stares. Mr Arrad takes his first mouthful; Manuel whips the plate away again. Basil sees this. Manuel peers at the plate.

Basil	*(taking the plate away from Manuel)* Will you stop that! *(he puts it in front of Mr Arrad)* I'm sorry about that.

Manuel whispers in Basil's ear. Basil peers over Mr Arrad's shoulder.

Basil	Excuse me. *(he takes the plate and examines it, puts it back and then removes it again just as Mr Arrad is about to start eating; he consults Manuel)* Where?
Manuel	*(pointing)* Look!
Basil	Thank you so much. *(he replaces the plate)* Enjoy your meal.

He moves off. The Arrads peer at the plate with suspicion. Manuel mimes whatever it is he has seen by flapping his arms. Basil passes the Johnstones' table.

Mr Johnstone	You haven't forgotten our lambs, have you?
Basil	No, no, they're coming, they're coming!
Mrs Arrad	*(calling Basil)* Excuse me. There is sugar in the salt-cellar.
Basil	. . . Anything else?
Mrs Arrad	I've just put it all over the plaice.
Basil	All over the place? What were you doing with it?
Mrs Arrad	All over the **plaice**.
Basil	*(catching Polly)* Polly – would you ask Terry not to finish yet – we need another one of these. *(hands her the plaice)* There is sugar on it.
Polly	What a sweet plaice.
Basil	What?
Polly	I'll have it re-placed.
Basil	What is sugar doing in this salt-cellar? What do you think we pay you for?
Polly	My staying power? *(goes into the kitchen with the offending plaice)*
Mr Johnstone	*(calling Basil)* The lamb!
Basil	I'm getting them, I'm getting them!

He goes into the kitchen. Sybil comes out; Miss Gurke gestures to her.

Miss Gurke	Er . . . excuse me.
Sybil	Yes?
Miss Gurke	I'm sorry, but do you think we could cancel our fruit salads?
Sybil	Well, it's a little tricky, Chef's just opened the tin.
Miss Gurke	Oh.
Miss Hare	Never mind, I'm sure it'll be very nice.

Sybil goes back to Mr Libson's table with his next course.

Sybil	There we are.
Mr Libson	Ah, thank you.
Sybil	Oh yes, I do like really beautiful places . . .
Basil	*(coming by carrying several things)* Busy this evening, isn't it.
Sybil	*(to Mr Libson)* I'll tell you a few of my favourites . . .
Basil	I said it's busy this evening.
Sybil	I'm talking to Mr Libson, Basil.
Basil	Good. Well, that's a help.
Sybil	I'm sure you can cope.
Basil	Oh, yes, I can cope. Coping's easy. Not puréeing your loved ones, that's the difficult part.

He is about to deliver the two plates of lamb to Mr Johnstone, who is relieved that the moment has at last come. However, the reception bell sounds.

Sybil	*(to Mr Libson)* Did you know Bideford bridge has all different . . .
Basil	There's someone at reception, dear. Shall I get it?
Sybil	Yes.
Basil	It's my turn is it? Fine. Oh yes! So it is. Funny, it's been my turn for fifteen years. *(he manages to get the door to the lobby open, still holding the plates)* Still, when I'm dead it'll be your turn, dear – you'll be 'it'.
Mr Johnstone	*(seeing his lambs disappear)* Excuse me, there are two lambs here.
Basil	I'll have them removed if they're bothering you.

He moves into the lobby. Mrs Hamilton is standing by the reception desk.

Basil	*(aggressively)* Yes?
Mrs Hamilton	Good evening.

Basil realizes she is rather attractive and slows down a bit.

Mr Johnstone	*(from the dining room)* Are those lambs ours?
Basil	*(over his shoulder)* Not yet. *(to Mrs Hamilton)* Good evening.
Mrs Hamilton	I reserved a room, by telephone, this morning . . . Mr and Mrs Hamilton.
Basil	Indeed yes. I remember it well. *(he goes behind the desk, putting down the plates)* Ah, excellent, Hamilton? . . .
Mrs Hamilton	That's right.

Basil	Well, may I welcome you to Fawlty Towers. I trust your stay will be an enjoyable and gracious one.
Mr Johnstone	*(appearing in the lobby and pointing at the plates)* Could we have those now?
Basil	Oh, by all means.
Mr Johnstone	Finished with them, have you?
Basil	Absolutely. *(Mr Johnstone takes the plates and turns.)* Bon apétitttttttttttt.

Mr Johnstone turns round. Basil beams.

Mr Johnstone	*(to Mrs Hamilton)* I recommend the self-service here. It's excellent.
Basil	That'll be all, thank you.
Mr Johnstone	What?
Basil	Your lambs will be getting cold, Mr Johnstone.
Mr Johnstone	Colder.
Basil	If you'd like them warmed up?
Mr Johnstone	Forget it. *(he exits angrily)*
Basil	You could get your wife to sit on 'em. *(to Mrs Hamilton)* I'm so sorry, but the rubbish we get in here. . . . Now, if you'd be so very kind as to fill that form out . . . *(turns to get the key)* Mr and Mrs Hamilton, ah yes, now we've put you in room twelve, which has a charming panoramic view overlooking the lawn.

Mr Hamilton has come in. He is aggressively American. He is also very wet.

Mr Hamilton	What a drive, eh? Everything on the wrong side of the road – and the weather, what do you get for living in a climate like this, green stamps? It's terrible.
Basil	*(to Mrs Hamilton)* I'm sorry about this.
Mr Hamilton	Took five hours from London. . . . Couldn't find the freeway. Had to take a little back street called the M5.
Basil	Well, I'm sorry it wasn't wide enough for you. A lot of the English cars have steering wheels.
Mr Hamilton	They do, do they? You wouldn't think there was room for them inside.
Basil	*(quietly, to Mrs Hamilton)* See what I mean?
Mrs Hamilton	What?
Basil	*(to himself)* Rub-bish. *(flicks a glance at Mr Hamilton and subtly holds his nose)*
Mrs Hamilton	May I introduce my husband?

Basil	*(rubs his nose hard, smiles at Mr Hamilton, then looks round)* The rubbish we get in here. *(picks up a sheet of paper)* Look at that. *(rolls it into a ball; Sybil appears at the kitchen door; Basil waves the ball at her)*
Sybil	Basil!
Basil	More rubbish, dear.
Sybil	What?
Basil	More of that bloody rubbish. Coh!
Sybil	Polly and Manuel are going, Basil.
Basil	Yes, just dealing with Mr and Mrs Hamilton, dear.
Sybil	Good evening.
Mr & Mrs Hamilton	Good evening.

Sybil goes into the dining room. Basil rings the bell.

Basil	Manuel! Manuel will bring your bags to your room. I hope you enjoy your stay.
Mr Hamilton	Thank you. Do we need to reserve a table for dinner?
Basil	Dinner?
Mr Hamilton	Yes. *(Basil does a lot of looking at his watch)* Is there a problem?
Basil	Well, it is after nine o'clock.
Mr Hamilton	So?
Basil	Well, yes . . . we do actually stop serving at nine.
Mr Hamilton	Nine.
Basil	Well, look – if you could go straight in I'm sure we could . . .
Mr Hamilton	Look, we've taken five hours to get here. We'd like to freshen up, maybe have a drink first, you know.
Basil	Yes . . . um . . . you couldn't do that afterwards?
Mrs Hamilton	Do what?
Basil	Well . . .
Mr Hamilton	You mean have our drink before dinner, after dinner, freshen up and go to bed?
Basil	If you could, it would make things a lot easier for us.
Mr Hamilton	Shall we go to bed now? Would that make it easier for you?
Basil	What?
Mr Hamilton	We're a little tired, fella. We want to clean up, relax. We'll be down in a few minutes.
Basil	Yes, well, the chef does actually stop at nine.
Mr Hamilton	Nine. Nine. Why does your chef stop at nine? Has he got something terminal?

Basil	No, no, but that's when he, in fact, stops.
Mr Hamilton	Now look, we drove from London to stay here, right? Are you telling me that you can't stay open a few minutes longer so that we can eat properly?
Basil	Well, we can do you sandwiches . . . ham, cheese . . .
Mr Hamilton	We want something hot.
Basil	Toasted sandwiches?
Mr Hamilton	You're joking.
Basil	Well . . . not really.
Mr Hamilton	Not really. *(to Mrs Hamilton)* Can you believe this? *(to Basil)* What the hell's wrong with this country? You can't get a drink after three, you can't eat after nine, is the war still on?
Basil	No, no, no, but it's the staff, you see.

Manuel comes from the kitchen to collect the bags.

Mr Hamilton	Oh, the staff . . .
Basil	We have to get the staff . . .
Mr Hamilton	How much?
Basil	What?
Mr Hamilton	*(pulling out a wad of notes)* How much of this Mickey Mouse money do you need to keep the chef on for half an hour? One . . . two . . . twenty pounds, uh? Is that enough?
Basil	*(pauses to think, then)* I'll see what I can do.
Mr Hamilton	Thank you.

The Hamiltons start up the stairs. Basil looks at the notes, pockets them and hurries across to the kitchen. Manuel, barging through the Hamiltons, leads them up the stairs.

Manuel	Excuse me, pardon, pardon, excuse me please, this way please . . .

The kitchen. Terry is washing his hands as Basil enters, sees a trifle and sniffs it.

Basil	Gosh, that does look absolutely marvellous, doesn't it. Um . . . oh, Terry, I almost forgot. Some guests have just arrived, right at the last moment as usual, typical . . . I'm sorry, but this puts us out just as much as it puts you out.
Terry	Don't put me out, Mr Fawlty.
Basil	Er, no, they want dinner, you see, and they insist first

on scraping off some of the filth that's somehow got
caked to them cruising down the M5.

Terry   Well, I got my class tonight, Mr Fawlty.

Polly   *(looking round the door)* We're ready, Terry.

Terry   Right-ho, Poll. *(Polly goes)*

Basil   Wait a minute, wait a minute . . . didn't I say? I mean
that I will make it up to you, did I? Out of my own
pocket.

Terry   It's not the money, Mr Fawlty. My karate means a lot
to me.

Basil   Half an hour's overtime and a taxi home.

Terry   If I miss a week, Mr Fawlty, next week I don't get out
in one piece.

Basil   An hour's overtime.

Terry   Sorry, Mr Fawlty.

Basil   What am I going to say to them?

Terry   . . . Two hours.

Basil   What?

Terry   Two hours' overtime.

Basil   I thought you said it wasn't the money.

Terry   It ain't, but I can't think what you're going to say to
your guests.

Basil   Look, Terry, I'd pay you two hours' overtime if I could
afford it!

A car horn sounds outside.

Terry   *(making to go)* Sorry, Mr Fawlty.

Basil   An hour and a half!

Terry   Cash?

Basil   Cash!

Terry   All right, Mr Fawlty, an hour and a half, but I go at
half-past nine, then I still get some of my class.

Basil   . . . And I do the washing up.

Terry   Well, you know how it is, Mr Fawlty.

Basil   Yes, I know how it is. I pay you for an hour and a half
and you clear off after half an hour, that's how it is.
(gives him some money) That's socialism.

Terry   Oh, no, Mr Fawlty, that's the free market.

Polly   *(looking round the door again)* Come on, Terry. Mustn't
keep the lady waiting.

Basil   The lady!

Polly   She's from Finland, Mr Fawlty, and very pretty. Tall,

	blonde . . . *(Terry gestures frantically at her from behind Basil)* um . . . *(she stops and exits)*
Basil	This Finnish floozie's your karate teacher, is she?
Terry	Well, it's a sort of karate, ain't it . . .
Basil	Right, give me that. *(grabs the money back)*
Terry	What?
Basil	I pay you overtime to miss a class, not to keep some bit of crumpet hanging around.
Terry	Yes, but she's . . .
Basil	No, it's all right, I'm doing the washing-up, I'll do the cooking too. You go off and enjoy yourself. Don't worry about me, you go and have a good time. I'll be all right. Go and have a bit of fun with a Finn.

Terry exits into the lobby. Polly is waiting.

Polly	Come on, Manuel.

Polly and Terry exit throught the main doors. Manuel comes in from the bar.

Manuel	Hey, where are you, Polly? Wait for me. *(he chases off after them)*

The dining room, a bit later. Sybil is sitting at a table near the door, reading a Harold Robbins novel. The door opens and Basil ushers in the Hamiltons.

Basil	Thank you. If you'd care to sit over there . . .
Sybil	Good evening.
Mr & Mrs Hamilton	Good evening.
Sybil	Is your room to your liking?
Mr Hamilton	Yes, it's very nice.
Mrs Hamilton	Very nice, thank you.
Sybil	Oh good. *(she rises and carries her finished starter back to the kitchen)*
Basil	I'll just get you tonight's menu . . . Oh, would you care for a drink before your meal?
Mr Hamilton	A scotch and water and screwdriver, please.
Basil	Um . . . and for you, madam?
Mrs Hamilton	The screwdriver's for me.
Basil	I see . . . um . . . would you like it now or after your meal?
Mrs Hamilton	Well, now, please.

Basil	There's nothing I can put right?
Mrs Hamilton	What?
Basil	Absolutely. So it's one scotch and one screwdriver.
Mr Hamilton	I think I'll join you. *(to Basil)* Make that two screwdrivers, will you?
Basil	You'd like a screwdriver as well?
Mr Hamilton	You got it.
Basil	Fine. So it's one scotch and you each need a screwdriver.
Mr Hamilton	No, no, no. Forget the scotch. Two screwdrivers.
Basil	I understand. And you'll leave the drinks.
Mr Hamilton	What?
Basil	Nothing to drink.
Mr Hamilton	What do you mean, 'Nothing to drink'?
Basil	Well you can't drink your screwdrivers, can you. Ha ha.
Mr Hamilton	What else would you suggest that we do with them?
Mrs Hamilton	Vodka and orange juice.
Basil	Ah, certainly madam.
Mr Hamilton	Make that two. And forget about the screwdrivers.
Basil	You're sure?
Mr Hamilton	We can manage without them.
Basil	As you wish, sir. *(he goes into the kitchen)*
Mr Hamilton	*(reading from a tourist magazine)* 'Relax in the carefree atmosphere of old English charm . . .' *(he sees Sybil who has just come back in)* I hope we're not intruding on your dinner hour.
Sybil	*(sitting at her table)* Not at all, no. You're American?
Mr Hamilton	That's right.
Sybil	Where are you from?
Mrs Hamilton	California.
Sybil	How lovely. **You're** English, though?
Mrs Hamilton	Yes, but I've been over there ten years now.
Sybil	**Ten** years. Do you ever get home-sick?
Mrs Hamilton	Oh, yes. But I love it there – the climate's so wonderful. You can swim and sunbathe and then after lunch drive up into the mountains and ski.
Sybil	How wonderful. *(Basil enters)*
Mr Hamilton	I like England and the English people, but I sure couldn't take this climate.
Mrs Hamilton	Harry finds it too gloomy.
Basil	*(putting the drinks on the Hamiltons' table)* Oh, I don't

	find it too gloomy. Do you, Sybil?
Sybil	Yes I do, Basil.
Basil	Well, yes, my wife finds it too gloomy. I find it rather bracing.
Sybil	What do you find bracing, Basil? . . . the damp, the drizzle, the fog . . .
Basil	Well, it's not always like this, dear. It changes.
Sybil	My husband's like the climate. **He** changes. This morning he went on for two hours about the 'bloody weather', ha ha ha.
Basil	Yes, well, it has been unusually damp this week, in fact, but normally we're rather spoiled down here on the English Riviera.
Sybil	Mr and Mrs Hamilton were telling me about California. You can swim in the morning and then in the afternoon you can drive up into the mountains and ski.
Basil	It must be rather tiring.
Mr Hamilton	Well, one has the choice.
Basil	Yes, but I don't think that would suit me. I like it down here. It's very mild all the year round. We have palm trees here in Torquay, you know. Do you have palm trees in California?
Mr Hamilton	Burt Lancaster had one, they say. But I don't believe them. *(he tastes his screwdriver)* What the hell is that?
Basil	Er . . . Vodka and orange juice . . .
Mr Hamilton	Orange juice?
Mrs Hamilton	I'm afraid it's not fresh.
Basil	Isn't it? *(he takes it and sniffs it)*
Mrs Hamilton	No.
Basil	We've just opened the bottle.
Mr Hamilton	Look, fresh means it comes out of an orange, not out of a bottle.
Basil	Ah! You'd like freshly **squeezed** orange juice.
Mr Hamilton	As against freshly unscrewed orange juice, yes.
Basil	. . . Leave it to me, I mean, I'll get chef on to it straight away *(he bustles off into the kitchen)*
Sybil	Sorry about that. A lot of English people are used to the flavour of the bottled . . .
Mrs Hamilton	Oh, that's all right. It's just that back home fresh orange juice comes like running water.
Sybil	Does it really? 'Course, it's so good for your skin, isn't

	it. I'd love to go to California some day. It looks so exciting. *(she indicates her book)*
Mrs Hamilton	Oh! *Never Love A Stranger.* Do you like it?
Sybil	Oh, I love Harold Robbins. I've read this one three times.
Mrs Hamilton	*The Pirate* is his best, I think. I read them when Harry's away. I just don't seem to have the time when he's home.
Sybil	Who needs Harold Robbins when you've got the real thing. *(she laughs; Basil enters)*
Mrs Hamilton	How long have you been married, Mrs Fawlty?
Sybil	Oh, since 1485.
Basil	*(putting the screwdrivers down)* There we are, fresh orange juice.
Sybil	But seriously though, his men are all so interesting. Ruthless and sexy and . . . powerful.
Basil	*(handing out the menus)* Who's this, then, dear? Proust? E. M. Forster?
Sybil	Harold Robbins.
Basil	Oh, of course, yes. My wife likes Harold Robbins. After a hard day's slaving under the hair-dryer she needs to unwind with a few aimless thrills.
Sybil	Basil! *(she exits to the kitchen)*
Basil	Have you ever read any? It really is the most awful American . . . well, not America, but trans-Atlantic tripe. A sort of pornographic muzak. Still, it keeps my wife off the streets.
Mr Hamilton	We both like him.
Basil	*(looks disturbed for a moment)* Oh! **Robbins!**
Mr Hamilton	What?
Basil	Harold Robbins. I thought you meant that awful man, what's his name, oh, Harold . . . Robinson. Have you read any Harold Robinson? Ah! Painful!
Mr Hamilton	How about Waldorf salad.
Basil	Was that one? Yes, you're absolutely right. Oh, that was a shocker, wasn't it.
Mr Hamilton	. . . Could you make me a Waldorf salad.
Basil	Oh . . . a . . . Wa . . . ?
Mr Hamilton	Waldorf salad.
Basil	. . . I think we're just out of Waldorfs.
Mr Hamilton	*(to Mrs Hamilton)* I don't believe this.
Mrs Hamilton	It's not very well known here, Harry.

Basil	Yes, may I recommend tonight the . . .
Mr Hamilton	Look, I'm sure your chef knows how to fix me a Waldorf salad, huh?
Basil	I wouldn't be **too** sure.
Mr Hamilton	Well, he's a chef, isn't he?
Basil	Yes, you wouldn't prefer . . .
Mr Hamilton	*(shouting)* Well, find out, will you? Just go out there and see if he knows how to fix me a Waldorf salad!
Basil	. . . Of course. *(he goes into the kitchen, but re-appears almost immediately)* He's not **absolutely** positive . . . he's almost got it. It's lettuce and tomatoes, walled in with . . . ?
Mr Hamilton	No, no, no, it's celery, apples, walnuts, grapes.
Mrs Hamilton	In a mayonnaise sauce.
Basil	Right. Incidentally, he did ask me to say that he does specially recommend the pâté tonight.
Mr Hamilton	I don't want pâté.
Basil	Or the . . . the grapefruit.
Mr Hamilton	Grapefruit?
Basil	The grapefruit.
Mr Hamilton	How's it done?
Basil	Well, it's halved, with a cherry in the centre. *(Sybil re-enters)*
Mr Hamilton	Look! I haven't paid you twenty pounds to have some guy cut a grapefruit in half and stick a cherry in the centre. *(Sybil reacts to the 'twenty pounds')*
Basil	Exactly.
Mr Hamilton	I want a Waldorf salad.
Basil	Absolutely. One Waldorf salad.
Mrs Hamilton	And a green salad for me.
Basil	And one green salad. Yes. And if we can't manage the Waldorf salad . . . ?
Mr Hamilton	*(loudly)* I want a Waldorf salad! And a couple of *filets mignons*. *(Basil is flummoxed)*
Mrs Hamilton	Steaks.
Mr Hamilton	Steaks!!
Basil	Steaks!
Mr Hamilton	Done rare.
Basil	Done rare!
Mr Hamilton	Not out of a bottle
Basil	Not out of a bottle. Right. *(he disappears into the kitchen)*
Sybil	Would you like to see the wine list? *(she gives it to them)*

Mr Hamilton	Thank you.
Sybil	May I ask, did you say you'd paid twenty pounds . . . ?
Mr Hamilton	Yes, but it's not the money, my wife and I, we wanted dinner and your husband said your chef usually leaves at nine o'clock . . .
Sybil	Well, this can't be right. There's no reason chef couldn't stay . . .
Basil	*(re-appearing from the kitchen)* I'm awfully sorry, he's forgotten already . . . walnuts, cheese . . .
Mr Hamilton	No! No cheese! It's celery, apples, walnuts, grapes!
Basil	Right!
Mr Hamilton	In mayonnaise.
Basil	Right! *(shouting into the kitchen)* Now come on! *(goes into the kitchen)*
Sybil	Um . . . would you excuse me one moment?
Mr Hamilton	Excuse me . . . a bottle of the Volnay, please.
Sybil	Of course. Thank you. *(she goes into the kitchen)*

In the kitchen, Basil is rummaging frantically in a large cardboard box.

Sybil	What's this about twenty pounds, Basil?
Basil	There's no celery. Would you believe it?
Sybil	I'll find the celery. What about this twenty pounds?
Basil	He gave me twenty pounds to keep the kitchens open, but chef wouldn't . . . I mean, where does he put things?
Sybil	If you'd just look . . .
Basil	I **have** looked. There's no celery, there's no grapes . . . walnuts! That's a laugh, easier to find a packet of sliced hippopotamus in suitcase sauce than a walnut in this bloody kitchen. *(he looks in the fridge)*
Sybil	Now, we've got apples. *(holding up some)*
Basil	Oh, terrific! Let's celebrate. We'll have an apple party. Everybody brings his own apple and stuffs it down somebody's throat.
Sybil	Basil, I'll find everything. Just go and get a bottle of Volnay.
Basil	What's a waldorf, anyway – a walnut that's gone off?
Sybil	It's the hotel, Basil. The Waldorf Hotel. In New York.
Basil	*(struck with an idea)* Wait, wait.
Sybil	*(warningly)* Basil.
Basil	*(going into the dining room)* Everything all right?

Mrs Hamilton	Yes thank you.
Mr Hamilton	Never been better.
Basil	Oh good. Um . . . by the way. I wonder . . . have you by any chance ever tried a Ritz salad?
Mr Hamilton	A Ritz salad?
Basil	Yes – it's a traditional old English . . . thing. It's apples, grapefruit and potatoes in a mayonnaise sauce.
Mr Hamilton	No, don't think I ever tried that.
Basil	Ah!
Mr Hamilton	Don't think I ever will, either.
Basil	No, well, that's probably pretty sound. Well, look, um . . . about this Waldorf salad of yours . . .
Mr Hamilton	Yes?
Basil	Um . . . I've had a bit of a tête-a-tête with chef, and the point is, we're all right on the apples. Absolutely no problem with them at all. Now . . . on the celery front, well, er . . . perhaps I should explain, we normally get our celery delivered on a Wednesday, along with our cabbages, onions, walnuts, grapes . . . that sort of thing, but this week the driver . . .
Mr Hamilton	Mr Fawlty.
Basil	Yes, he was putting the crate into the van . . .
Mr Hamilton	I'm not interested.
Basil	. . . and he sort of slipped forward and the van door caught his arm, like that, and he may have fractured it . . .
Mr Hamilton	You don't have any.
Basil	They did the X-rays and we'll know tomorrow whether they're going to have to operate, and to cut a long story short . . . we don't have any, no. But . . . um . . . still . . . it makes you think how lucky you are, doesn't it. Here we are, with all our limbs functioning. I mean, quite frankly, if you've got your health, what else matters?
Mr Hamilton	What a bunch of crap!
Basil	*(interested)* Oh, do you think so? I always feel . . .
Mr Hamilton	What the hell's going on here!? It says hotel outside – now, is this a hotel or isn't it?
Basil	Well . . . within reason.
Mr Hamilton	You know something, fella – if this was back in the States I wouldn't board my dog here.
Basil	Fussy, is he? Poodle?
Mr Hamilton	*(standing up and facing Basil)* Poodle! I'm not getting

	through to you, am I. You know, I stay in hotels all over the world and this is the first time I've had to bribe a chef to cook me a meal and then found out he doesn't have the basic goddam ingredients. Holy Cow, can't you see what a **crummy** dump this is?
Basil	*(shouting towards the kitchen)* You're listening to this, are you, Terry?
Mr Hamilton	I'm talking to **you**!
Basil	*(to kitchen)* It's all right, Terry, you can get on with . . .
Mr Hamilton	Shut up, will you, and listen to me. Can't you see this ain't good enough?
Basil	Yes, I see what you mean.
Mr Hamilton	And then you give me some half-assed story about some delivery guy busting his arm. Now look, Fawlty, if your chef couldn't find the ingredients from that guy, why didn't he get them from somebody else, uh?
Basil	Exactly. Hopeless.
Mr Hamilton	*(amazed)* What?
Basil	He's hopeless. Absolutely hopeless.
Mr Hamilton	Right. You're the manager, aren't you? You're responsible. So what are you going to do about it, uh?
Basil	*(confidentially)* . . . I'll have a word with him.
Mr Hamilton	Have a word with him? Man, you've got to tell him. Lay it on the line.
Basil	Lay it on the line?
Mr Hamilton	Tell him, if he doesn't get on the ball you're going to bust his ass.
Basil	Bust his . . .
Mr Hamilton	I'll tell him. *(makes for kitchen)*
Basil	*(restraining him)* No, no!! No, I'll tell him. Leave it to me.
Mr Hamilton	Tell him!
Basil	I will. I've got it. I've got it. I've got it. Bust his . . . ?
Mr Hamilton	Ass!!
Basil	Oh, that! Right! . . . And two green salads?

He goes into the kitchen. As he does so Sybil comes out with a Waldorf salad and a green salad. She puts them on the table.

Sybil	Here we are. One green salad, and one Waldorf salad.
Mr Hamilton	*(confused)* But I thought that . . .

Sybil	Yes? *(the reception bell rings)* Oh – would you excuse me one moment?
	She exits. The Hamiltons peer at the salads. At this moment Basil's voice is heard from the kitchen.
Basil's voice	No, it's not good enough, do you hear me, it's not good enough! *(pretending to be Terry)* But Mr Robinson hurt his arm! *(as himself)* That's a bunch of arse, that's what that is!
Mrs Hamilton	*(tasting her salad)* It's fine.
Basil's voice	Why can't you make a Waldorf salad?
Mr Hamilton	*(to Mrs Hamilton)* Waldorf salad?
Mrs Hamilton	*(surprised)* Yes.
Basil's voice	First thing tomorrow you get the ingredients for a Waldorf salad or I'm going to break your bottom. *(as Terry)* Oh no, no, you can't do that. *(as himself)* No, I mean it. I mean it!
Sybil	*(coming back in from the lobby)* Everything all right?
Mrs Hamilton	Yes, thank you.
Sybil	You're sure there's nothing . . . ?
Mr Hamilton	No, really. It's very good.
Sybil	Oh, good.
Mr Hamilton	Oh . . . your chef?
Sybil	Yes?
Mr Hamilton	Has he been with you long?
Sybil	About six months. He used to work at Dorchester.
Mrs Hamilton	At the Dorchester?
Sybil	No, **in** Dorchester. About forty miles away . . .
Basil	*(entering with two green salads)* Here we are, two green salads.
Sybil	Basil!
Basil	Yes, dear?
Sybil	Mr Hamilton **has** his Waldorf salad, dear.
Basil	No, dear, chef couldn't make it. He didn't have the ingredients. I've just smashed his backside about it.
Sybil	*(pointing to the salad)* But there it is.
Basil	What!?
Sybil	There's the Waldorf salad. Chef found the ingredients. *(she takes the two green salads)*
Mr Hamilton	It's fine.
Basil	*(to Sybil, between his teeth)* Well, if he found the ingredients, why didn't he **tell** me? It would have been

perfectly simple, wouldn't it? Has he been struck dumb? Or has somebody torn his tongue out in the last two minutes?

Sybil	Basil.
Mr Hamilton	Maybe Robinson's arm got better.
Basil	I'm sorry about this.
Mr Hamilton	It's all right.
Basil	No it isn't.
Mr Hamilton	It doesn't matter.
Basil	Well, it matters to me.
Mr Hamilton	Not to me. I've got my Waldorf salad.
Basil	*(snatching it away)* Would you excuse me.
Mr Hamilton	For God's sake!
Basil	*(screaming)* Chef!! What's the meaning of this? *(he exits into the kitchen)*
Sybil	Basil, would you bring that back immediately. *(to Mr Hamilton)* I'm sorry, I'll just get it back for you. *(she goes towards the kitchen)*
Basil's voice	*(from the kitchen)* Sorry! I'll give you sorry! Get off your knees! *(Sybil enters the kitchen)* Leave this to me, Sybil, I'll handle it.
Sybil's voice	Basil!
Basil's voice	I haven't finished with Chef yet, Sybil, I mean, why didn't you tell me, why didn't you tell me, you stupid cow. Eh, Chef? No, no, I haven't finished, I haven't finished, you can have it in a . . . *(there is a loud bonk)* . . . Oooh!
Sybil	*(coming back in with the salad)* Sorry about that little confusion, Chef hasn't been with us very long and we've just reorganized the kitchen. *(she gives Mr Hamilton his salad)*
Mr Hamilton	Thank you.
Sybil	Oh, you haven't got your wine yet. Basil! . . . Won't be a moment. Basil!

The kitchen door opens and Basil, holding a cloth to his forehead, looks wanly out.

Basil	*(subdued)* Yes, my sweet?
Sybil	Mr and Mrs Hamilton haven't got their wine yet.
Basil	Oh.
Sybil	And Basil – has Chef put the steaks on yet?
Basil	No – I'll tell him. *(he disappears into the kitchen)*

Mrs Hamilton	Is your husband all right?
Sybil	Oh yes. He's just had rather a long day.
Mr Hamilton	There's just the two of you here, right?
Sybil	We haven't had a proper holiday for eight years.
Mrs Hamilton	Eight years?!
Sybil	Yes, I have to get away occasionally, just for a few hours, even if it's down to the hairdresser or a round of golf or a bridge evening with some of the girls, or a drive in the country sometimes, just on my own, pop down to Cornwall for the day, sometimes it's so beautiful down there . . .

Basil appears with a hat pulled down strangely over his temple.

Sybil	*(to the Hamiltons)* Yes, you must visit Cornwall while you're here. *(goes to the kitchen)*
Basil	Your Volnay, sir.
Mr Hamilton	Oh, thank you. *(tastes the wine)*
Basil	Oh, incidentally, I've been talking to Chef and we've sorted out what happened. Apparently he thought he'd already got . . .
Mr Hamilton	*(approving the wine)* That's very nice, thank you.
Basil	. . . Thank you . . . got . . . got **two** for Waldorf salad you see, and in fact he had the ingredients, but . . .
Mr Hamilton	No, that's fine, it doesn't matter.
Basil	. . . until he'd made one he didn't realize that he didn't have enough for the second one, you see . . .
Mr Hamilton	Look, don't let it bother you.
Basil	*(pulling a letter out of his pocket)* Anyway, this will explain everything.
Mr Hamilton	What's that?
Basil	It's a letter.
Mr Hamilton	A letter?
Basil	A letter from the chef. It explains everything.
Mr Hamilton	A letter from the chef!?
Basil	He wanted to apologize personally, but I didn't want him wasting your time, so I thought . . .
Mr Hamilton	Oh, just forget about it, will you?
Basil	I'll read it for you.
Mr Hamilton	I want my steak!
Basil	It won't be a moment. *(opens the letter and reads)* 'Dear Mr and Mrs Hamilton, I hope you are well. This is just

a brief note to say I take full responsibility for the dreadful mess-ups tonight. If I'd only listened to Mr Fawlty none of this fiasco would have happened.' *(feigning spontaneity)* Oh! *(smoke starts to pour into the room from the kitchen; not seeing it, Basil goes on reading)* 'I'd just like to tell you that such a cock-up . . . *(the Hamiltons have seen the smoke)* . . . has never occurred in my career before, but now that everything has been sorted out I'll be back to my very best form. Signed, Terry.'

Basil smiles at the Hamiltons, catches their line of vision and sees the smoke. Emitting a strange angry moan, he moves towards the kitchen, looks at the Hamiltons, punches his palm three times meaningfully, and then hurriedly enters the kitchen. Sounds of banging and screaming emerge.

Basil's voice   What are you doing? What do you mean, you've burnt it?

Mr Hamilton   I've had just about enough of this. *(he rises and goes towards the kitchen)*

Basil's voice   How could you forget about it?

Mr Hamilton enters the kitchen and stands behind Basil, who is haranguing empty space.

Basil   *(pretending to be Terry)* Well, I was making another Waldorf salad. *(as himself)* Making another Waldorf salad? What are you making another Waldorf salad for? *(he takes his hat off and belabours the fridge; as Terry)* Careful, Mr Fawlty! I'm only a little fellow! *(as himself)* What do you think Mr and Mrs Hamilton must think . . . *(he gestures towards the dining-room door; this brings Mr Hamilton into his field of view; he stops dead, then recovers and smiles welcomingly)* Mr Hamilton, may I introduce Terry, who . . . *(indicates the empty space, then jumps)* Where did he go? *(to Hamilton)* Where's he gone? Did you see him?

Mr Hamilton   Maybe he went to get something to eat.

He leaves the kitchen decisively and goes to his wife in the dining room.

Mr Hamilton   Come on, honey.

Mrs Hamilton   What is it, Harry?

Mr Hamilton	We're leaving.
Mrs Hamilton	Well, what's happened?
Mr Hamilton	I'll tell you later.

They both leave the dining room, go into the lobby and make for the stairs. Basil sticks his head out of the kitchen door.

Basil	Your steak will be ready in a moment, Mrs Hamilton . . . *(Hamilton checks but Mrs Hamilton goes on upstairs.)* He must have heard you coming and panicked and slipped out into the yard, you know, after all the problems . . .
Mr Hamilton	How big a butterball do you take me for?
Basil	. . . Butter . . . ?
Mr Hamilton	Do you think I don't know what's been going on out there?
Basil	Oh – it's a bit of a débâcle, I'm afraid . . .
Mr Hamilton	I'm talking about you taking twenty pounds off me to keep the chef on, letting him go, cooking the meal yourself and then pretending he's still out there.
Basil	Oh, that.
Mr Hamilton	Yes, that. And I'd be interested to know what you've got to say about it.

By this time some guests have gathered within earshot. They include the Major, Mr Arrad and Misses Tibbs and Gatsby.

Basil	*(to them)* Good evening.
Mr Hamilton	I asked you a question!
Basil	Yes – I'm sorry that your meal has not been fully satisfactory this evening . . .
Mr Hamilton	*(addressing the guests)* Hah! What I'm suggesting is that this is the crummiest, shoddiest, worst-run hotel in the whole of Western Europe.
The Major	No! No! I won't have that! There's a place in Eastbourne . . . what's its name . . . ?
Mr Hamilton	*(to Basil)* And that you are the British Tourist Board's answer to Donald Duck.
Basil	No, look, I know things have gone wrong this evening, but you must remember we've had thousands of satisfied customers . . .
Mr Hamilton	All right, let's ask them, eh?
Basil	What?
Mr Hamilton	Let's ask them. *(to the spectators)* Are you all satisfied? *(a*

	pause; to Mr Arrad) You – are you satisfied?
Basil	*(to the Major)* Yes, Major, are you satisfied? I mean, you've been here seven years, are you satisfied?
The Major	Oh, yes, I love it here.
Basil	*(to Misses Tibbs and Gatsby)* Ladies, are you satisfied?
Misses Tibbs & Gatsby	Oh yes, thank you, Mr Fawlty.
Miss Gatsby	And thank you for asking.
Basil	Not at all . . . Mr Arrad – are you satisfied?
Mr Arrad	Er, well, yes, I . . .
Basil	Miss Gurke?
Miss Gurke	Oh, very nice, yes . . .
Basil	*(to Mr Hamilton)* You see . . . satisfied customers! Of course if this little hotel is not to your taste, then you are free to say so, that is your privilege. And I shall of course refund your money. *(he looks for the £20; unseen by him, Mr Johnstone comes up and stands behind him)* I know how important it is to you Americans. But you must remember *(he hands the money over)* that here in Britain there are things that we value more, things that perhaps in America you've rather forgotten, but which here in Britain are far, far more important . . .
Mr Johnston	I'm not satisfied.
Basil	. . . in our . . . what?
Mr Johnstone	I'm not satisfied.
Mrs Johnstone	No, we're not satisfied.
Basil	Well, people like you never are, are you.
Mrs Johnstone	What?
Basil	There is nothing I could do would please a pair like you, short of putting straw in the rooms.
Mrs Johnstone	I think you're the rudest man I've ever met.
Basil	I haven't started yet . . .
Mr Hamilton	*(taking over)* And you're not going to. You're going to stand here nice and quiet while these people say whether or not they're satisfied. And if you move off that spot, Fawlty, I'm going to bust your ass.
Basil	Everything's bottoms, isn't it.
Mr Hamilton	*(to Johnstone)* Yes, sir?
Mr Johnstone	I think this is probably the worst hotel we've ever stayed in.
Mrs Johnstone	Yes it is. The service here is an absolute disgrace.
Mrs Arrad	I agree.
Mr Hamilton	You do?

Mrs Arrad	Yes. Do you know that we had to wait nearly half an hour for our main course and when it arrived it was wrong.
Mr Arrad	And when I complained he completely fobbed me off with some rubbish about . . .
Mrs Johnstone	My prawns were off and when I told him there was an argument.
Miss Gurke	And her meat was awfully poor.
Mr Libson	And I asked you to fix my radiator three times and nothing's been done.
Mr Hamilton	*(grabbing Basil by the tie)* Satisfied customers, huh? Hot dog! *(releases him and goes off upstairs)*
Basil	This is typical, absolutely typical . . . of the kind of . . . *(shouting)* ARSE I have to put up with from you people. You ponce in here expecting to be waited on hand and foot, well I'm trying to run a hotel here. Have you **any** idea of how much there is to do? Do you ever think of that? Of course not, you're all too busy sticking your noses into every corner, poking around for things to complain about, aren't you. Well, let me tell you something – this is exactly how Nazi Germany started, you know. A lot of layabouts with nothing better to do than to cause trouble. Well I've had fifteen years of pandering to please the likes of you and I've had enough. I've had it. Come on, pack your bags and get out!

Mr and Mrs Hamilton come back down the stairs.

Mrs Hamilton	*(to Basil)* They're packed.
Mr Hamilton	And order ten taxis, will you, I'll pay for 'em. *(he and Mrs Hamilton go upstairs)*
Basil	Come on! Come on!
Miss Gurke	What?
Basil	Out, everybody out.
Mrs Arrad	Out?
Basil	Come on. Upstairs. Pack your bags. *Adios!* Out!
Mr Johnstone	It's raining.
Basil	Well, you should have thought of that before, shouldn't you. Too late now. Come on, out! *Raus! Raus!*

The guests start to go upstairs. Sybil has appeared in the lobby.

Sybil	Basil – what are you **doing?**

The guests stop on the stairs.

Basil	Well, let me explain, my little workhorse. The guests and I have been having a bit of an old chin-wag, and the upshot of it all is, they're off.
Sybil	*(disbelieving)* Off!?
Basil	Well, let me put it this way, dear – either they go or I go. *(Sybil just looks at him)* Right! Come on back everybody. My wife's had a better idea. Come on back. **I'm** going instead. *(the guests come back into the lobby)* Well, goodbye dear. It's been an interesting fifteen years but all good things must come to an end. *(kisses her)* I hope you enjoy your new work here, helping to run a hotel. Goodbye, Major. Goodbye, ladies, give my regards to Polly and Manuel. 'Bye, dear.

He makes to leave. The Hamiltons come downstairs with their bags.

Sybil	You've forgotten your keys, Basil.
Basil	So I have dear, yes. *(he gives them to her)* Oh, and goodbye to all the rest of you. I hope you enjoy your stay here. Don't forget – any complaints, don't hesitate to tell my wife. Any hour of the day or night – just shout! 'Bye!

He stalks out through the main doors. Outside it is pouring with rain. He keeps going but after a few yards comes to a halt and stands there getting soaked. He looks up and thinks. . . . Back in the lobby Mr Hamilton is on the telephone and the other guests are still clustered around.

Mr Hamilton	*(to phone)* Ten minutes, that'll be fine.

He puts the phone down. Basil comes back in.

Basil	*(to Sybil)* Hallo dear, I'm back.
Sybil	What do you want, Basil?
Basil	A room, please. Number twelve is free, I think. I'd like breakfast in bed at half past nine in the morning please, that's eggs, bacon, sausage and tomato, Waldorf salad washed down with lashings of hot screwdrivers . . .

The Kipper and the Corpse

Fourth of second series, first broadcast on 12 March 1979, BBC2.

Mrs Chase   Mavis Pugh
Major Gowen   Ballard Berkeley
Basil Fawlty   John Cleese
Sybil Fawlty   Prunella Scales
Manuel   Andrew Sachs
Dr Price   Geoffrey Palmer
Guest   Len Marten
Mr Leeman   Derek Royle
Mr Xerxes   Robert McBain
Mr Zebedee   Raymond Mason
Miss Young   Pamela Buchner
Polly   Connie Booth
Terry   Brian Hall
Miss Tibbs   Gilly Flower
Miss Gatsby   Renée Roberts
Mr White   Richard Davies
Mrs White   Elizabeth Benson
Mr Ingrams   Charles McKeown

The hotel bar; evening. Sybil is at the bar, Manuel is serving guests. The Major is sitting at a table with Mrs Chase, who is fondling a little lap dog.

Mrs Chase	And he loves pecans and walnuts and he simply adores those little cheese footballs . . . don't you, my darling . . . isn't he beautiful?
The Major	*(who is not that interested)* Very attractive little feller . . . what is it?
Mrs Chase	He's a little Chitzu.
The Major	Is he really? . . . Oh dear, dear, dear. What breed is it?
Mrs Chase	Well, they're lap dogs, aren't they.
The Major	A Lapp dog? Oh, hard to imagine him stalking a reindeer, what?
Basil	*(coming up to the table)* Ah, Major, can I get you another one?
The Major	Ah . . . *(looks at watch)* Why not, why not?
Basil	For you, Mrs Chase?
Mrs Chase	Oh, nothing for me, thank you, but Prince would like a little saucer of warm milk as it's nearly our bed-time . . .
Basil	Yes . . . Manuel! *(to Mrs Chase)* Manuel will attend to its heart's desires. I'm afraid I'm lumbered with the people tonight . . . *(he moves off; Manuel hurries up)* Manuel – *por favor, el perro microscópico . . .*

Dr Price comes into the bar.

Sybil	Oh, good evening, Dr Price.
Dr Price	Good evening.
Sybil	What can I get you?
Dr Price	Scotch, please . . . and I suppose it's too late to get anything to eat, is it? – I missed dinner.
Sybil	What did you have in mind?
Dr Price	Well, I rather fancy some sausages.
Sybil	Oh, I'm afraid Chef would have locked them away. We could do you sandwiches – ham, cheese, tomato . . .
Dr Price	Er . . . ham, thank you.
Sybil	I'll just arrange it for you. Basil . . .
Basil	*(who is serving drinks)* Yes, dear?
Sybil	Would you make some ham sandwiches, please.
Basil	Look, I'm trying . . .
Sybil	For Dr Price. *(the phone rings in the lobby)*

Basil	Oh . . . of course. Yes, one moment, Doctor. *(delivers the drink)* There we are, Major.
Sybil	Excuse me . . . the phone. *(she leaves)*
Basil	*(to Manuel, who is trying to close the window)* Ah, found another draught, have we?
Mrs Chase	We have to be very careful, Mr Fawlty, he's not very strong.
Basil	Indeed yes. A rapid movement of air could damage him irreparably. If only one could keep them in air-tight containers.
The Major	Wouldn't be able to breathe, would he, Fawlty?
Basil	Well, he could try, Major, he could try. *(he sweeps on to the next table, where sit a short balding man and a rather obviously sexy redhead)* Anything else for you?
Man	Er, no thank you . . . it's a bit late and we'd better . . . get upstairs.
Basil	Quite, quite. *(to himself)* Sorry to have kept you. *(to Dr Price)* Um . . . doctor . . . one round? Two?
Dr Price	Oh, just one, please.
Basil	My pleasure. *(he leaves for the kitchen)*

In the lobby Sybil is on the reception phone, definitely gossiping.

Sybil	No, no, she was the one he had with him the third time, the first time was the dowdy one, then his wife, then her, and now this red . . . *(the man and the redhead approach the desk)* . . . Oh yes, that must have been lovely. *(to man)* Number twelve . . . let's see . . . *(gets the key)*
Man	Thank you. *(he and his companion go upstairs)*
Sybil	*(to phone)* . . . How very lovely, yes that was them . . . not much, they get less fussy as they get older.

A party comes in through the main doors: Miss Young, Mr Leeman, Mr Xerxes and Mr Zebedee; they are business associates. Mr Leeman is apologetic.

Mr Leeman	Sorry about this.
Mr Xerxes	Please. It couldn't matter less, we're meeting in the morning anyway.
Mr Zebedee	You've had a long journey.
Mr Xerxes	You get a good night's sleep.
Miss Young	You're sure you're feeling all right?
Mr Leeman	Oh, fine, fine, just a little . . .

Miss Young	Oh yes, of course.
Mr Xerxes	Well, you get straight to bed, and we'll pick you up here at nine-thirty.
Mr Zebedee	We'll have a coffee and go in to the MD at ten.
Mr Leeman	Fine, thanks, OK.
The Others	Goodnight. See you in the morning . . . sleep well . . .
Mr Leeman	See you at nine-thirty . . . sorry . . . *(they leave and he turns towards Sybil)*
Sybil	*(to phone)* Harris . . . oh no, on his own again . . . oh, no, I wouldn't have thought so, he watches the football. *(to Mr Leeman)* Number eight, isn't it? . . . Where are we . . . *(gives him the key)* Are you feeling all right?
Mr Leeman	Er . . . not too good, no . . .
Sybil	Oh dear. Would you like a little hot something?
Mr Leeman	Oh, no, no . . . I'm fine, thank you.
Sybil	Oh, well, if there's anything you need . . .
Mr Leeman	*(moving away)* Yes. Thank you.
Sybil	*(to phone)* No, that wasn't him, that was a new one.
Basil	*(appearing from the kitchen with a plate of sandwiches; to Leeman)* Good night. *(Leeman does not respond, moving past towards the stairs)* I said 'Good night.'
Mr Leeman	Oh, good night.
Basil	That didn't hurt, did it.
Sybil	Basil!

Mr Leeman disappears uncertainly as Basil crosses the lobby.

Basil	Good manners cost nothing, dear.
Sybil	He's not feeling very well, Basil.
Basil	He only had to say 'Good night', dear. It's not the Gettysburg address.
Sybil	Basil, when you're not feeling well . . .
Basil	*(going into the bar)* Just two little words, dear, to bring a little happiness into the world.
Mr Leeman	*(coming down again)* Excuse me.
Sybil	Yes, Mr Leeman. What can I do for you?
Mr Leeman	Do you think I might have breakfast in bed in the morning?
Basil	*(coming back in)* . . . In bed?
Mr Leeman	Yes.
Sybil	Of course, Mr Leeman.
Basil	Yes, we can manage that, can we dear?

Sybil	Yes, we can. *(to phone)* I'll call you back. *(puts the phone down)*
Basil	Is it your legs?
Mr Leeman	. . . I'm sorry?
Basil	Well, most of our guests manage to struggle down in the morning.
Sybil	A full breakfast or the continental?
Mr Leeman	Oh, er . . .
Sybil	Our chef does a very good full breakfast, eggs, bacon, sausage, tomato, fried bread . . .
Mr Leeman	The continental.
Sybil	You wouldn't care for kippers?
Mr Leeman	Oh . . . fine, kippers, yes, thank you.

Basil departs resignedly.

Sybil	Toast, butter, marmalade . . .
Mr Leeman	Yes, thank you.
Sybil	Tea or coffee?
Mr Leeman	*(not feeling at all well)* Yes, er . . . tea, thank you.
Sybil	A newspaper?
Mr Leeman	Er . . . *Telegraph.*
Sybil	Thank you . . . Good night.

Mr Leeman starts to move off. Sybil goes into the office; Basil comes back in.

Basil	Rosewood, mahogany, teak?
Mr Leeman	. . . I beg your pardon?
Basil	What would you like your breakfast tray made out of?
Mr Leeman	I don't really mind.
Basil	Are you sure? Fine, well you go along and have a really good night's sleep then – I'm hoping to get a couple of hours later on myself . . . *(shouting after Mr Leeman as he goes up the stairs)* but I'll be up in good time to serve you your breakfast in bed. *(Leeman has now gone)* If you can remember to sleep with your mouth open you won't even have to wake up. I'll just drop in small pieces of lightly buttered kipper when you're breathing in the right direction, if that doesn't put you out. *(imitates Sybil)* Basil! *(slaps his own wrist)*

The dining room at breakfast the next morning. Dr Price is at the centre table; Polly is taking his order.

Dr Price	Sausages, please.
Polly	Just sausages?
Dr Price	Just sausages.
Polly	Tea or coffee?
Dr Price	Coffee, please.

There are sounds of a minor fracas at Mrs Chase's table. Polly moves over there. The dog is seated on a chair at the table.

Manuel	But is . . .
Mrs Chase	No, no, not a saucer.
Manuel	*Como?*
Mrs Chase	I said a bowl.
Manuel	. . . a ball?
Mrs Chase	Yes. And not cold like this, that's too **cold**. I said tepid, didn't I?
Polly	*Mas grande*, Manuel – *de agua caliente.*
Manuel	Ah. *(he and Polly move off)*
Mrs Chase	He could catch pneumonia from that. And bring another cushion. He's not quite high enough.

Polly and Manuel go into the kitchen. Terry is cooking and Sybil helping.

Polly	Sausages on six, Terry.
Terry	Coming up
Polly	*Mas grande*, Manuel.

She hurries into the lobby, passing Basil as he comes in looking at the paper.

Basil	Another car strike. Would you believe it.
Sybil	*(handing him a packet)* Put these kippers back, would you, Basil.
Basil	They ought to get Butlin's to run our car factories.
Sybil	In the fridge.
Basil	*(looking at the kippers)* . . . These should have been eaten by . . . when was the sixth?
Sybil	Oh, that's all right.
Basil	It says on the packet, Sybil.
Terry	They're all right, Mr Fawlty.
Basil	*(checking with the paper)* The sixth?
Sybil	That's just to cover themselves.

Polly hurries in and hands Manuel a cushion. He goes into the dining room with it.

Terry	Eggs and sausages, Poll.

The dining room. Manuel approaches Mrs Chase's table with bowl and cushion. He puts the bowl on the floor.

Mrs Chase	On the table . . . on the table. *(Manuel puts the cushion on the table)* No! **That!** *(Manuel puts the bowl on the table uncertainly; Mrs Chase picks up the dog)* Now put that under him. *(Manuel puts the bowl on the chair)* The cushion! The cushion!

Manuel puts the cushion under the dog, but the dog snaps at him, scoring a hit.

Manuel	He bite me!
Mrs Chase	You frightened him.
Manuel	*Qué?*
Mrs Chase	You make sudden movements like that, of course he's going to bite. Don't you have dogs in Calcutta?
Polly	*(coming up)* Excuse me, but I have an order for eggs and sausage for this table.
Mrs Chase	Oh, yes. The sausages are for him. *(Polly puts the food down)*
Manuel	Ooh!
Polly	What's the matter, Manuel?
Manuel	He bite me.
Mrs Chase	Cut them up. Cut them up into little pieces. *(Polly starts cutting up her eggs)* No, not my eggs, not my eggs. The sausages!
Polly	Oh, sorry. *(she goes to cut them up but the dog takes a bite at her, too)*
Manuel	He bite Polly, too. You see?
Mrs Chase	If dogs are allowed in the dining room at least the staff should know how to handle them.
Polly	*(charmingly)* I'll cut them up in the kitchen, Mrs Chase.
Mrs Chase	**Little** pieces.

The kitchen. Terry is finishing the kippers.

Terry	Kippers ready!

Polly and Manuel enter. She puts the plate down, hard.

Manuel	He hurt you, Polly?

Basil is peering at the kippers.

Sybil	Basil, what are you doing?
Basil	. . . Do you know when the sixth **was**, Sybil?
Sybil	Will you just take it upstairs.
Terry	They're all right, Mr Fawlty.
Basil	Are they supposed to be that colour?
Sybil	Basil, will you just take it up. What's the matter, Manuel?
Polly	That hairy mosquito just bit us both.
Sybil	What?
Manuel	Is not right in dining room like that.
Sybil	Well, she pays extra for the dog, Manuel, you see . . . Basil, it's **after** eight.
Basil	*(still peering at the kippers)* Poisoning is still an offence in this country, you know, Sybil.
Sybil	Oh **do** get a move on, we've got a busy day, I've got the laundrymen coming . . .
Basil	The laundrymen! My God! A woman's work is never delegated, is it. *(he exits)*
Sybil	What are you doing, Polly?
Polly	Just preparing some sausages. *(she adds some tabasco sauce to them)* Bangers à la Bang.

The upstairs corridor. Basil comes along with the tray, looking at the paper as he goes. He arrives at Mr Leeman's door and knocks.

Basil	Good morning! Breakfast!

Inside the room Mr Leeman is sitting up in bed, his eyes open. He is dead. The room light is on. Outside, Basil knocks again.

Basil	Breakfast! *(he opens the door and goes in; he puts the tray down in front of Mr Leeman)* Here we are. *(he picks up a book from the floor; Mr Leeman slumps forward and appears to be staring at the newspaper; Basil puts the book down on the bedside table)* Another car strike. Marvellous, isn't it. *(goes to the window and draws the curtains)* Taxpayers pay 'em millions each year, they get the money, go on strike. It's called Socialism. I mean if they don't like making cars why don't they get themselves another bloody job designing cathedrals or composing viola concertos? The British Leyland Concerto in four movements, all of 'em slow, with a four-hour tea break in between. I'll tell you why, 'cos they're not interested in anything except lounging about on conveyor belts stuffing themselves with

my money. You don't mind if I turn the light off? *(he does so and turns to Mr Leeman as he opens the door)* Well, enjoy your breakfast . . . I'm sorry, I didn't catch that . . . oh, not at all, thank you for mentioning it. *(he exits, closing the door, and starts off down the corridor)* Unbelievable. Un-be-lievable. Not a single bloody word. You get up at five-thirty so they can lounge around in bed till midday and do you get so much as a word of thanks? *(he gets to the bottom of the stairs as Polly comes out of the kitchen carrying a little silver jug)* What's that?

Polly   Forgot the milk.

Basil   Well, don't get talking to him, you'll never get away. *(he goes into the kitchen; Polly disappears up the stairs)*

The kitchen. Sybil is working on her laundry list.

Basil   Would you believe it? I get him his breakfast, I take it all the way upstairs, I lay it in front of him, hand him his newspaper, I tidy the rom, draw the curtains, guess what he says? *(Sybil is absorbed with her list)* I said, 'Guess what he says?'

Sybil   Mmmmm?

Basil   Nothing! *(no reaction)* Your friend, the one in eight. Nothing . . . not a word! Are you listening to me? . . . Hello, hello . . . can anyone hear me? Have I ceased to exist? Have I become invisible? Sybil, Sybil, Sybil . . . can you see me?

Sybil   *(looking round at him)* No. *(she returns to her list)*

Basil   Oh good. Well, I'll go and lie down then. No I won't, I'll go and hit some guests. *(he exits into the dining room)*

The dining room. He is sneaking up behind a guest when there are strange strangled death-rattle noises from Mrs Chase's table.

Mrs Chase   Poor little boy . . . poor little toma-woma . . . ah . . . let me see . . .

The kitchen. Terry gives Manuel a plate of sausages.

Terry   Dr Price's sausages.

Polly runs into the kitchen, rather upset.

Sybil   What is it, Polly?

Polly   He's dead.

Sybil	. . . Dead? Who?
Polly	. . . Number eight.
Sybil	Leeman. But Basil just took him his breakfast.
Polly	He's cold.
Sybil	Oh no.

Sybil and Polly run out into the lobby. Manuel and Terry stare at each other. Basil enters.

Basil	What's the matter with that dog?
Manuel	. . . He is dead.
Basil	Well, he's certainly struggling for life at the moment. A dead dog in the breakfast room, eh? Egon Ronay'd knock off a star for that.
Manuel	No, no . . . Mr Leeman is dead.
Basil	Well, that would explain a lot.
Terry	No, Mr Fawlty, really . . . Poll just said so.
Basil	What are you on about? I just took him his kippers. . . . Oh my God! *(he turns and runs out at full speed)*

The lobby. Basil runs upstairs, passing Sybil.

Sybil	Leeman's dead. I'm getting Dr Price.
Basil	Wait! . . . Wait! *(but she's gone; he runs on up)*

Mr Leeman's room. Polly is there; Basil rushes in. He stares at the body.

Polly	I just put the milk down on the tray . . . *(Basil picks up the plate of kippers and looks around feverishly)* . . . What are you doing? *(Basil grabs the kippers and throws the plate under the bed)* . . . What are you **doing**?
Basil	*(running to the window)* I told her. I told her the sixth. We could get twenty years for this. *(he is having trouble opening the window)*
Polly	What?
Basil	The kippers! The kippers! Oh my God. *(he moves the window up a bit)*
Polly	Mr Fawlty, he's been dead for hours. *(Basil is still struggling with the window)* Mr Fawlty! He's cold. He's been dead for hours. He must have died in his sleep. Mr Fawlty!
Basil	What, what?
Polly	He hasn't touched those kippers. Well, look! Feel him!
Basil	What?

Polly	Feel him!
Basil	*(feeling the body)* He's stone cold.
Polly	Yes.
Basil	Oh joy!! Oh, **thank** you God! Isn't it wonderful!!! Oh, I'm so happy! Hooray! *(Polly is trying to restrain him)* Hoo . . . *(he turns and sees Dr Price standing there with Sybil)* Sad, isn't it. Tch tch tch. *(he hides the kippers inside his cardigan)*
Dr Price	May I ask who . . . *(looks at Basil; he has smelt the kipper)*
Basil	Bit stuffy, isn't it. I'll open a window.
Sybil	*(prompting Dr Price)* Who . . . ?
Dr Price	Who found the body?
Sybil	Polly did.
Polly	I was bringing him up the milk . . . and . . . we'd forgotten it.
Dr Price	You brought the milk with the breakfast?
Sybil	No, the breakfast had been brought up.
Dr Price	Well, who brought the breakfast? Who found him?

Basil is at the window; he tries to flip one of the kippers out but it hits a pane and falls back. He puts his foot on it. Dr Price looks at him.

Basil	Oh, I brought the breakfast.
Dr Price	*(seeing the kipper)* What's that?
Basil	Er . . . that's a bit of it.
Dr Price	Bit of what?
Basil	A bit of the breakfast.
Dr Price	You brought him his breakfast.
Basil	Yes.
Dr Price	So you told her he was dead.
Basil	Yes.
Dr Price	*(to Polly)* Well, then, why did you bring him . . . *(Basil tries to get the other kipper out of his cardigan but Dr Price looks at him; Dr Price returns to Polly)* Why did you bring him the milk, then?
Polly	Why?
Dr Price	Yes, why?
Polly	Well, when he said Mr Leeman was dead, I thought he'd said he's still in bed.
Sybil	Well, he didn't actually say he was dead, Dr Price.
Basil	Well, I said he was pretty quiet.
Dr Price	Quiet?

Basil	Exactly.
Sybil	What were you talking to him about, Basil, car strikes, was it?
Basil	Thank you, Sybil.
Dr Price	I don't understand. He's been dead for about ten hours.
Basil	Yes, it's so final, isn't it.
Sybil	Basil!
Basil	Well, wouldn't you say it was final dear, I'd say it was pretty bloody final.
Dr Price	Do you mean to tell me you didn't realize this man was dead?
Basil	People don't talk that much in the morning . . . well look, I'm just delivering a tray, right? If the guest isn't singing 'Oh What A Beautiful Morning' I don't immediately think, 'Oh there's another one snuffed it in the night.' Another name in the Fawlty Towers Book of Remembrance. I mean, this is a hotel, not the Burma Railway.
Sybil	Basil!
Basil	Well, I mean it does actually say 'Hotel' outside, you know. Perhaps I should be more specific. 'Hotel for people who have a better than fifty per cent chance of making it through the night' . . . what are you looking at me like that for?
Sybil	*(goes over to him; quietly)* Basil, there's a kipper sticking out of your jumper.
Basil	Ah, there it is. I've been looking for that. That's the other one.
Sybil	We'll be downstairs, doctor. *(starts propelling Basil out of the room)*
Polly	Shall I ring the undertaker?
Sybil	Would you, Polly.
Basil	*(shouting back over his shoulder)* I've been up since five-thirty, you know. *(he is borne out of the room; Dr Price starts his examination)*
	The lobby. Sybil, Basil and Polly come downstairs. Basil still has the kipper in his hands.
Sybil	He was leaving today. Some people are coming at lunchtime.
Basil	Well, we'll put him in another room.
Sybil	We're full tonight. Oh do put that away. *(he throws the*

	kipper into the kitchen) Get the body into the office until the undertaker comes.
Basil	Now?
Sybil	When doctor's finished. *(she goes to the reception desk, where Polly is dialling)*
Basil	What are you doing?
Sybil	Making up his bill.
Basil	Who are you going to give it to?
Sybil	We'll put it in his wallet, they're bound to look there. Better not charge him for breakfast.

Miss Gatsby appears at the dining-room door.

Polly	*(to phone)* Mr Simkins? Fawlty Towers here. I'm afraid somebody's died during the night. . . . When could you collect the body? *(she sees Miss Gatsby coming up)* . . . Somebody . . . anybody, really . . .
Basil	*(takes Miss Gatsby's arm gallantly to move her on)* Good morning, good morning!
Miss Gatsby	You're very cheerful this morning, Mr Fawlty.
Basil	*(cheerfully)* Yes, well one of the guests has just died.
Miss Gatsby	Oooh, you are wicked. *(she goes)*
Basil	Manuel! Manuel! *(Manuel runs out of the kitchen dusting off the kipper; Basil grabs it)* Manuel, we're going to get the body. *(to Polly)* Polly . . . Polly . . . *(he nods his head towards upstairs)*
Polly	*(to phone)* Yes, if you can. *(she puts the phone down)*
Basil	*(waves the kipper, then sees Dr Price coming down the stairs)* Would it be all right to . . .

Dr Price nods. Basil, Manuel and Polly hurry upstairs.

Dr Price	*(to Sybil)* Could I use the phone please, I have to call the coroner.
Sybil	The coroner?!
Dr Price	I can't give him his death certificate because I'm not his doctor. I have to report his death to the coroner . . .
Sybil	Oh, I see. Of course. Do come this way, doctor. *(she leads him into the office)*

The upstairs corridor. Polly is watching down the stairs. Basil's head appears from Mr Leeman's room.

Basil	All clear?
Polly	All clear . . .

*Basil and Manuel appear carrying the body, covered with a
sheet with some folded towels on top.*

Manuel	Is heavy.
Basil	Come on, come on!

Miss Tibbs appears behind them and is about to overtake.

Miss Tibbs	Good morning, Manuel.
Manuel	Good morning.

Some towels fall off the body.

Miss Tibbs	Oh . . . I'll pick it up. *(she picks up the towels and tries to replace them)*
Basil	No, it's all right. Leave it. No, leave it. It's heavy.
Miss Tibbs	No, it's quite all right, I'll put them like that.
Basil	Look, don't bother. We can manage.
Miss Tibbs	Oh, it's no bother.
Basil	No, no, leave it alone!
Miss Tibbs	I know, if I just fold them like this. *(Manuel groans under the weight)*
Basil	Go away! Move, Manuel! Move, move, move!
Polly	*(taking Miss Tibbs by the arm)* I'll do it, Miss Tibbs.
Miss Tibbs	No, it's all right. *(they move off with the body, but she is standing on the sheet; it comes off; Miss Tibbs screams)* Aaahh! He's dead!
Basil	Serves you right.
Polly	*(trying to calm the screaming Miss Tibbs)* Sshh! Sshh! It's all right, Miss Tibbs.
Miss Tibbs	Aaaah! Oh my God!
Basil	Shut up!

Polly tries to muffle Miss Tibbs, but fails.

Miss Tibbs	Aaaaaaggggggghhhh!
Basil	Slap her!
Polly	What?
Basil	She's hysterical. Slap her.

*Polly tries to put her hand over Miss Tibbs' mouth but she gets
bitten and withdraws the hand very fast. Manuel groans.*

Miss Tibbs	Murder! Murder!!
Basil	Slap her!

Polly does so. Miss Tibbs folds up and falls to the floor. Manuel drops the body.

Basil *(to Polly)* Oh, spiffing! Absolutely spiffing! Well done! Two dead, twenty-five to go. *(he hears a noise from downstairs)* Quick, Polly!

Polly runs to the top of the stairs. Basil drags the body into the nearest room and then gets Manuel to help him carry Miss Tibbs into the same room. Polly is on her knees, stalling Mr and Mrs White, who are coming up.

Polly I just dropped my ring. Oh . . . there it is. *(she hears the door slam)* Oh, sorry, I'm in your way. *(she gets up)*

Mr White That's quite all right. *(they pass her and make for the room into which Basil and Manuel have taken the bodies)*

Polly *(getting between them and the door)* Oh! Is this your room?

Mr White Yes.

Polly It's lovely, isn't it.

Mrs White Yes.

Polly Did you enjoy your breakfast?

Mr White Oh, yes, thank you, yes, yes. Excuse me . . . do you think we could just go inside and get our . . .

Polly Not really.

Mr White Pardon?

Polly Well, it's being cleaned at the moment. Mr Fawlty's doing it . . .

Mrs White But we want to get our things.

Mr White Yes, we're going out, you see.

Polly Oh, well, it'll only take a couple of minutes.

Mrs White I'm sorry, we're a little late. *(she moves to take the door handle)*

Polly Excuse me . . . Mr Fawlty! *(she knocks)* Mr Fawlty!!!

Basil's voice All clear?

Polly Er . . . Mr Fawlty . . .

Basil's voice Anybody about?

Polly Mr and Mrs White want to come into their room.

Basil's voice Ooooh, no! Wait a minute. *(a pause, then the door opens a crack)* Hallo.

Mr White Can we come in?

Basil Er . . .

Polly I was just explaining you were finishing the room.

Basil Yes, won't be five minutes.

Mr White Well, could you finish it later?

From inside, Manuel groans and there is a heavy thump.

Basil	*(to Manuel)* Pick up that ashtray, will you Manuel, please. *(to the Whites)* Could we do it later?
Mrs White	When we've got our things.
Polly	Well, it'll only be a couple of minutes.
Mr White	Look, Fawlty, we want our things.
Basil	Oh, right, yes, thank you so much. *(he disappears, closes the door and bolts it)*
Mr White	He's locked it!
Polly	Well, that's just a precaution.
Mr White	*(banging on the door)* Have you locked this?
Basil's voice	Only slightly.
Mr White	*(banging)* Will you let us in.
Basil's voice	In a minute.

In the bedroom, Basil and Manuel are putting Miss Tibbs into the wardrobe.

Basil	Get the coats . . . get the coats . . .

Outside the room the Whites are waiting.

Mrs White	What's going on?
Polly	Well, he's a bit of a perfectionist.

In the bedroom, Basil unbolts the door.

Basil	Readyyyyy!

The Whites come in. Manuel is holding two coats. Basil is polishing the wardrobe with his handkerchief.

Mr White	What's been going on in here?
Basil	Well, we tried rearranging the furniture but it didn't really work. Manuel has your coats.

Manuel gives them their coats. They look around suspiciously. They are about to leave when a moan is heard. They stop. Manuel starts singing loudly. Polly joins in. The Whites stare at Manuel.

Basil	It's all right. He's from Barcelona.

The moaning is heard again. Polly simulates pain.

Polly	Ooooh!
Mrs White	What's that noise?
Polly	Oh, just my back.

Mrs White	No, that moaning.

A loud moan from the wardrobe. Basil goes to the window and looks out.

Basil	Oh yes. That's odd.
Mr White	No, no, it's coming from the cupboard.

Basil listens. Another moan.

Basil	Well, we'll get some oil. *(more noise)* Have a nice day.
Mrs White	There's someone in there.
Basil	What?
Mr White	Yes, listen.
Basil	No, no. no. *(shrieking and hammering starts)* Good Lord, so there is!
Mrs White	Let them out!!
Basil	Good idea. Right . . . well . . . um . . .
Mr White	Well, go on.
Basil	Yes, we're going to. It's the next thing on the list. If you do get a chance to see the museum it's well . . .
Mr White	Open it. Now. Now!
Basil	All right, yes, right. Oh, it's locked. Damn.
Mr White	Where's the key?
Basil	Yes, where is the key? Do you have any idea, Polly, Manuel . . . ?
Polly	I expect we've left it downstairs somewhere.
Manuel	*Qué?*
Basil	Where's the key?
Manuel	. . . In your pocket.
Basil	No it isn't.
Manuel	Yes it is.
Basil	No, no, it's not.
Manuel	*Si.* Look, look! *(despite Basil's attempts to stop him, he reaches in Basil's pocket and produces the key)* Look!
Basil	Oh, well done, Manuel. Thank you very much. Thank you. Right, well, we've got it now.
Mr White	Give it to me. I'll do it.
Basil	All right, I will, I will! *(he opens the wardrobe door and Miss Tibbs emerges gibbering and crying; Polly comforts her)* Now, I've warned you about this before! You can hide in your own cupboard but not in other people's! *(behind him the wardrobe door opens slightly and an arm flops out; Basil turns to the Whites)* I'm sorry about this, you can't really blame

	her. She doesn't have much in her life, she has to make her own entertainment.
Polly	*(seeing the arm)* She has trouble with her arm. That's why she goes **in the cupboard**.
Basil	Exactly.
Mrs White	Are you feeling better?
Polly	Her arm gets stuck there!
Basil	It's always happening to her.
Miss Tibbs	*(crying)* He's dead!
Basil	Yes, it's her husband. She hasn't got over it. Died thirty years ago . . .
Polly	*(shouting)* She doesn't mean any **arm**!!

Basil glances back and sees the arm.

Miss Tibbs	In the cupboard!!
Basil	No more today, you've had enough. *(suddenly points to the other side of the room by the door)* Oh my God, look at that!

The Whites look. Basil runs to the door and starts stamping on something. Polly nips across, flings the arm in the wardrobe and shuts the door. She returns to Miss Tibbs. Manuel stares at Basil, thinks he's got the point of what Basil's doing and starts Spanish dancing. Basil picks up an imaginary dead spider and throws it away. Manuel is still dancing.

Basil	Thank you, Manuel. That's enough. *(to the Whites)* Anything else we can do for you?

Miss Tibbs' bedroom. Miss Tibbs is on her bed. Sybil is making some tea.

Miss Tibbs	Oh, it was so horrible, Mrs Fawlty, you've no idea.
Sybil	Oh, I know.
Miss Tibbs	It was pitch black in there . . . and that thing . . . with its hand . . .
Sybil	Oh, I know. *(gives Miss Tibbs the tea)* Now you have a little rest and try to think of something else.
Miss Tibbs	But **anything** could have happened.
Sybil	Well, he **was** dead, dear.
Miss Tibbs	A man is a man, Mrs Fawlty.
Sybil	*(slightly thrown)* Oh, I know . . .
Miss Tibbs	I shall speak to him about it.
Sybil	**Speak** to him?
Miss Tibbs	To Mr Fawlty. We're his oldest residents . . .

Sybil	Well, have a little rest first.
Miss Tibbs	Frightening me like that. I shall speak to him.
Sybil	Have a word with him in a little while when you're feeling better. *(she leaves)*

In the lobby, the Whites are standing by the reception desk. Mr White is on the phone.

Mr White	I see; thank you. *(rings off; to Mrs White)* It's all right, dear – they've got rooms at the Seaview.
Mrs White	Tonight?
Mr White	Yes.
Mrs White	Well, let's have a look at it.
Mr White	And if that's no good we'll try the one up by the prophylactic emporium.

They leave by the main door. Polly's head appears round the bottom of the stairs.

Polly	OK.

Basil and Manuel hurry down the stairs carrying Mr Leeman, and into the office. The Major, coming from the bar, sees them. They put the body on the swivel chair. The Major comes into the office carrying his newspaper.

The Major	Morning, Fawlty.
Basil	Ah, hello, Major.
The Major	Any sign of the papers?
Basil	Well, you've got it, Major.
The Major	Have I? So I have, yes. Oh, I say, I say Fawlty . . . *(indicating Mr Leeman)* he doesn't look quite the ticket.
Basil	Major, don't say anything to anybody, but he's dead.
The Major	Ah! . . . Shot, was he?
Basil	No, no, no. Died in his sleep.
The Major	In his sleep? Ah, well, you're off your guard, you see.
Basil	Yes.
The Major	Fawlty . . . I shouldn't let him lie around here, you know.
Basil	No, no, the undertakers are coming to get him.
The Major	Ah! 'Cos they attract the flies, you see. *(he moves off)*

Basil goes out into the lobby. Dr Price has just come out of the dining room.

Dr Price	Look, I've been waiting in there.
Basil	What?

Dr Price	I haven't had any breakfast yet.
Basil	Oh, right. Sorry. Coming, coming . . . *(he hurries towards the kitchen)*
Dr Price	*(to himself)* It's only sausages. *(he goes into the dining room)*

The kitchen. Basil rushes over to the fridge and gets some sausages out. In the background, Miss Tibbs goes to the reception desk and sounds the bell.

Miss Tibbs	Mr Fawlty, I want a word with you, please.

She rings the bell again. Basil closes the door to the lobby and starts frying the sausages. Then he goes into the dining room, where Dr Price is sitting at his table.

Basil	Sorry about the delay, doctor. Normal service has been resumed as soon as possible, ha ha ha. *(a scream is heard from the direction of the office)* . . . More coffee? *(another scream)* Tea? Tea? *(Dr Price looks at him, puzzled)* I'll turn the radio down.

He goes into the kitchen, then rushes across the lobby to the office. Miss Tibbs is lying flat out on the floor; Mr Leeman's arm is swinging slightly.

Basil	Oh! *(Manuel and Sybil appear at the door)*
Manuel	Miss Tibbs.
Sybil	Oh no.
Basil	Would you believe it?
Sybil	What d'you put him **there** for?
Basil	Well, he wouldn't fit in the safe and all the drawers were full. Come on, Manuel. *(they start carrying the body out)* Wonderful, isn't it? Our guests. They give us trouble even when they're dead.
Sybil	Where are you taking him?
Basil	Kitchen.

They hurry off towards the kitchen with the body, but Miss Gatsby appears down the stairs.

Sybil	Polly.
Polly	*(diverting Miss Gatsby)* Just a moment.

Basil and Manuel swerve out of the main doors to avoid Miss Gatsby. Outside they see the Whites about to drive off. Mrs White sees them and nudges her husband.

Basil   Hallo!

Mr White looks at them. Polly appears and waves. They all disappear inside. The Whites drive off and there is the sound of a car crash.

In the lobby, Basil and Manuel hurry back in with the body. Polly picks up the sheets and towels from the floor and waves them towards the kitchen; but the dining-room door opens and Mrs Chase appears carrying a moribund poopie which emits occasional dying noises. She goes upstairs, passing Basil and Manuel who stand there helplessly with the body.

Mrs Chase   He's seriously ill.
Basil   Oh dear.
Mrs Chase   Well don't just stand there. Call a vet!
Basil   Right.
Mrs Chase   He's been poisoned.

She disappears upstairs. The three stare after her, then jerk into action. They hustle the body into the kitchen, which is filled with smoke.

Basil   On the table! On the table! *(they put the body down on the table)* Open the back door.

Manuel does so. Polly dumps the sheets and towels into a large laundry basket which is by the door, then goes into the lobby. Basil grabs the cremated sausages off the stove. Dr Price looks in from the dining room.

Basil   *(showing him the sausages)* Sorry about them. Bit overdone, I'm afraid. We'll send 'em down to the crematorium.
Dr Price   *(staring at the body)* What in the . . . !!!???
Basil   Oh.
Dr Price   You can't keep a dead body in here, where there's food.
Basil   Can't we?
Dr Price   Of course not.
Basil   Oh, right, OK. Sorry. Manuel!

They lift the body again.

Manuel   Where? Where?
Basil   Put it there, in the basket.

They put the body into the laundry basket.

Dr Price	Not in here . . . not in the kitchen.
Basil	Oh, right.

In the lobby, the Whites are coming in through the main doors. Mrs White is badly shaken. Mr White is holding a handkerchief to his head. They go upstairs as Basil and Manuel carry the basket out and dump it in front of the hatstand, which is against the wall between the kitchen and dining-room doors. Basil does not see the Whites, but notices a new visitor, Mr Ingrams, standing at the reception desk.

Basil	Sybil!

In the bar, Sybil is sitting with a very shaky Miss Tibbs.

Sybil	*(calling)* I'm looking after Miss Tibbs, Basil. *(to Miss Tibbs)* How are you feeling, dear? *(Miss Tibbs just stares fixedly ahead)*

In the lobby.

Basil	*(to Mr Ingrams)* Won't be two minutes. *(he hurries back into the kitchen)*

In the kitchen, Dr Price is waiting for him.

Basil	Sorry about that. *(he hurries towards the sausages)*
Dr Price	Wash your hands first, please.
Basil	Oh, right.
Dr Price	And make sure this area is scrubbed before any more food is prepared in here.
Basil	Absolutely.
Dr Price	Sausages excepted. You may cook them immediately. I'll take the risk.
Basil	But of course. *Tout de suite.*

Dr Price goes back into the dining room, where Manuel is clearing away his table. Dr Price puts his hands on the tablecloth just as Manuel tries to remove it.

Dr Price	Leave it.
Manuel	No, I take it.
Dr Price	Leave it.
Manuel	No, no, is not time, please. *(Dr Price starts moving salt and pepper from an adjoining table)* No, no, no, please.
Dr Price	I'm sitting here.
Manuel	Is no lunch till twelve.

Dr Price	I'm still having breakfast.
Manuel	. . . Is finished . . . all gone . . . breakfast kaput.
Dr Price	*(sitting)* I'm having sausages.
Manuel	*(confiscating the cruet)* Is not allowed.
Dr Price	Put that back. Look, I'm a doctor. I'm a doctor and I want my sausages.
Manuel	I tell you, is finished. Bye-bye, please, bye-bye.

Dr Price rises, gets salt and mustard from another table. As he returns, Manuel pinches his knife and fork and darts off. There is no other cutlery around.

Dr Price	Now look.
Manuel	Is finish.
Dr Price	*(getting really angry)* Give those to me. *(pursues Manuel round the room)* Come on, come on.
Manuel	No, is no possible.

They circle the table. Basil comes in from the kitchen.

Basil	Is everything all right?
Manuel	He want to eat now.
Dr Price	I've been trying to sit down, he keeps moving things from my table.
Basil	I'm so sorry.
Dr Price	He doesn't seem to understand that I haven't finished breakfast.
Basil	Manuel? Manuel – let me explain. *(he pokes Manuel in the eye)* You understand? Good. *(to Dr Price)* They'll be with you in just a couple of minutes.

In the lobby, Sybil is checking in a guest, an ordinary businessman.

Sybil	There we are, Mr Ingrams, number eight. At the top of the stairs on the right. Excuse me not coming with you but one of our guests has been taken ill.
Mr Ingrams	*(taking the key)* Thank you.

He goes upstairs and Sybil hurries back into the bar. Miss Young, Mr Xerxes and Mr Zebedee come in through the main doors. Mr Zebedee hangs his hat on the hatstand. Basil and Manuel appear from the dining room and go to the laundry basket, not noticing that it is in a slightly different position.

Mr Xerxes	*(to Basil)* Ah, excuse me.

Basil	*(lifting the basket with Manuel)* In the office.
Miss Young	Excuse me.
Basil	Yes?
Miss Young	We have an appointment with Mr Leeman. *(Basil and Manuel drop the basket)* Do you know where he is?
Basil	*(sitting casually on the basket)* . . . Where he is? Um . . .
Miss Young	Would he be in the dining-room? *(Basil indicates a negative)*
Mr Xerxes	Might he be in his room?
Basil	Now let me think . . . where is he . . .

Manuel puts his foot on the basket and imitates Basil's pose of deep thought.

Miss Young	We've come to collect him, as we're taking him to . . .
Basil	I'm sorry?
Miss Young	We've come to collect him.
Basil	Oh – you've come to **collect** him.
Miss Young	Yes.
Basil	*(standing up)* Oh, I'm sorry. I didn't realize. *(indicating their clothes)* Modern dress.
Miss Young	What?
Basil	Your dress is very modern. I didn't realize women did it.
Miss Young	Did what?
Basil	Ssh. *(points down at the basket)*
Mr Zebedee	He's downstairs?
Basil	*(quietly)* No, no – in the basket.
Mr Xerxes	. . . I **beg** your pardon?
Basil	He's in the basket.
Miss Young	In the **basket**?
Basil	Yes. *(to a passing guest)* Hallo.
Mr Zebedee	What's . . . what's he doing in the basket?
Basil	*(with a minimal shrug)* Well . . . not much.
Mr Xerxes	What are you talking about?
Basil	Don't you believe me? Look. Look. *(he opens the lid a little; they hesitantly look in; he glances round and opens it more; they look in and look at Basil, mystified; he looks at them, looks in the basket, and reacts with horror. Polly comes downstairs)* Oh my God! He's gone! Where is he?
Polly	*(pointing into the basket)* Fresh laundry.
Basil	They've taken him!

Basil, Manuel and Polly rush outside. The laundry van is just pulling away.

Basil, Manuel & Polly   Stop, stop . . . wait, wait . . .

> *They manage to stop the van. Meanwhile, in the dining room Dr Price is sitting at his table, his arms folded. He catches the scent of something . . . there is smoke coming through the kitchen doors. In the bar, Sybil is sitting with a staring Miss Tibbs. The reception bell sounds.*

Sybil   *(calling)* Basil!

> *In the lobby, Messrs Xerxes, Zebedee and Young are standing there, shaken. Xerxes is ringing the reception bell. Basil and Manuel appear just outside the main door with the basket.*

Basil   *(calling back to van)* If you could just hang on a couple of minutes Sorry to keep you. *(he and an increasingly flagging Manuel drag the basket in and park it by the desk)* It's all right. It's all right. We sorted it out. He's in this one.

> *Xerxes and company stare at him. Polly intervenes.*

Polly   *(confidentially)* The doctor didn't want him in the kitchen . . . so we put him in the basket.

Basil   It's more hygienic.

> *Mr Xerxes rings the reception bell.*

Sybil's voice   *(from the bar)* Basil!
Polly   *(getting to the reception desk; to Mr Xerxes)* Yes.
Miss Young   *(to Polly, warily)* You do **work** here?
Polly   Yes.
Miss Young   Well, we'd like to speak to the manager. *(Polly looks blank)*
Basil   I'm the manager. Is there a problem?
Polly   *(in confirmation)* He is . . . really.
Mr Xerxes   No, er, there seems to be some kind of misunderstanding here. *(to Polly)* We've come to collect one of your guests, Mr Leeman, to take him into town for a meeting.
Basil   A meeting?
Miss Young   Yes, a meeting.
Mr Xerxes   With our managing director.
Basil   *(realizing)* Oh, I see. Oh, Mr **Leeman**!
Miss Young   Yes.
Polly   We thought you said the **linen**.
Basil   *(to himself, but too loudly)* Brilliant! *(out loud)* Sorry! Sorry . . . oh, that's it . . . *(he leans on the basket)*

Sybil	*(coming in from the bar)* Sorry to keep you . . .
Basil	Oh, hallo, my sweet.
Sybil	What are you doing, Basil?
Basil	Well, it's a bit involved, dear, but we thought that these gentlemen thought that we thought that they had . . .
Polly	*(to Basil)* No, no.
Basil	No, that's not it.
Polly	*(to Sybil)* Well they were coming for Mr Leeman, and we thought they were coming to collect the **linen**.
Sybil	Mr Leeman.
Basil	So if you'll just sort that out, dear, I'll take the linen upstairs.
Sybil	I see. Thank you, Basil.
Basil	Not at all, my sweet. *(he and Manuel carry the basket upstairs; Manuel is sagging badly and groaning with the effort)*
Sybil	*(to Xerxes, Young and Zebedee)* Would you mind coming into the office for a moment. *(she goes into the office; they follow her uncertainly)*

In the upstairs corridor, Basil and Manuel appear at the top of the stairs. Manuel is getting the worst of it. They stagger along and put the basket down outside number eight.

Basil	Come on, Manuel. One last effort.
The Major	*(walking past)* Another one, Fawlty?
Basil	No, no, same one, Major.

The Major moves on. Polly has followed them upstairs and she opens the door to number eight as they take the body out of the basket and carry it into the room – where Mr Ingrams is sitting on the bed inflating a life-size rubber sex-aid-type doll. Basil and Manuel turn round and go out again rapidly.

Basil	Sorry! Sorry, coming in like that. Sorry.

Ingrams releases the doll and it deflates. Outside in the corridor Basil and Manuel dither. Polly points to the Whites' room.

Polly	They've gone into town.
Basil	Oh. Yes.

They open the door and carry the body in. Inside the room is dark. They lay the body on one of the two beds just as Polly opens the curtains. The light reveals Mrs White lying on the other bed. As she stirs Polly flips the eiderdown over her and

Basil and Manuel pick the body up again and disappear out of the door. Mr White comes out of the bathroom holding a pad of cotton wool to his head. Mrs White, struggling to escape from the eiderdown, falls off the bed.

Polly Sorry . . . wrong room. *(she exits)*

In the lobby, Basil and Manuel rush down the stairs. Manuel is moaning exhaustedly. They go into the kitchen, but Dr Price is standing by the stove frying himself some sausages. Before he can see them they back out into the lobby. Manuel is totally exhausted.

Basil Back in the basket. *(tries to shove Manuel towards the basket by the dining-room door)* Come on, come on.

Manuel Can't lift.

Basil Come on!

Manuel Too tired.

Basil There's somebody coming!

Manuel Mr Fawlty, I no want to work here any more.

Basil Open the basket.

Manuel No.

Basil Open the basket! *(Manuel opens the basket)* Now inside. *(Manuel starts climbing inside it)* Not you!

Manuel I quit.

Basil Get out.

Manuel I on strike.

Basil I'm warning you . . .

Manuel I stay here. Is nice. *(he climbs in and closes the lid on himself)*

Basil *(nearly berserk)* You see this . . . *(indicating Mr Leeman)* You're next!

He hears a sound from the office and drags the body away. Messrs Zebedee, Xerxes and Young come out of the office with Sybil.

Sybil I really am so sorry.

Miss Young Thank you.

Sybil Goodbye.

All Goodbye.

Sybil moves towards the bar. Zebedee, Xerxes and Young move towards the main door, then see Basil. He has sat Mr Leeman on the umbrella-stand part of the hatrack, and is standing in front of him, keeping him in place and hiding him from their view. Basil stands nonchalantly with his arms folded. The others are a bit taken aback.

Basil	Goodbye.
Mr Xerxes & Miss Young Goodbye.	
Basil	Goodbye. *(Mr Zebedee moves over to Basil)* Yes?
Mr Zebedee	Could I get my hat?
Basil	Your hat?
Mr Zebedee	Yes. It's just the . . .
Basil	Yes, I'll have it sent on. Do you have a card with your address? I'll send it on.
Mr Zebedee	Well . . . could I just get it?
Basil	Well, do you have to have it **now**?
Mr Zebedee	Yes.
Basil	Well, supposing you lose it? It's very windy.
Mr Zebedee	I'd like to have it.
Basil	*(sighs to the basket)* Oh, right . . . Manuel! Manuel! *(the others look alarmed)* He's in the basket. He is . . . *(Polly comes downstairs)* Polly, would you get Manuel out of the basket, please.
Polly	*(looking at the basket)* Manuel?
Basil	Yes – come on, girl, come on, what's the matter?
Polly	*(opening the lid cautiously)* No, he isn't in there.
Basil	Yes he is.
Polly	He isn't.
Basil	He is . . . look for him!
Polly	*(rummaging in the laundry)* . . . Oh . . . sorry.
Manuel	*(getting out, to Polly)* You . . . big scab.
Basil	*(to the others)* See! *(he unfolds his arms, revealing Mr Leeman's hand on his arm; hurriedly he releases it and refolds his arms)* Manuel, would you get this gentleman his hat please.
Manuel	Where?
Mr Zebedee	*(pointing)* There! On the rack.
Manuel	*(seeing Mr Leeman)* Ugh! *(he stands next to Basil to hide the evidence and, rather awkwardly, passes a hat over)*
Basil	What colour was it?
Mr Zebedee	Brown. No, that's not it . . . *(Polly reaches over and gets the correct hat)* Thank you.

Miss Tibbs has emerged unsteadily from the bar and now confronts Basil.

Miss Tibbs	Mr Fawlty! I want a word with you in your office.
Basil	Yes, when would be convenient for you?
Miss Tibbs	*(to the others)* I'm seventy-nine!!

The Whites come down the stairs.

Mr White	What on earth is going on here?
Basil	Oh, sorry about the eiderdown, it got a bit caught.
Mrs Chase	*(coming downstairs minus dog)* My baby! My baby's dying! *(general consternation)* They poisoned him!
Miss Young	Your **baby**?
Mrs Chase	He said he'd gone for a vet.
Miss Young	A **vet**?
Basil	Sybil!

Dr Price comes in from the dining room holding a plate of sausages.

| Dr Price | I've just cooked these sausages myself and they're **off**! They should have been eaten by the third. *(goes back into the dining room)* |

Miss Gatsby comes down the stairs. Basil sees Sybil behind the reception desk.

| Basil | Ah, there you are dear. You **do** look nice. Ladies and gentlemen . . . ladies and gentlemen . . . *(calling out through main door)* Laundry's ready . . . *(to his audience)* Ladies and gentlemen, there have been a lot of cock-ups this morning, you all deserve an explanation, and I'm happy to say that my wife will give it to you. Thank you, thank you so much. |

He gestures extravagantly towards Sybil. The throng turns towards her; he leaps into the basket and pulls the lid down. Two laundry men come in. Polly and Manuel move away from the still-seated Mr Leeman. The laundrymen pick up the basket and carry it out. Sybil is surrounded by the throng, all complaining noisily. The Major comes downstairs and sees the corpse.

| The Major | *(to Mr Leeman)* What's going on, old boy? |

Miss Tibbs sees the corpse and screams. Miss Gatsby holds her up. Further pandemonium ensues as the others see it.

| Sybil | Basil! Basil! Basil! Basil! |

The basket is loaded on the back of the van, which drives off.
Sybil's voice wafts furiously after it.

Sybil's voice Basil! Basil! Basil! . . .

The Anniversary

Fifth of second series, first broadcast on 26 March 1979, BBC2.

Polly   Connie Booth
Terry   Brian Hall
Manuel   Andrew Sachs
Sybil Fawlty   Prunella Scales
Basil Fawlty   John Cleese
Roger   Ken Campbell
Alice   Una Stubbs
Virginia   Pat Keen
Arthur   Robert Arnold
Reg   Roger Hume
Kitty   Denyse Alexander
Major Gowen   Ballard Berkeley
Audrey   Christine Shaw
Miss Tibbs   Gilly Flower
Miss Gatsby   Renée Roberts

The kitchen. Terry is clearing things up; Polly is drying the washing-up.

Polly	I mean, it's only a hundred.
Terry	Yeah, nothing for them.
Polly	And I said I'd pay it back in six weeks.
Terry	Well, knock it off your wages.
Polly	And she said she thought it would be all right. *(she starts to dry a vase of flowers without looking)*
Terry	Poll!
Polly	*(realizes and puts it down)* I mean, if he'd said 'No' three weeks ago when I asked him I could have got the money somewhere else.
Terry	Ask him this morning.
Polly	Well, I've asked him three times, it's embarrassing.
Terry	Well, tell him. Say if he won't let you have it you'll go.
Polly	I've got to have it this weekend.
Terry	Well, **ask** him. I mean, me and you practically run the bleeding place for 'em.

He goes out. Manuel comes in with a couple of carrier bags.

Manuel	Ah, Polly. Your paintings brushes.
Polly	Thank you, Manuel. *(she examines them)*
Manuel	Here. And the change is 44p.
Polly	Ah . . . what's all that?
Manuel	Oh, I make a paella, a surprise tonight. My mother's recipe. Is . . . *(indicates top-hole)*
Polly	But does Terry know?
Manuel	Oh . . . perhaps Mr Fawlty say?

Sybil comes in, obviously cross about something. Polly looks at her.

Polly	. . . Anything wrong?
Sybil	*(heavily martyred)* Nothing you could do anything about, thank you, Polly.
Polly	Are you sure?
Sybil	Our fifteenth wedding anniversary today . . . guess who's forgotten.
Polly	Oh, no.
Sybil	I didn't **think** he'd forget this year, not after what happened when he forgot last year . . . I shouldn't be so thin-skinned about it. I'm just cursed with a sensitive

	nature, I'm afraid. Still, that's the way I am. I suppose we all have our cross to bear.
Basil	*(coming in cheerfully humming the end of Beethoven's Ninth)* Do you know what poem that's based on, Polly?
Polly	No.
Basil	Ode to Joy. *(to Sybil)* Hallo, dear. *(to Polly)* Oh, Polly, you won't forget to put some more splits in the bar, will you.
Polly	No, I'll do it later.
Sybil	I don't expect Polly will forget, Basil.
Basil	No, just reminding her, dear.
Sybil	Oh, were you.
Basil	I thought so, yes.
Sybil	Really?
Basil	Well, it sounded like it to me.
Sybil	You don't have to worry about Polly forgetting anything important, Basil.
Basil	Don't I?
Sybil	No, you don't.
Basil	Oh good, how splendid.
Sybil	No, **she** doesn't forget things.
Basil	. . . Doesn't she?
Sybil	Well, can you remember the last time she did?
Basil	No, I can't . . . but then my memory isn't very good.
Sybil	You can say that again.
Basil	Oh, can I dear? Oh, thank you. *(clears his throat)* I've forgotten what it was.
Sybil	Well, don't worry, Basil, provided you can remember the things that matter to **you**. *(she leaves in a huff)*
Basil	Do I detect the smell of burning martyr?
Polly	*(hurrying up to him)* Mr Fawlty, it's your anniversary.
Basil	*(nodding)* Mmmm . . . but don't let on.
Polly	What?
Basil	I'm pretending I've forgotten. . . . Well, I forgot last year and I got flayed alive for it, so we've got some friends arriving in about *(glancing at his watch)* ten minutes for a surprise drinks party. Manuel's making a special paella for tonight, got some champagne . . . but don't tell her I've remembered yet . . . let her have a bit of a fume.
Polly	Wouldn't it be simpler to boil her in oil?
Basil	Yes, but not as economical.
Manuel	*(coming up)* Ah, Mr Fawlty, what time for the paella?
Basil	. . . Er . . . nine o'clock . . . but secret, mmm?

Manuel	Ah, *si, si.*
Polly	Oh Mr Fawlty . . .
Basil	Hmmm?
Polly	Have you decided about the car?
Basil	. . . The car?
Polly	The money for the car.
Basil	Ah! . . . Um . . .
Polly	I spoke to Mrs Fawlty and she said it was all right.
Basil	Yes, I don't think she quite understands the cash-flow situation vis-à-vis the frozen assets . . .
Polly	But it's only a hundred.
Basil	Yes, well . . .
Polly	I said I'd pay you back in six weeks.
Basil	Let me think about it, hmm?
Polly	But I've got to know this weekend – they won't hold it any longer.
Basil	**This** weekend? You should have told me.
Polly	I told you three weeks ago.
Basil	Look, it's my anniversary, right? I've got some friends arriving in a few minutes. We'll discuss it later. Oh, and when they get here, give me a hand with the coats and drinks, will you. *(he goes out)*
Polly	I scratch your back, you scratch mine, eh?
Terry	*(coming in and seeing Manuel's ingredients)* What's this,then?

The lobby. Basil comes out of the kitchen looking slightly relieved. Miss Tibbs and Miss Gatsby come downstairs.

Miss Tibbs & Miss Gatsby	Good morning, Mr Fawlty.
Basil	Good morning, ladies.

They exit. Sybil is standing at the door to the office. Basil senses her and looks round.

Sybil	Can I have a word with you, Basil?
Basil	Er, could it wait just a few minutes, dear?
Sybil	No. *(she goes into the office; he follows)*
Basil	Is everything all right, dear? You seem just a little bit tense.
Sybil	Do you know what day it is today, Basil?
Basil	Um . . . it's the sixteenth today, dear.
Sybil	It's the seventeenth, Basil.
Basil	No, it's the sixteenth today, dear.

Sybil	*(quietly, very angry)* It's the seventeenth, Basil.
Basil	We'll soon settle this, dear. *(he goes out to the reception desk and picks up the paper; Sybil comes to the office door)* Oh. Yes, you are right. The seventeenth of April. Well, well, well . . .
Sybil	Does that stir any memories in you, Basil?
Basil	. . . Memories? . . . *(his face lights up)* . . . Agincourt!
Sybil	. . . What?
Basil	Anniversary of the Battle of Agincourt? *(Sybil slaps him and walks into the office; he is pleased)* . . . Trafalgar? Crécy? Poitiers? Yom Kippur?

The office door slams. Terry is approaching fast from the kitchen.

Terry	Mr Fawlty. Manuel says he's cooking a paella for you.
Basil	Sssh. It's for Mrs Fawlty. Anniversary . . .
Terry	I **can** do paella you know.
Basil	Yes, I know.
Terry	I have been to catering school.
Basil	Oh yes, I know . . . but he **is** Spanish, you know, and I thought it'd be rather nice . . .
Terry	Gazpacho, Chicken Andaluse, Eggplant Espagnole, Franco Fritters . . . I **can** do it you know.

Manuel comes up behind Terry.

Basil	Yes, of course you can, but he's been wanting to do it ever since he got here, so I thought it would be rather nice, you know, just tonight to give him the chance . . .

Sybil leaves the office by the other door and walks out through the main doors, passing Manuel who looks rather agitated.

Terry	I don't want to cause trouble, Mr Fawlty.
Basil	Yes you do.
Manuel	*(pointing after Sybil)* Mr Fawlty . . .
Basil	Now, don't you start. I don't want an argument . . .
Manuel	No, no, please.
Basil	Be quiet! I've told him I want you to do it.
Manuel	No, no – Mrs Fawlty. She go.
Basil	. . . What?
Manuel	She leave. She leave. She go out.
Basil	. . . What? *(he goes out through the main door, breaking into a run as he goes down the steps)* Sybil! Sybil! Sybil! *(he tries to*

stop her as she drives off, fails, and runs after the car as it disappears down the drive) Sybil! No! No no no! You don't understand! I remembered, Sybil! There's a party, Sybil, I've asked people over. Come back, it's our anniversary, you stupid . . . bird-brained . . . *(he runs out of the gate a few paces but Sybil has definitely gone)* Oh my God.

He turns, sinks to the ground, and beats the ground for a moment with both his fists. A car comes up the drive and brakes quite sharply beside him. The occupants are Roger and Alice, one of the couples invited for drinks.

Roger	*(leaning out of the window)* Everything all right?
Basil	*(getting up and indicating the area he's been hitting)* Bit of a bump. Just smoothing it out. *(he stamps on it)*
Alice	Are we too early?
Basil	Oh, no, not at all. Come on in. *(the car moves on; he races ahead of them into the lobby)*

In the lobby, Manuel is explaining to Polly as Basil rushes in.

Basil	They're here, they're here, what do I say . . . what am I going to say?
Polly	Oh . . . say she's er . . . um . . .
Basil	She's 'er, um' . . . oh, brilliant! Problem solved, she's 'er, um'.
Manuel	Is surprise party.
Basil	Yes.
Manuel	She not here.
Basil	Right.
Manuel	That is surprise.

Basil would hit him but Roger and Alice enter at this moment.

Roger	Hallo, Bas.
Polly	*(to Basil)* Say she's ill.
Basil	She's ill!!
Roger	What?
Basil	She's ill, Sybil, how are you. What would you like to drink.
Roger	Syb-ill?
Basil	Yes.
Alice	Oh dear, what's the matter?
Roger	Did you hear that? I said 'Syb-ill'.
Basil	Yes.

Roger	Got it?
Basil	. . . No, no, I'm fine.
Roger	No, no, no, I call her 'Syb', right? So, Syb-ill. Bas-well. Ha ha!
Manuel	*(joining in)* Man-well! Ha ha! *(he goes into the kitchen)*
Alice	What's the matter, Basil?
Roger	Yes, what have you done to her, eh, Bas?
Alice	Roger?
Roger	She knows my name – she's been learning it all night.
Alice	What's the matter, Basil?
Basil	Nothing . . . *(Alice stares)* Nothing.
Alice	With **Sybil**.
Basil	Oh, with Sybil. Oh . . . quite a bit actually.
Alice	Oh dear.
Basil	No, no, she's fine. She's absolutely fine . . . well, I mean she's feeling dreadful, but she'll live and that's what counts in the long run, isn't it. Ha ha.
Alice	Well I'll pop up and see her, then.
Basil	Oh, you don't want to bother with that. Come on through and have a drink.

He starts moving towards the bar. Alice stays put. He stops.

Alice	No, you go on. I'll see you in a moment.
Basil	*(hurrying back to her)* No, er, Alice . . .
Alice	Yes?
Basil	I . . . I wouldn't, actually.
Roger	Let 'em have a natter, old boy.
Basil	No, no, I mustn't.
Alice	Oh, but she's up there on her own, I'm sure she'd like a little company.
Basil	Uh-huh.
Alice	I know I would.
Basil	Well you wouldn't if you looked like her. You know, she's very swollen up . . . you know . . . *(he indicates the eyes)* . . . And she looks fairly . . . you know what Sybil's like about her appearance. *(he grabs Alice's hand)*
Alice	Oh, don't be silly, Basil, she won't mind **me** seeing her.
Basil	*(restraining her)* Oh she would! I think she would.
Alice	But it's her anniversary and she's all on her own.
Basil	Aah! *(he grabs his leg)* The old leg . . . bit of gyp. Ooh! Better have a drink. Come on through. *(he tries to guide Alice towards the bar)*

Alice	Poor old Basil! Well, look, let me call her, then.
Basil	. . . What?
Alice	Let me call her from down here and see what she says about it.
Basil	Er . . .
Alice	*(pointing to phone on reception desk)* There's the phone.
Roger	Come on, Bas, let's have a drink.
Basil	*(to Alice)* No, no, please.
Roger	Come **on**!
Basil	Please.
Alice	Why not?
Basil	Well, she's having a bit of a sleep . . . you know.
Alice	Well, she can sleep all day, Basil, she won't mind me just . . .
Basil	No, but she's . . . lost her voice.
Alice	. . . Lost her **voice?**
Basil	Poor thing! Gone . . . just like that.
Roger	Come on.
Basil	Just coming, Roger. After you, Alice . . . in here.

They move into the bar.

Basil	Right, Alice . . . What would you . . . what would you like to drink, Alice?
Alice	Gin and It, please Basil.
Basil	Right.
Alice	Has the doctor been?
Basil	Er . . . what's yours, Rog?
Roger	*(surprised Basil has to ask)* Gin and tonic.
Basil	Oh yes of course. Right.
Alice	Basil, has the doctor been?
Basil	Nuts?
Roger	*(sotto voce to Alice)* They've had a row. She's refused to come down.
Basil	Um . . . you were just asking about the doctor.
Alice	Yes.
Basil	You see, he hasn't been yet in fact.
Alice	Oh.
Basil	I expect we'll get him over this afternoon.
Roger	What a shame, eh? Poor old Syb. On your anniversary too.

Polly comes in from the lobby.

Alice	Ah! Hallo, Polly.
Polly	Oh, hallo, Mrs Tarry.
Alice	Isn't it a shame about Mrs Fawlty.
Polly	Isn't it – I'm afraid the doctor says she's going to have to be quiet in bed for a couple of days.
Basil	Yes, but the doctor hasn't actually been yet Polly . . . I don't know who you were thinking of . . .
Polly	But that man this morning . . . he looked like a doctor.
Basil	Yes, yes, he did actually, yes, that's true . . . but he wasn't. Unfortunately.
Roger	He wasn't a doctor.
Basil	No, no. He was a dentist.
Roger	A **dentist?**
Basil	. . . Yes.
Roger	What's a dentist doing here?
Basil	Staying in the hotel . . . he's a guest, you see. Dentists do stay at hotels, you know.
Roger	Yes, but they don't go around telling other people's wives to stay in bed, do they.
Polly	Oh, he must have been talking about **his** wife.
Roger	**His** wife.
Basil	Well, jolly good luck. Nice to see you both. Cheers!
Alice	Cheers.
Roger	Up yours, Bas. *(they drink)*
Alice	Well, I hope she's better soon.
Basil	Oh, yes, yes.
Roger	Who, Syb or the dentist's wife?

A pause.

Basil	*(gives a forced laugh)* Well, you're both keeping well, are you?
Roger	Oh, yes, yes, couldn't be better.
Alice	And you, Basil?
Basil	Oh, can't complain. Well, I could, but it wouldn't do any good, would it. Ha ha.
Alice	No . . . a shame, and on your anniversary as well.
Basil	Yes. Still, it all comes out in the wash, doesn't it. We're thinking of having this room done up as a matter of fact.
Alice	Really?
Basil	Yes. Sort of captain's cabin, you know, put a couple of

	charts on the wall, few ropes, wheel in the corner, that sort of thing.
Roger	Yes, give it a bit of **class**.
Basil	Wasn't **my** idea, Roger.
Alice	Poor Sybil.

Arthur and Virginia come in. The others greet them.

Virginia	Hallo Basil.
Basil	Hallo, Virginia. Hallo, Arthur.
Virginia	Happy anniversary!
Basil	Oh, thank you, thank you, yes.
Virginia	We've brought you a little surprise. *(she takes a cake-tin from Arthur)*
Alice	Oh, can I see? *(Virginia lifts the lid)* Oh, a cake! Lovely!
Basil	Jolly nice.
Alice	Did you make it?
Virginia	Lots of extra marzipan.
Basil	She's not well.
Virginia	Mmm?
Basil	Sybil.
Virginia	Not well?
Alice	She's in bed.
Virginia	That's not like Sybil.
Alice	She's lost her voice.
Virginia	What is it?
Basil	Well, we're not absolutely sure.
Roger	I bet she'd like a bit of that marzipan.
Basil	*(warningly)* Roger.
Roger	Cheer her up, Bas.
Virginia	Good idea. We'll take her up a slice.
Basil	Yes, I don't think we'd better.
Virginia	Well, why not?
Basil	She really ought not to be disturbed.
Virginia	Just for a minute, Basil.
Basil	It's not a very good idea. Tomorrow, perhaps.
Virginia	What on earth's the matter with her?
Basil	Er . . .
Virginia	Has the doctor been?
Roger	No, but the dentist's had a good look.
Virginia	The **dentist?**
Basil	No, well, we called the doctor, we described the symptoms to him over the phone and he says she ought to

stay very quiet. *(Polly has appeared)* Ah, Polly. *(to Virginia)* What would you like to drink, Virginia?

Virginia   Oh, medium sherry, please.

Virginia and Alice sit down at a table. Manuel appears and tries to attract Basil's attention.

Manuel   Mr Fawlty!

Virginia   What **are** the symptoms?

Basil   Well, she's lost her voice, and she's very puffed up. *(to Manuel)* Yes, what is it?

Manuel   Is Terry, he being very difficult . . .

Virginia   Puffed up?

Basil   *(to Manuel)* What?

Manuel   He move my pot. He put his pot where my pot is . . .

Arthur   Beer for me.

Basil   Well, put your pot somewhere else.

Manuel   I put it somewhere else, he move it again.

Polly   *(out of the side of her mouth as she passes Basil with the drinks)* What's puffed up?

Basil   *(through clenched teeth)* Th'eyes. *(to Manuel)* Just . . . tell him I said not to do it, all right?

Polly   What?

Basil   Th'eyes.

Manuel   I tell you he want to make trouble, he push mop in my feet . . .

Polly   *(to Virginia)* . . . Her thighs.

Virginia   Thighs!?

Polly   Well, most of her legs, actually. *(to Manuel)* Now just tell him. Go on. *(Manuel exits)*

Virginia   Basil – Polly says her legs are puffed up.

Basil   *(leans down and looks at Polly's legs)* Are they?

Virginia   . . . No, Sybil's.

Basil   . . . What?

Virginia   Sybil's legs.

Basil   Sybil's **legs?**

Polly   Her **thighs!**

Basil   . . . Oh, er, yes, just a bit. A tiny bit . . . but mainly round the face. Round the eyes, you know.

Polly   *(realizing her mistake)* Oh!

Virginia   Her face is puffed up, she's lost her voice, and her legs are a bit . . .

Basil   . . . Expanded. Sad, isn't it. Poor old sow.

Virginia	Well, when's the doctor coming?
Basil	Later. Soon. Soon.
Virginia	When?
Basil	Well, I don't know exactly.
Virginia	Well, I'd better go up and have a look at her. *(she gets up and makes to go)*
Basil	*(amazed)* What?
Virginia	She sounds **ill**, Basil.
Basil	She **is** ill. That's why we don't want people going up there and talking to her.
Virginia	I'm not going to talk to her, Basil. I'm going to look at her.
Basil	Look at her? She's ill, isn't she? What's the bloody point of looking at her?
Virginia	I am a **nurse**, Basil. *(she moves off past him)*
Basil	*(to himself)* Oh, no! *(he rushes after her)* I know, I know. I know that. *(he leads her back)* Did you hear that, everyone, all the years I've known old Virginia and she thinks I've forgotten she's a nurse. You're a marvel, you know that? *(he grasps her and kisses her)*
Virginia	Please let me go, Basil.
Basil	What?
Virginia	I want to look at Sybil.
Basil	Well, you can't.
Virginia	Why not?
Basil	Because . . . because . . . you've lost weight, haven't you . . . isn't that absolutely marvellous.
Polly	Mr Fawlty, I think you ought to tell them.
Basil	Oh, right . . .
Polly	. . . About the doctor coming this morning.
Basil	He came this morning. First thing.
Virginia	Well, why didn't you **say** so?
Polly	. . . He didn't want to worry you.
Basil	I didn't want to worry you . . .
Virginia	. . . Is it serious?
Basil	Well, it might be . . . *(there is a slight gasp from the others)* I mean, not completely serious but slightly serious.
Alice	Oh, Basil.
Basil	*(bravely)* It's all right, I'd just rather we didn't . . . you know . . . talk about it.

A pause. Suddenly the atmosphere is jarred by the merry entry of Reg and Kitty.

Reg & Kitty	Hallo everyone. Hallo, Basil.
Basil	*(with dignity)* Hallo, Reg. Hallo, Kitty.
Kitty	Sybil's not here, is she?
Basil	Er, no, I was just . . .
Kitty	*(to Reg)* There you are, you see. I told you. *(to the others)* I just saw her in the town.
Roger	What?
Kitty	In her car. In the High Street.
Basil	. . . Oh, no, no, that's the other woman.
Kitty	What other woman?
Basil	That woman who looks slightly like Sybil. You know her, don't you? You know?
Virginia	Like Sybil?
Basil	Well, yes . . . very broad. From the North.
Reg	Drives a red Maxi, does she?
Basil	Well, her husband does, I think. I expect she's borrowed it.
Roger	Perhaps she stole yours, old boy. It's not out there.
Basil	It's at the garage, Rog.
Virginia	She looks like Sybil?
Basil	Yes.
Virginia	And she comes from the North?
Basil	Well, she has a Northern accent, you know. I assume she's from the North.
Virginia	You've spoken to her!
Basil	Mmm.
Virginia	What's her name?
Basil	Well, I don't know her name, I mean, I only met her **once!** At a fête.
Virginia	. . . Sorry, Basil, I didn't mean . . .
Reg	No, no, no, of course. By the way, Basil, where **is** Sybil?
Basil	She's in bed.
Kitty	Oh dear.
Basil	Yes, she's really not well. She really mustn't see anybody. Now . . .
Reg	What, not at all?
Basil	No.
Kitty	Can't we just put our heads round the corner?
Basil	No, I'm afraid not. She mustn't have any excitement.
Reg	Oh, **Basil** . . .
Basil	What d'you mean, 'Oh, Basil'?
Arthur	Well, we are her oldest friends, old man. I mean, it can

	only do her good, and we have all come over here to see you both . . .
Basil	Well, I'm sorry if you've been put out . . . *(getting worked up)* I mean, you'll have some drinks, plenty of nuts, see your old friends, have a few laughs, but if that isn't good enough, I'll . . . I'll refund your petrol for you.
Arthur	No, no.
Reg	Steady on, Basil.
Basil	*(calming down)* Well, I'm sorry . . . but . . .
Virginia	Of course. We understand. You're a bit upset.
Basil	Well, you know . . .
Reg	Yes, of course. But you know us well enough. You should have called it off. Waited till she's better.
Basil	I would have done, Reg, but there just wasn't time, you know.
Roger	. . . Wasn't time?
Basil	*(a bit fiercely)* She only began to puff up an hour ago.
Roger	You said the doctor came first thing this morning.
Basil	Yes, yes, that's right. That was for the throat. The puffing up started up after he'd gone, OK?
Virginia	**After!?**
Basil	Yes, after. Are you taking notes? *(to Virginia, who is setting off)* Where are **you** going?
Virginia	I'm going to see her, Basil. *(he grabs her and leads her back)* But, Basil, there's something very peculiar about this, and I'm not standing here while an old friend like Sybil . . .
Basil	Look! Look!!! It's perfectly Sybil! Simple's not well. She lost her throat and her voice hurt. The doctor came and said it was a bit serious, not a lot, a bit. He went away, she started to puff up, he's coming back later this afternoon and it's best for her to be on her own now, what is so peculiar about that?
Roger	Her driving round in the town.
Basil	. . . What did you say?
Roger	Er, no, sorry, just a joke, Bas – can I have another gin, please?
Basil	Just a joke? She's down there in the town driving around, is that what you think?
Alice	'Course it isn't, Basil.
Basil	No, no, no, no, obviously I've been standing around here making up crackpot stories about my wife being seriously ill upstairs – is that it, Roger?

Roger	No, no, no, of course not . . . it was just that it **was** a bit funny, Kitty . . . seeing that Northern woman in the car.
Basil	Funny? . . . Oh, I **see**, you mean you think that that was **Sybil** in the car and she's not upstairs, is that it? Oh, I understand. I've got it now. Right, well, what are we all waiting around here for? Come on, everybody upstairs. *(he motions them; nobody moves)* Come on. All of you.
Alice	No, Basil.
Reg	No, no.
Basil	Come on, everyone who thinks I'm a liar, come on up.
Kitty	No, of course we don't, Basil.
Basil	Come on.
Arthur	Hang on, old man.
Virginia	*(kindly)* Don't get like that, Basil.
Basil	Come and see Sybil.
Reg	No, we don't want to.
Arthur	No, it'd be best to leave her. We'll see her another time.
Virginia	Yes, when she's feeling better.
Basil	But Roger wants to **now**.
Roger	No, we mustn't disturb her.
Basil	No, no, no, no, if Roger wants to . . .
Alice	He **doesn't**, Basil. *(they all look to Roger)*
Roger	Well, we could just say hello.
Alice	*(furious)* Oh, **Roger**!!
Basil	Right. All right. Fine! All right, OK then, fine!! No problem. No problem. Suits me. Good idea. I'll just pop upstairs and ask her to stop dying and then you can all come up and identify her.
Alice	*(embarrassed)* Basil.

Basil moves off towards the lobby, grabbing Polly by the arm as he goes past her.

Basil	Polly, would you give me a hand. *(he draws her out of the bar and shouts over his shoulder to the others)* Help yourself to another drink, please make yourself at home, relax . . .
Roger	Any more nuts?

The lobby. Basil pulls Polly along.

Polly	What are you doing?
Basil	You won't have to say anything.
Polly	What? *(they have reached the stairs; as he starts pulling her up them the penny drops)* Oh, no. No. No. No.

Basil	Come on. *(he grabs her round the waist and half carries her up the stairs)*
Polly	*(resisting)* No!
Basil	Come on.
Polly	I won't.
Basil	Yes you will.
Polly	I won't, I won't.
Basil	It's easy. You just put on her dark glasses and one of her wigs.
Polly	Let me go!

They have got to the top of the stairs. Basil hustles Polly along the corridor.

Basil	I'll keep them away from you.
Polly	Mr Fawlty, will you listen to me?
Basil	We'll draw the curtains.
Polly	Oh come on, they'd never believe I was . . .
Basil	Seeing is believing.
Polly	But I don't **look** like her!
Basil	You're a woman, aren't you?
Polly	My face is too long.
Basil	We'll shorten it. You've lost your voice, all you have to do is wave.
Polly	Wave?
Basil	*(holding her firmly)* You just put one hand up and jiggle it about. You'll soon get the hang of it. *(he kicks the door to the bedroom open and pushes her in)*

In the bedroom, he runs to the wardrobe, pulls out a wig and throws it to her.

Polly	Mr Fawlty, I know you're very excited, you might even be having a nervous breakdown, I don't know, I'm no expert – but you must really try and see that this isn't going to work.
Basil	*(throwing her a negligée)* Get that on.
Polly	It isn't going to work!
Basil	What's the matter, what's the matter?
Polly	I'm not **doing** it! You want to be in a Marx Brothers film, that's **your** problem. I'm not interested.
Basil	Not interested?
Polly	No.
Basil	This is all your fault.

Polly	**My** fault?
Basil	You said she was ill.
Polly	You were the one who invited them to come up here. They didn't want to. **You** pretend to be Sybil. *(throws him the wig)* **You** get into the bed! *(throws him the negligée)*
Basil	I'm too big! I've got a moustache! What's this supposed to be, a great hairy bogey?
Polly	It's something you get when you're puffed up.
Basil	. . . I'll ruin you. You'll never waitress in Torquay again.
Polly	Waitress? That's a joke. I help out at receptions, I clean the rooms, I deal with the tradesmen, I change the fuses, I mend the switchboard, and if you think my duties now include impersonating members of your family you have got one more screw loose than I thought. I'm not doing it. Do you understand? You get yourself out of it. It's nothing to do with me.

There is a knock at the door. Basil hears it and mimes a heart attack, clutching his chest, emitting gurgling noises and sinking to the floor.

Polly	A hundred for the car.
Basil	. . . All right.
Polly	Now! *(another knock at the door)*
Basil	What?!
Polly	Now!
Basil	Now?
Polly	Now.

Outside in the corridor, Manuel is standing by the door bridling. After a moment Basil comes out.

Basil	Hallo? *(he sees Manuel)*
Manuel	Is not possible.
Basil	What?
Manuel	Is not possible for me. Please come. *(he takes Basil's sleeve)*
Basil	What is it?
Manuel	Is Terry, please come.
Basil	Look, I'm busy.
Manuel	He tell me I not know to make a paella. He tell me.
Basil	You tell him . . .
Manuel	I tell him, paella is Spanish, not Cockney stinking eel pie. I make paella like my momma . . .
Basil	I'm not interested!

Manuel	My momma's recipe is big in Barcelona.
Basil	Go away! Go on!
Manuel	No, no, you come – he call me ignorant wog motherboy crump.
Basil	*(getting loose from Manuel)* Let go of me! Now look!
Reg's voice	*(calling up the stairs)* Basil!
Basil	Yes? *(to Manuel)* You tell Terry – let you alone.
Reg	*(appearing at the top of the stairs)* Basil?
Basil	Yes, Reg? *(to Manuel)* Go on . . . go away! Not you, Reg!
Manuel	*(going, reluctantly)* Is big in Barcelona, big, big.
Reg	Are we supposed to come up now?
Basil	Er, yes, in a moment, Reg. No, no, no, come on up now, you know, yes, come on up . . . yes, she's just, you know, touching up the worst bits.

Reg comes forward tentatively, followed by the others straggling behind.

Virginia	How is she feeling, Basil?
Basil	Well, um, I woke her and told her that you'd come over – she was very very pleased, of course, but she's very weak and her throat, you know, and she has great difficulty expressing herself. *(they all nod and make concerned noises)* Makes a change. Hah! *(an embarrassed pause)* She should be able to see you in a moment. She's pretty quick with the old . . .
Virginia	She's not bothering to make up for us, is she?
Basil	Oh, no, no, no . . . just . . . you know. *(a pause)* She asked me to thank you and say how much she's looking forward to seeing you all.
Arthur	Good.
Virginia	She can speak a little then, can she, Basil?
Basil	Um . . . not really, no. No, I see what you mean . . . she wrote that down, actually, on one of the . . . um, postcards she keeps by the side of the bed.
Roger	Did she stamp it? *(Basil glares)*
Alice	Basil – do you have an ashtray anywhere?
Basil	Oh, yes, I'll get one, Alice. *(he sets off past them)*
Alice	Oh, Basil, there's no need to . . .
Basil	No, it's no bother, not at all. I shan't be a second . . .

He hurries down the stairs, across the lobby and into the bar. He grabs a bottle, uncorks it and swings it up to take a swig from it just as Manuel arrives and plucks at his arm.

296 The Complete Fawlty Towers

Manuel	Mr Fawlty! Mr Fawlty! *(Basil takes his eye off the bottle, most of which goes over him)* He put mince in it! He put bloody mince in it!!
Basil	*(indicating soaking jacket)* Look what you've done!
Manuel	Oh, sorry! Sorry! *(he starts trying to wipe Basil dry)* Look, I tell him, paella is a fish dish.
Basil	*(pushing him away)* Go away. Go away.
Manuel	What I do?
Basil	Go away! *Arriba* – vamoose!!

In the upstairs corridor the crowd has started to bicker.

Roger	Well, this is fun, isn't it.
Alice	Roger!!
Roger	No, I mean, who wants to go to the boozer or play golf when you can come to one of Basil's do's.
Virginia	Oh, come on, Roger. It can't be easy for him with Sybil lying there ill.
Roger	. . . Well, you know what I think about that.
Virginia	What?
Alice & Kitty	Sssh!
Basil	*(coming up with ashtray, nuts and crisps)* Here we are – I brought some nuts.
Alice	Oh, Basil, you shouldn't have.
Basil	*(to Reg)* If you could just take the ashtray. *(there is a sudden flurry as he drops the nuts)* Sorry.
Alice	Oh, never mind.
Basil	I'll get some more, shall I?
Reg	No, no, we've got the crisps.
Basil	Sure? I don't mind . . .
Virginia	No, no, crisps will be lovely.
Basil	Really? OK, OK. *(he offers them round)* Crisp, Alice?
Alice	Thank you.
Basil	Arthur?
Arthur	Not for me, thank you.
Basil	Kitty, would you like a crisp?
Kitty	Thank you, lovely, thank you.
Basil	Just hold them – I'll just get a brush.
Roger	A Basil Brush.
Basil	Ha ha, oh very good, Rog. *(he runs off again down the corridor; the others stare after him, surprised)*
Roger	Broom broom! *(Basil disappears)*
Virginia	Roger? . . . What did you mean?

Roger	Well, they've had a row. She refused to come down.
Kitty	*(shocked)* Roger.
Roger	And he's embarrassed her into seeing us.
Basil's voice	*(from downstairs)* I'm not interested!

In the lobby, Basil is being hampered by Manuel.

Basil	I'm not interested! *(he throws Manuel into the kitchen, and runs back upstairs)*

In the upstairs corridor Alice and Kitty are trying to pick up the nuts. Basil runs up and starts helping them.

Basil	Oh, don't you bother, leave it to me.
Reg	Basil. *(Basil continues working)* Basil?
Basil	Mmmm?
Reg	Perhaps she's ready now?
Basil	Oh yes. Er . . . good idea. Yes, I'll just have a look. Right. *(he opens the door and puts his head inside for a moment)* Not quite. Nearly. Anyone care for another crisp?
All	No, thank you, no.
Roger	Have you got a choc ice?
Basil	*(putting the bowl on the floor near them)* Well, I'll put them there . . . just help yourselves . . . *(he looks awkward and flinches at the carpet with his foot)*
Roger	Nice carpet, Bas.
Basil	Thank you, yes, it's a bit worn now.
Roger	Oh, I thought it was part of the pattern.
Alice	Nice paper, Basil.
Basil	Oh, thank you, Alice. Yes, we got it to go with the carpet, you know . . .
Roger	To go with it?
Basil	That's right, Roger.
Roger	Well, one of 'em'll have to go. My money's on the carpet . . .
Basil	You read a lot of Oscar Wilde, do you, Rog? *(pointing up)* I don't know if you've ever seen the moulding up there. *(he treads into the crisp bowl, slips, and sits down abruptly)*
Alice	Oh, dear.
Basil	It's all right, it's all right, don't worry. I'll clean it up. *(he stands up)*
Roger	What time's the main feature?

Basil ignores him. The Major walks by.

The Major	Morning, Fawlty. Lovely day for a round of golf.
Basil	Oh, morning, Major. Yes.
The Major	Anyone care to make up a four?
Basil	No, no. We're going to see Sybil, Major.
The Major	Playing a match, is she?
Basil	No, no, she's ill. Really quite ill.
The Major	Oh . . . she should be in bed, you know.
Basil	She is. We're going in to see her.
The Major	Another lot in with her, is there?
Basil	May I introduce Major Gowen, our oldest resident . . . I don't know if you know everyone, Major?
The Major	*(shaking hands with everyone)* Good morning . . . delighted to meet you . . . Welcome to Torquay.
All	Good morning, Major.
Basil	*(peeps inside the bedroom)* Yes, all right. She's ready now, come on in. *(the Major starts to go in; Basil steers him out)* Yes, not you.

They go into Sybil's bedroom. The curtains are drawn and it is very dark.

Alice	Sybil?
Virginia	Hallo darling, don't try and speak.
Kitty	The gang's here.
Alice	Sorry you're not well.
Kitty	Such a shame.
Virginia	So we thought we'd come and visit you. . . . Happy anniversary.
All	Yes, happy anniversary.

There is a crash and a cry. Someone has fallen over. Cries of alarm from the women; a moan.

Virginia	What's the matter?
Arthur	Reg has fallen over. You all right, Reg?
Reg	Done my ankle.
Alice	Oh dear.
Basil	You all right, Reg?
Virginia	Careful!
Kitty	It's so dark in here.
Roger	The bloody light's not working.
Reg	I tripped over something.

There's another crash and a cry. General alarm.

Arthur	Who's that?
Kitty	Me.
Alice	It's Kitty.
Virginia	Where are you, dear?
Arthur	Can't we have some light in here, Basil?
Basil	Yes, all right, hang on. *(there is the sound of a metal wastepaper-basket being kicked across the room)* Here we are. OK?

He switches on a small table lamp on the other side of the room. Sybil's bed, on which Polly is lying, is almost surrounded by screens, with a gap at the foot and a small gap near the head.

Roger	Well, now the light's on we can see the screen.
Basil	Oh dear.
Virginia	Are you all right, Kitty?
Kitty	I think so.

Reg is getting up gingerly, helped by Arthur.

Roger	You shouldn't have gone to all this trouble, Basil.
Alice	Roger! *(she elbows him)*
Basil	Come on up here. OK? You both all right? Come on round here, you can see her from there. *(to the hidden Polly)* Everything all right, dear? *(to the others)* Here she is!

They move to the foot of the bed and look round it towards 'Sybil'. Basil moves to the gap in the screen at the head of the bed.

All	Hallo, Sybil. Hallo.

Polly is wearing a wig and dark glasses, and has stuffed something in her mouth to puff her cheeks up. She is in deep shadow. She waves a beringed hand at them.

Roger	There's something there – I can see it moving.
Virginia	It's a bit dark, Basil.
Basil	Yes, well, her eyes are very sensitive.
Virginia	She's got her glasses.
Basil	Yes, well, I'll just draw the curtains a bit . . . *(he goes to do so but Polly makes frantic noises and grabs his leg)* Yes, I know they are sensitive, dear . . . it's all right, trust me, dear . . . trust me, trust me. *(he draws the curtains open a little)*

All	That's better. Hallo, dear. Happy anniversary. Hallo, Sybil.
Alice	You poor dear.
Virginia	How are you feeling, dear?

Polly gives the thumbs down.

All	Oooh.
Virginia	You're very swollen. *(Polly points to her cheeks and then her legs)*
Basil	. . . Her thighs! The thighs.
Kitty	We've brought you a cake.
All	Yes.

Basil takes it and shows it to Polly, who gives the spot-on signal.

Basil	Would you like a little bit, dear? *(Polly shakes her head firmly)* Oh, have a little bit? Go on . . . *(Polly points to her cheeks)* Oh, yes! Well . . . fifteen years, eh?
All	Fifteen years, yes! Well, well. Happy anniversary.
Arthur	Well done, both of you.

Polly does the Royal Wave for a bit.

Basil	Thank you. *(a pause; Polly waves again; Basil stares at her, then gets the point)* . . . Ah, yes . . . well, I think she's feeling a little bit tired.
Roger	All that waving'd wear anyone out. *(Polly stretches)*
Basil	So perhaps we'd better all . . . er . . . *(Polly yawns)*
Virginia	What's that in her mouth, dear . . . the white stuff?

Polly indicates 'It's nothing'.

Basil	Just foam . . . you know, from the excitement. Fifteen years, eh? Um, well . . . *(he puts the cake down, chancing to look out of the window; to his horror he sees Sybil's car drive up)* Aaaaaaagh!!
Virginia	What is it?
Basil	*(in panic)* I've just remembered something! Downstairs! You stay here, have a chat with Polly, **Sybil!** Sybil!! And I'll just . . . shan't be a moment. *(he rushes off)*
Roger	A chat? Does anyone know semaphore?

The lobby. Basil rushes downstairs just as Sybil walks in.

Basil	*(calmly)* Hallo, dear.

Sybil	I came back for my clubs, Basil, I'm not staying.
Basil	Oh, aren't you? OK.
Sybil	What?
Basil	Well, I'm sure you know best, dear.
Sybil	You don't even want me to, do you.
Basil	Um . . . *(picks a bit of thread off his jacket)* Oh, what's that?
Sybil	*(slapping him in the face)* Fifteen years I've been with you. When I think what I might have had.
Basil	Fifteen years! Coh!
Sybil	. . . You want me to go, don't you.
Basil	Oh, no! But . . . well, you've obviously made up your mind, so . . .
Sybil	I won't forget this, Basil.
Basil	Won't you dear?
Sybil	No, I won't. *(a little pause; she starts to cry)* I'm going now, Basil. I think it's best, don't you?
Basil	All right, dear.
Sybil	Goodbye, Basil.
Basil	. . . Cheerio, dear. *(she leaves; just outside she turns and looks back)* Drive carefully, dear. *(she goes and Basil rushes back up the stairs)*

In the bedroom the guests are taking their leave.

Arthur	Get well soon.
Reg	Look after yourself. *(Polly waves)*
Kitty	We'll have a little party when you're feeling better.
Virginia	You know, I really don't like leaving you like this, dear. *(Polly indicates 'It's all right')* Let me just have a little feel . . . *(she advances with her hands out)* Just to see if . . . *(Polly waves her away)* Now, now don't be frightened, I'm not going to hurt you . . . just feel your glands, dear. *(she comes very close; Polly fends her off)* No, don't be silly Sybil. It's for your own good, now, don't be silly. *(Polly hits her quite hard)* Aagh!

Virginia falls back quite startled. The others are amazed. Basil hurries in.

Basil	What's going on?
Virginia	*(holding her eye and crying)* She hit me, Basil.
Basil	What?
Virginia	I was just trying to examine her, she lashed out . . .
Basil	*(hitting Polly)* Don't. Don't hit our friends. I know you're

not feeling a hundred per cent, but control yourself! *(to Virginia)* I'm sorry. She's not herself today. Don't worry, the doctor'll be over here soon. I'll give you a call, tell you what he says. So . . . um . . . anyone care for another drink, or . . . ?

All   No, no thank you Basil, we ought to be going . . .

Outside in the forecourt, Sybil and Audrey are sitting in the car. Sybil, genuinely upset, is crying. Audrey is comforting her.

Audrey   They're all the same, dear. They're all the same, believe me.

Sybil   Oh, I know, I know.

Audrey   Now, you forget all about it. We're going to have a nice game of golf and go out to dinner. *(Sybil puts the car into gear)* Did you get your clubs?

In the lobby, the gang are coming down the stairs. They are the walking wounded. Reg limps with support from Arthur, Kitty walks unsteadily, and Virginia, still holding her eye, is being helped by Alice. Basil follows them.

Basil   Well, awfully nice to have seen you all. Thanks for coming over.

Roger   No, not at all. We must do this more often. You know, when they're fit again.

Basil   Yes, yes, I'm sorry about all the injuries . . . still, perhaps when Sybil's a bit better . . . you know, perhaps we can all get together and have a . . .

Sybil has come in behind him. The guests are staring past him at her; he turns and sees her. She looks at them, then at him. There is a long moment.

Basil   *(to Sybil)* How extraordinary. We were just talking about you. *(offers his hand)* Basil Fawlty. We met once . . . at a fête. *(she stares at him; he starts to lead her into the kitchen)* Let me show you where it is. How's the North, then? Have you been up there at all recently?

The kitchen. Basil leads Sybil, who is too stunned to resist, in. Manuel and Terry are fighting on the floor. He ignores this, steers her past them, opens a cupboard and puts her inside.

Basil   I'll explain everything in a moment, dear. *(he closes the door and locks it)*

He goes back, stepping over the fight. In the lobby, the whole gang are utterly stunned. Basil comes back out of the kitchen, from which the noises of the fight continues.

Basil   What a coincidence – she's thinking of buying one of our fridges. Well – lovely to have seen you all . . . and sorry about the ankle . . . keep the head right back . . .

The gang, speechless, move off out of the main door, ushered by Basil. Roger is the last to go.

Roger   Great fun.

He hands Basil his glass and leaves. Polly has come down the stairs.

Basil   *(to Polly)* Piece of cake. *(he braces himself and makes for the kitchen)* Now comes the tricky bit.

Basil the Rat

Sixth of second series, first broadcast on 25 October 1979, BBC2.

Sybil Fawlty   Prunella Scales
Basil Fawlty   John Cleese
Mr Carnegie   John Quarmby
Polly   Connie Booth
Terry   Brian Hall
Manuel   Andrew Sachs
Miss Tibbs   Gilly Flower
Miss Gatsby   Renée Roberts
Guest   Stuart Sherwin
Major Gowen   Ballard Berkeley
Mr Taylor   James Taylor
Mrs Taylor   Melody Lang
Ronald   David Neville
Quentina   Sabina Franklyn

The hotel forecourt. The Fawltys' car drives up. Basil and Sybil get out and walk towards the hotel.

Sybil	You said you'd go.
Basil	I didn't say I'd go, I said I might. I've got to do the accounts tonight.
Sybil	You don't have to do the accounts tonight.
Basil	I **do**.
Sybil	It's always the same. Whenever I want to go out, you've always got some excuse.
Basil	It's not an excuse. It's just that tonight . . .
Sybil	It's not just tonight, it's any night I want to go out with any of my friends, anyone at all, any other members of the human race.
Basil	Yes, well, I wouldn't call the Sherrins members of the human race, dear.

They enter the lobby.

Sybil	I'm cooped up in this hotel all day long, you never take me out, the only bit of life I get is when I get away with some of my friends.
Basil	Well, you must get away more often, dear.
Sybil	. . . They all think you're peculiar, you know that, don't you. They've all said at one time or another, how on earth did the two of us ever get together. Black magic, my mother says. *(she stalks off into the office)*
Basil	Well, she'd know, wouldn't she. Her and that cat. *(he goes into the kitchen)*

In the kitchen, Basil comes in and sees a man kneeling down by the fridge peering at a plate of meat. It is Mr Carnegie, a stranger to Basil.

Basil	Shall I get you the wine list?
Carnegie	Mr Fawlty?
Basil	Mister? Oh, please, call me waiter. Look, I'll go and get a chair and then you can really tuck in – there's some stuff in the bin you might like, you know, potato peelings, cold rice pudding, that sort of thing – not exactly *haute cuisine* but it'll certainly help to fill you up. *(Sybil comes in)* Ah, Sybil, may I introduce you to the gentleman who's just opened the self-service department here . . . Mr . . . ?
Carnegie	Carnegie.

Basil   Mr Carnegie the scavenger gourmet from . . . ?
Carnegie   The Public Health Department. *(he puts the meat back in the fridge and stands up)*
Basil   Yes, but where were you born, Scavenger or down here in the West Country . . .
Sybil   Public Health Department?
Polly   *(entering with an invoice)* Oh . . . here's the invoice for the meat, Mr Carnegie . . . *(to Sybil)* It's the six-monthly check-up.
Sybil   Oh yes, the meat was delivered on Wednesday . . .
Carnegie   *(having examined the invoice)* Yes . . . that would appear to be satisfactory.
Basil   Oh, good. Hope you didn't mind my little joke just now. Thank God we English can laugh at each other, eh?

Mr Carnegie makes a note on his clipboard. Terry walks in, stops, and looks at Polly.

Polly   *(to Terry, mouthing silently)* Public Health Department.

Terry leaves. Carnegie sees him.

Basil   That's our new chef just left . . . just popped out for a quick prayer, I expect, ha ha ha.
Carnegie   *(ignoring this sally)* Mr Fawlty.
Basil   *(waving)* Hallo.
Carnegie   These premises do not come up to the standard required by this authority. Unless appropriate steps are taken instantly, I shall have no alternative but to prosecute or recommend closure to the appropriate committee of the Council. Specifically, lack of proper cleaning routines, dirty and greasy filters, greasy and encrusted deep fat fryer, dirty cracked and stained food preparation surfaces, dirty cracked and missing wall and floor tiles, dirty marked and stained utensils, dirty and greasy interior surfaces of the ventilator hoods.
Basil   Yes, about the fat fryer . . .
Carnegie   Inadequate temperature control and storage of dangerous foodstuffs, storage of cooked and raw meat in same trays, storage of raw meat above confectionery with consequent dripping of meat juices on to cream products, refrigerator seals loose and cracked, icebox undefrosted and refrigerator overstocked.
Basil   Yes, say no more . . .

Carnegie	Food handling routine suspect, evidence of smoking in food preparation area, dirty and grubby food-handling overalls, lack of washhandbasin which you gave us a verbal assurance you'd have installed on our last visit six months ago, and two dead pigeons in the water tank.
Basil	. . . Otherwise OK?
Carnegie	As I said, I shall refrain from serving a food hygiene notice today, but I shall return tomorrow. If the items on this list have not been rectified I shall take immediate action. I have not had time to inspect the bedrooms and common passageways but I shall be doing so tomorrow.
Sybil	*(ushering him out)* Yes, of course.
Carnegie	*(as he leaves, to Basil)* The only gourmets you'll find scavenging in this kitchen will be kamikaze ones. *(he and Sybil exit)*
Terry	*(opening the back door at which he has been listening)* I thought we was in trouble there for a minute.
Basil	. . . We **are** in trouble.
Terry	*(glancing at the list)* Piece of cake.
Basil	Have you **read** this piece of cake?
Terry	Oh, they got to do that, ain't they, it's part of their job.
Basil	Terry, this kitchen is filthy.
Terry	Filthy Towers, eh?
Basil	Now, look . . .
Terry	Look, all kitchens are filthy, Mr Fawlty – in fact the better the kitchen the filthier it is. Have you ever read George Orwell's experiences at Maxim's in Paris?
Basil	No, do you have a copy? I'll read it out in court!
Sybil	*(coming back in)* Don't just stand there gossiping. Go upstairs . . .
Basil	I am not gossiping, I am trying to point out to our alleged chef . . .
Sybil	Go upstairs and get Manuel, and check the bathrooms for soap and paper and get those pigeons out of the water tank.
Basil	Yes, my little commandant.
Sybil	And see how many fire extinguishers are missing. Come on, Polly, we'll start in here.

She leaves. Polly spots the cat.

| Polly | Not in here, puss. *(she puts the cat out of the back door)* |

Basil makes his way upstairs. Singing and vague guitar strumming are emerging from Manuel's room. Basil goes in; Manuel is sitting on his bed strumming and singing.

Basil	Manuel, I'm sorry, this is an emergency. Important, *si?* The Health Inspector's just been, things wrong with hotel. We put them right by tomorrow, all right? Now, Manuel, go up to the roof . . .
Manuel	The roof? *Si* . . . *(makes to go)*
Basil	No, no, come back – I haven't **told** you yet! Now, go to the water tank . . .
Manuel	Water?
Basil	Water **tank**. Water on roof in tank, yes?
Manuel	*Si, si.*
Basil	Two dead pigeons in tank. Take out. *(Manuel stares suspiciously)* It's not difficult, Manuel. This is not a proposition from Wittgenstein. Listen. Two dead pigeons . . . water tank . . . *(Manuel begins to break up)* What's funny?
Manuel	. . . How they get up there?
Basil	How . . . they **flew** up there! *(Manuel gets slightly hysterical and flaps his arms)* That's right. That's right.
Manuel	*(collapsing with laughter on the bed)* Oink, oink? Oink, oink!
Basil	Will you stop . . . will you just pull yourself together . . . Not **pigs**! **Pig**eons!
Manuel	*Qué?*
Basil	*(grabbing a Spanish–English dictionary off the shelf)* Pigeon! Pigeon! . . . Like your English! *(he shows Manuel the entry)*
Manuel	Pig . . . gy . . . on.
Basil	*(noticing a cage containing a rodent, on the bedside cabinet)* What is that?
Manuel	Is my hamster. 'Piggy-on'.
Basil	. . . Hamster?
Manuel	*Si. Si.* No. pidge-**on**.
Basil	Manuel, that's a rat.
Manuel	Pidgin.
Basil	It's a rat!
Manuel	No, no, is hamster.
Basil	Well, of course it's a rat! You have rats in Spain, don't you? – or did Franco have them all shot?
Manuel	No, is hamster.
Basil	Is rat.

Manuel	No, I think so too.
Basil	What?
Manuel	I say to man in shop, 'Is rat.' He say, 'No, no, is special kind of hamster. Is Filigree Siberian hamster.' Only one in shop. He make special price, only five pound.
Basil	*(calmly)* Have you ever heard of the bubonic plague, Manuel? It was very popular here at one time. A lot of pedigree hamsters came over on ships from Siberia . . . *(he takes the cage)*
Manuel	What are you doing?
Basil	I'm sorry, Manuel, this is a rat.
Manuel	No, no, is hamster.
Basil	Is not hamster. Hamsters are small and cuddly. Cuddle this, you'd never play the guitar again.

He walks out of the room with the cage. In the corridor, Manuel comes after him in pursuit.

Manuel	*Qué?* Where you go? Where you go? Where you take him?
Basil	I'm sorry, Manuel, he's got to go.
Manuel	Go? No!
Basil	Yes.
Manuel	No, no, he mine. He stay with me.
Basil	Now, look! This is a hotel! The Health Inspector comes tomorrow. If he finds this, I . . . closed down . . . no warning . . . closed down. *Finito.* You, out of work. Back to Barcelona.
Manuel	He do no hurt. He in cage, he safe, please . . .

He hangs on to Basil's leg. Miss Tibbs and Miss Gatsby appear at the top of the stairs.

Basil	Good morning, ladies.
Miss Gatsby	What's the matter?
Manuel	He take my hamster. Please, no, Mr Fawlty.
Miss Tibbs	*(reproachfully)* Mr Fawlty!!
Manuel	I love him, I love him.
Miss Tibbs	How **could** you.
Basil	Excuse me.
Manuel	He take it from my room.
Miss Tibbs	*(comforting Manuel)* Ah, there there . . .
Miss Gatsby	Never mind, it'll be all right.
Miss Tibbs	You can keep it in our room.
Miss Gatsby	Yes. *(to Basil)* That's right – we'll keep it in our room, Mr

Fawlty. We'll look after it.

Basil holds the cage out at them. They scream.

Misses Tibbs & Gatsby Aaah! A rat! A rat! A rat!! *(they scurry off)*

Manuel No, is Siberian hamster . . . filigree . . . *(but Basil has disappeared downstairs)*

The lobby. Basil comes down the stairs with the cage. A couple approaching the stairs see the cage and the woman starts back.

Basil It's all right – it's only a Siberian hamster, just getting rid of it.

He goes into the kitchen. Manuel comes downstairs and sees Polly, dithers, and runs to her at reception.

Manuel Polly, Polly – he take my hamster.

Polly What?

Manuel Mr Fawlty take my hamster. He crazy – he thinks is rat.

Polly . . . Manuel . . . prepare yourself for a shock . . .

In the kitchen, the cage is on the table. Basil and Sybil are discussing it.

Sybil Well, why didn't you check?

Basil What?

Sybil Well, you mean he's had it a whole year and you've only just found out?

Basil Yes.

Sybil Well, supposing the Health Inspector had seen it.

Basil I **know**.

Sybil He could have closed us down. . . . Well, what are you going to do with it, Basil? You can't keep it here.

Basil I know.

Sybil And don't let it loose in the garden, he'll come back in the house.

Basil Can't we get you on 'Mastermind', Sybil? Next contestant Sybil Fawlty from Torquay, special subject the bleeding obvious. I wasn't **going** to let it go in the garden.

Sybil Well, what **are** you going to do with it?

Basil I don't know. I'll take it away, let it go. Give it its freedom.

Sybil You can't do that, Basil – he wouldn't be able to defend himself.

Basil He's a rat, isn't he?

Sybil He's domesticated *(to the rat)*, aren't you.

Basil	Well, you're domesticated. You do all right. Look, he's not going to get mugged by a gang of field-mice, is he?
Sybil	Basil, he's Manuel's pet. We have a duty to it . . . perhaps we could find a home for him.
Basil	All right! I'll put an ad in the papers! Wanted, kind home for enormous savage rodent. Answers to the name of Sybil. Look, I'll take it out into the country, let him go . . .
Sybil	No! I cannot abide cruelty to living creatures.
Basil	Well, I'm a creature, you can abide it to me.
Sybil	You're not living. *(Manuel comes in)* Look Manuel, we were just wondering what we ought to do . . .
Manuel	Mrs Fawlty, please understand. If he go, I go.
Basil	*(putting out his hand)* Well, goodbye.
Sybil	*(to Manuel)* **Please** listen. You know we **really** can't keep him here. The Health Inspector wouldn't . . .
Manuel	Mrs Fawlty. He here one year. He do no harm.
Sybil	But, Manuel, listen . . . if they see your rat they could close the hotel down. *(to Basil)* Perhaps it would be simplest to have him put to S-L-E-E-P.
Basil	Who, him or the rat? We might get a discount if we had 'em both done.
Manuel	'Spleep'?
Polly	*(coming in)* Manuel, I've rung my friend – it's all right – she'll take him.
Manuel	*Qué?*
Polly	She has lots of animals, and it's not far away. You can go and see him whenever you want. So come on, we'll take him over there now.
Manuel	But he forget me.
Basil	*(giving him the cage)* Well, rats are like that, Manuel. Don't get involved with 'em.
Polly	Come on, Manuel.
Sybil	I think it's the best solution, Manuel.
Polly	Oh, he'll be happy, you'll see. *(she and Manuel leave the kitchen with the cage)*
Sybil	Sad, isn't it.
Basil	Well . . . look at it from the point of view of the rat.
Sybil	What?
Basil	Would you want to spend the rest of your life with Manuel waiting on you?

Outside, Polly and Manuel walk down the drive with the cage between them.

The kitchen. General bustling. Terry is at the hoods over the stove, Polly is wiping the walls, Sybil is moving round checking. The cat is in the corner.

Sybil   Now, we've been through the cupboards, you're doing the walls, Terry the filters, checked the fridges . . . oh . . . *(she sees the cat)* Come here . . . *(she puts it out of the back door)*

Basil   *(coming in from the lobby)* Right, that's done. Now, Sybil, everything done here?

Sybil   Have you put the lid on the tank, Basil?

Basil   That's why I've been on the roof the last forty minutes, dear, yes.

Sybil   And you took the pigeons out?

Basil   No, I left them in, they're nearly done. Now, the walls . . .

Sybil   I've checked everything.

Basil   Terry the hoods . . . have we done the cupboards?

Sybil   It's **all** been done, Basil.

Basil   The fridge. Have we got it separate?

Sybil   Basil, I told you, it's all been done.

Basil   The seals on the old fridge . . . the floor . . .

Sybil   I've checked it.

Basil   . . . Just running over the bleeding obvious, dear. So, all ship-shape and Bristol fashion, eh? All ready for old snoopy-drawers. *(Manuel comes into the kitchen looking terribly depressed; he wears a black armband and walks with a slow droop; Basil watches him go by and into the dining room)* Is this about that rodent?

Sybil   Just leave him alone, Basil. He's upset.

Basil   Well, he's not going to cheer up moping about like that, is he.

Sybil   Just let him be.

Basil   It doesn't help him you encouraging it, you know. You've got to get his mind off it. *(to Manuel, who has returned, indicating the kitchen)* Well, Manuel, what do you think? Looks good, doesn't it, eh? All clean and shining bright, eh?

Manuel   Is so empty without him.

Basil   Yes, yes – those walls look good, too, don't they. And the hoods gleaming like that. Isn't that a marvellous sight.

Manuel   Please leave me alone . . . I get over it.

Basil   Yes, yes, you'll get over it. No point in letting it get you down. Plenty more fish in the sea, eh? *(he claps Manuel on the back)*

Manuel   Don't!

Basil   What?

Manuel   Don't hit me. Always you hit me.

Basil   I'm not hitting you – I'm trying to cheer you up.

Sybil   Let him **be**, Basil.

Basil   Look, look, look . . . don't look at me with those awful cow eyes! Why don't you go to the cinema tonight? Why don't you and Polly go to the ice rink tonight. Why . . . why . . . why don't you cheer up, for Christ's sake!

Sybil   Basil.

Basil   I cannot stand this awful self-indulgence.

Sybil   Oh, leave him alone, Basil. He's just depressed.

Basil   Manuel . . . my wife informs me that you're . . . depressed. Let me tell you something. Depression is a **very bad thing**. It's like a virus. If you don't stamp on it it spreads throughout the mind, and then one day you wake up in the morning, and you . . . you can't face life any more.

Sybil   And then you open a hotel. *(exits)*

Basil   We didn't win the war by getting depressed, you know. *(exits)*

Polly   Manuel!

Manuel   *Como?*

Polly   Not so **sad**.

Manuel   . . . No?

Polly   No, no, it's too much.

Manuel   *(cheering up)* Too much?

Polly   Much too much. Just a **little** bit sad.

Terry   *(handing Manuel a saucer)* There's the food.

Manuel   Ah. *Gracias.*

Polly   Don't forget the water. *(she fills a bowl at the sink)*

Manuel   Oh, Terry, Terry, let me have a bit of that.

Terry   That's fillet.

Manuel   *Si, si*, he like it. Please.

Terry   *(cutting off a bit)* Want some Bearnaise with it?

Manuel   No, no, no. Is chostelerol.

He gets the fillet and the water and hurries out of the back door. Outside, he looks round to make sure the coast is clear, and then makes for an outbuilding not far away. As he reaches it he shoos away the cat, who is nosing round the door. He goes inside, puts the food down, and calls in a whisper . . .

Manuel	Basil . . . *(he squeaks)*

In the lobby, Polly is at the desk dealing with a guest. She takes his cheque.

Polly	Thank you, Mr Higgins.
Guest	Thank you.
Polly	*(producing a wrapped picture)* And here's the picture.
Guest	What?
Polly	The picture. The one in your room. You said you liked it.
Guest	Er . . .
Manuel	*(coming in)* Polly! Polly!
Polly	Sssh.
Manuel	Polly.
Polly	Wait.
Guest	No, I'm sorry, I really don't . . .
Polly	Oh, just a fiver. You can have it on approval.
Guest	*(moving off)* Sorry . . .
Polly	It's for my sister's eye operation . . . *(the guest has gone)* You bastard.
Manuel	Polly.
Polly	Oh, **what?!**
Manuel	He gone . . . He gone. He escape.
Polly	But how did he get out of the cage?
Manuel	I leave the door open so he exercise in shed.
Polly	*(grabbing him by the lapels)* You dago dodo! *(Basil appears from the dining room; Manuel can't see him but Polly can; she starts brushing his lapels)* You . . . got . . . it all over your front.
Manuel	*Qué?*
Polly	*Mucho salo.*
Manuel	What you do?
Polly	Is dirty.
Manuel	No matter. What about Basil?
Polly	Mr Fawlty to you. *(Basil is watching, rather surprised)*
Manuel	No, no, no, no . . . Basil.
Polly	*Esta aqui. (Manuel sees Basil)* Now go and clean it.
Manuel	*Si, si. (he runs off towards the kitchen)*
Basil	Jolly good, Polly. That's the way to snap him out of it.

The Major approaches, carrying a cup of coffee.

The Major	Morning, Fawlty.
Basil	Hallo, Major. Here are the papers.
Polly	That's where I left it . . . *(she makes off towards the kitchen)*
The Major	*(taking the paper)* Strike, strike, strike. Why do we bother, Fawlty? *(exits to the bar)*
Basil	*(to himself)* I didn't know you did, Major.

The bar is empty. The Major comes in, sits down and stares at his paper.

The Major	*(loudly, but to nobody)* Boycott made the century. *(he glances up and sees the rat; it is sitting on the next table eating peanuts out of a bowl; the Major stares at it, then gets up)* Stay where you are, old chap . . . don't move. *(he puts another bowl by the rat and moves slowly out of the bar)*

In the lobby, Basil is looking at some flowers on the centre table. The Major hurries by behind him and goes up the stairs. Basil takes the flowers into the kitchen.

Basil	Terry, give these a rinse, will you.
Terry	I have.
Basil	Well, they're still dirty. Put them in the dishwasher.

He goes back into the lobby. The Major appears at the bottom of the stairs and passes Basil carrying a shot-gun. He goes into the bar. Basil does a double-take and follows him. In the bar, the Major is stalking round the room with the gun. There is of course no sign of the rat.

Basil	*(genuinely unsettled)* Do you need any help, Major?
The Major	Don't move! *(he points the gun in Basil's direction; Basil puts his hands up)* Vermin!
Basil	We haven't got any this week, Major.
The Major	Hmmm?
Basil	No Germans staying this week, Major . . . may I have the gun?
The Major	Going to shoot him, Fawlty.
Basil	Yes . . . Major . . .
The Major	Mmm?
Basil	Not . . . not legal, actually, any more . . . murder . . .
The Major	But they're **animals**, Fawlty!
Basil	Oh, yes, yes. . . . Still, forgive and forget, eh, Major? *(he takes the gun)*

The Major	Forgive 'em?
Basil	Well, pretend we do.
The Major	But they spread disease, Fawlty . . . he was sitting there on that table, eating the nuts if you please.
Basil	*(to himself)* He's really gone this time.
The Major	About that size. That with the tail . . .
Basil	*(realizing)* Tail . . . what did you say it was?
The Major	Vermin. . . . A dirty rat!
Basil	*(glares in the direction of the lobby)* . . . How long ago?
The Major	Oh, about two minutes ago.
Basil	Stay there, Major, stay there. If you see him, give me a shout.
The Major	Will do.

Basil strides out of the bar, parking the gun behind the bar itself, and goes into the kitchen, where Terry is looking behind the fridge which he has pulled out from the wall.

Terry	I'm just cleaning behind the fridge, Mr Fawlty.

Basil looks at him and pushes the dining-room door open. He looks in, comes out, checks, and goes back in. In the dining room, Polly is kneeling under a table, only her rear and legs visible. Basil walks quietly up behind her.

Polly	Basil . . . Basil . . . cheesies . . . Basil . . .
Basil	Yes? *(there is a thump and the table jerks upwards, Polly appears)* Here I am!
Polly	Oh, hallo, Mr Fawlty . . .
Basil	Oh, that's for me, is it? Thank you.
Polly	Oh . . . *(he takes the piece of cheese from her hand and eats it)* Shall I get you some more, there's plenty . . .
Basil	He's called Basil, is he? . . . Don't play dumb with me, I trusted you, you're responsible for this. 'Oh, I've got a friend who'll look after him, Mr Fawlty'! *(he is about to hit her when he sees Manuel crawling out from under another table; Basil runs after him and Manuel scuttles back under the table)* Come on. Come on out, come on, Basil's here. *(he makes kiss-kiss noises)*
Terry	*(coming in from the kitchen)* Have you got him?
Basil	. . . He's under there.
Terry	Right. I'll get him. *(he goes towards the table and then stops, rather sheepish)*
Basil	Cleaning behind the fridge, hmm?

Terry	Well, we didn't want to worry you, you've got a lot on your mind Mr Fawlty.
Basil	What, you mean a Public Health Inspector coming after a twenty-four-hour warning and a rat loose in the hotel, is that what you mean?
Polly	He must have escaped, Mr Fawlty, and come back . . .
Basil	Come **back?**
Polly	*(desperately)* They home.
Basil	Oh, I see, he's a **homing** rat, is he?
Terry	. . . Oh yeah, rats are amazing creatures, Mr Fawlty. I read about one once, his owner had gone down to Penzance . . .
Basil	Yes, yes, I read about that. When the chef got filleted with his own carving knife . . .
Terry	No, honest, Mr Fawlty, scout's honour.
Polly	We'll find him, Mr Fawlty!
Basil	Well, if you could, that would be lovely. Before they close us down. Super. Well, let's have a little Basil hunt, shall we, and then we'll deal with the sackings later.
Terry	I'll do the cellar.
Polly	I'll do this floor. Manuel, you check your room.
Basil	Start in the bar, Polly, it was there two minutes ago. I'll do the kitchen. *(he goes into the kitchen and starts checking the cupboards)*
Terry	I've done all them. *(he goes out of the back door)*

Basil remembers another cupboard, goes and gets rat poison from it, then runs to the fridge where he finds a plate of veal fillets. He takes one, sprinkles some poison on it, puts it on the floor, leaves the poison on top of the fridge and washes his hands. He goes into the lobby, and goes behind the reception desk. Mr Carnegie comes in and Sybil, coming down the stairs, greet him.

Sybil	Oh, Mr Carnegie. Good morning.
Carnegie	Good morning, Mrs Fawlty.
Basil	Oh, hallo. Nice to see you.
Sybil	Would you like some coffee before we adjourn to . . .
Carnegie	No thank you. If we start upstairs with the water tanks . . .
Basil	Ah, good idea.
Carnegie	What?
Basil	Good thinking. About starting upstairs. Sybil, would you like to show Mr Carnegie upstairs?

Sybil	I was just going to, Basil.
Basil	Yes, and I'll keep an eye on things down here, shall I, see if I can find something to be getting on with . . .

The gun goes off in the bar. They all jump.

Carnegie	Good God, what was that?
Basil	Bloody television exploding again. I'll deal with it. You go upstairs. *(he hurries towards the bar)*
Carnegie	That was a gun!
Sybil	Yes, it did sound like it, didn't it.

Polly runs in carrying a large net. She sees Mr Carnegie; he sees her.

Polly	Moths.
Carnegie	What is going on here? *(he goes towards the bar)*

In the bar, Basil is trying to get the gun away from the Major. They tussle as Mr Carnegie walks in.

The Major	I'll get him! *(Basil gets the gun away from him and sees Mr Carnegie)* He'll come back for the nuts, you know. He was sniffing around here just now . . .
Basil	*(kneeing him in the balls)* Sorry, sorry Major. *(to Mr Carnegie)* It wasn't the television, it was just this gun. I'll put it under lock and key straight away.

He goes into the lobby followed by Mr Carnegie.

Carnegie	Why was he firing it in the hotel?
Basil	Starlings . . . shooting starlings.
Carnegie	In the bar?
Basil	Through the window. I'll lock it away.
Carnegie	Is it licensed?
Basil	Oh, yes, oh yes. *(he goes into the office)*
Carnegie	*(to Sybil)* You do realize that under the Health and Safety Act it is your responsibility?
Sybil	Oh yes, I'm terribly sorry. It's never happened before, Mr Carnegie.
Carnegie	Well, I shall have to notify the police, of course. They will take steps.

Manuel comes flying down the stairs in a panic.

Polly	It's all right, it's all right, Manuel.
Manuel	Is he all right?

Polly	Yes, he's all right.
Manuel	He not dead?
Polly	No, no, no! It was just the Major letting the gun off . . .
Manuel	The Major try to kill Basil?
Sybil	Kill Basil?
Manuel	No, no, not Mr Fawlty, I mean Basil my little . . .
Polly	Ratatouille!
Carnegie	Basil . . . the little . . .
Polly	Ratatouille. The chef calls the ratatouille Basil, because he puts quite a lot of Basil in it.
Manuel	*(horrified)* He put Basil in ratatouille?
Polly	Yes . . .
Manuel	Aaahh! *(he runs towards the kitchen and goes in, followed by Polly, still clutching her net)*
Sybil	*(to Mr Carnegie)* He's from Barcelona. You know, typical Latin, really. Would you like to . . . *(she indicates the stairs)*

In the kitchen, Manuel is shouting at Terry.

Manuel	Why you do this?
Terry	I haven't, I haven't.
Manuel	Polly say you put Basil in ratatouille.
Terry	I haven't **made** any bleeding ratatouille.
Polly	Manuel!
Manuel	*(to Polly)* Why you say he put Basil in ratatouille?
Polly	I had to say something, that was the Health Inspector. Now will you calm down.
Manuel	Where is he?
Polly	I don't know.
Manuel	Perhaps he dead.
Terry	Oh, he's all right. Give us the veal, Poll, I've got to get lunch ready.

Polly gets the veal out of the fridge.

Manuel	But how you know he all right? Major fire his gun. Perhaps he hit . . . I must find him. *(he dashes forward, knocking the veal out of Polly's hands onto the floor)* Oh, sorry, Polly! *(he runs out)*
Terry	Oh, pick 'em up quick, before he gets in here. *(they start piling the veal back on the plate frantically)*

In the lobby, Basil and the Major are coming in from the bar.

Basil	That's right, Major. You've got it. Well, you've nearly got

it. Anyway, the thing is, not a word about rats. You were shooting **starling**. All right?

The Major	A starling?
Basil	Yes.
The Major	Through the window.
Basil	Right.
The Major	But, Fawlty, how did the starling get in the bar?
Basil	No, no, **you** were in the bar.
The Major	I was in the bar?
Basil	Yes!
The Major	So I was!
Basil	Yes, and the starling was in the garden and the rat was nowhere at all.
The Major	Well, I didn't see him.
Basil	*(moving off)* Say goodnight to the folks, Gracie.

He goes into the kitchen. Terry is preparing the veal.

Basil	All right, Terry, everything under control?
Terry	Yeah . . . is he still . . . ?
Basil	No, he's started upstairs. God knows where the rat is . . . *(he sees the cat on the fridge; it has got at the plate of veal)* Oh, puss . . . *(he picks up the cat and the piece of veal it was nibbling and puts it out of the back door)* Come on puss, out you go . . . *(he hides the piece of veal on top of a high cupboard, and rinses his hands)* Oh! And I put some, er . . . *(he looks around the floor but cannot see the poisoned veal)* Terry . . .
Terry	Yes?
Basil	There was a piece of veal down here.
Terry	Yes, we got 'em all up, Mr Fawlty.
Basil	What?
Terry	We picked 'em all up.
Polly	*(coming in)* Got the veals, Terry?
Terry	Here we are, Poll. *(he gives her two plates)*
Basil	Terry, listen to me. What do you mean you picked them all up?
Terry	Well, Manuel knocked 'em over. We picked 'em all up.

Polly goes out with the veal.

| Basil | . . . Oh my God. |
| Terry | . . . What's the matter? |

Basil	One of them's got rat poison on it! *(he rushes into the dining room)*

In the dining room, Manuel is taking an order. Polly is returning from Mr and Mrs Taylor's table. Basil flies past her and grabs both plates.

Basil	Sorry! Sorry! *(they stare at him)* Veal's off! Sorry.
Mrs Taylor	That's veal.
Basil	No, no, this is veal substitute – we're giving it a try, and it's a bit of a disappointment, I'm afraid. In fact it's no substitute at all . . . Polly, would you take this order again, please? *(he whispers an explanation in her ear)* Thank you, thank you so much. *(he goes towards the kitchen)*
Polly	I'm sorry about that – would you like the lamb or the plaice?
Mrs Taylor	Veal substitute?
Polly	It's Japanese, actually – soya bean and essence of cow. *(Basil exits)*

In the kitchen, Mr Carnegie is talking to Sybil. Basil enters with the plates, sees Mr Carnegie, and moves back into the dining room.

Carnegie	Seals.
Sybil	We've moved all the meat into this one and put all the confectionery in the new one over here.

Back in the dining room, Basil dithers, trying to decide where to put the plates.

Taylor	*(calling to him)* A bottle of the Beaujolais, please.
Basil	Ah, certainly. *(he goes back into the kitchen)*

In the kitchen.

Carnegie	And the washhandbasin?
Sybil	We ordered it yesterday. Here's the acknowledgement of the order.

Basil comes in and takes a bottle of wine from a rack in the corner.

Carnegie	Well, it would now appear that this kitchen is now in a satisfactory condition. I shall be writing to confirm the . . .

Basil sees the box of rat poison on top of the fridge. He grabs at it, dropping the bottle, which smashes.

Basil	Sorry. It slipped. *(he hides the poison behind his back)*
Carnegie	. . . outstanding points and someone will be dropping in to carry out a future random inspection to make sure these standards are being maintained . . .
Sybil	Thank you.
Basil	Marvellous. Marvellous. *(he puts the poison out of the back door and gets another bottle of wine)*
Carnegie	It's ten to one, I'd like to take lunch here if I may.
Sybil	Oh, certainly, Mr Carnegie.
Carnegie	I couldn't help noticing you had some veal over here.
Basil	*(dropping the bottle)* Veal?
Sybil	Yes, it's Dutch.
Basil	It's not Dutch, actually. It's Norwegian.
Sybil	Norwegian?
Basil	Yes – not the absolute apex quite honestly.
Sybil	Terry, the veal is Dutch, isn't it?
Terry	Norwegian, Mrs Fawlty.
Carnegie	I've been in this business twenty years, I've never heard of Norwegian veal.
Basil	No, they've only just branched into it, you know. I don't think it's a winner, frankly – more of a veal substitute. It's got a lot of air pockets in it, that sort of thing. The lamb is Dutch.
Carnegie	Dutch?
Basil	Well, English. I mean, we call it Dutch because it's as good as the Dutch veal. It's better, quite honestly.
Carnegie	I'd prefer the veal.
Basil	Yes . . . how about the lobster? Would you prefer lobster? A couple of lobsters? Oh, it's **frightfully** good at the moment, and it's not expensive this week, we've got so much we're having a lobster sale at the moment to try and shift it all. 75p each. You can't say better than that, can you?
Carnegie	Just the veal. *(he moves to the lobby door)*
Basil	*(following him)* Well, if you like the veal, perhaps you'd prefer the chicken.
Sybil	*(getting in front of Basil)* Basil, he wants the veal.
Carnegie	Could I make a phone call?
Sybil	Yes, of course. Through here. *(they go out)*
Polly	*(coming in from the dining room)* What's all this about rat poison on the veal?
Terry	He's put rat poison on one, they've got mixed up and

	nobody knows which is which now. What happened to the one the cat had?
Polly	The cat?! *(rushes out of back door)*
Basil	That's no good. That might have poison on it, too.
Terry	Well, where is it?
Basil	What?
Terry	Where's the cat's slice?
Basil	*(gets it)* Up there.
Terry	Right now, how's the cat?
Basil	. . . How's the cat. How's the **cat**? We're just about to take the life of a Public Health Inspector and you want to know 'how's the cat'. It's gone to London to see the Queen. What are we going to do?
Polly	*(bringing the cat in)* He's all right.
Terry	Great!
Basil	*(leaping about in mock joy)* Hooray! Hooray! The cat lives! The cat lives! Long live the cat! What are we going to **do**?
Terry	Mr Fawlty. If the cat is all right . . . that means that slice is all right.
Polly	Well . . . how long would it take to work?
Terry	That stuff, two minutes. He had this ten minutes ago at least.

They all peer at the veal.

Polly	It's a bit chewed there.
Terry	I'll give it a trim. *(he does so)*

In the dining room, Mr Carnegie is just sitting down. Sybil is standing by him.

Sybil	So you're driving over to Babbacombe this afternoon?
Carnegie	Yes, we're . . . *(he realizes he has sat down on something; he gets up slowly holding a plate of veal)* What is a plate of veal doing there?
Sybil	I'll just relieve you of it, shall I? *(she takes it and brushes off Mr Carnegie's jacket)*
Basil	*(coming in from the kitchen)* Do sit down, Mr Carnegie.
Sybil	He just has, Basil.
Carnegie	On a plate of veal.
Basil	Has it put you off?
Carnegie	What?
Basil	Has it put you off the veal at all?

Carnegie	Well, I'm not eating **that** one if that's what you mean. *(goes to sit at another chair at the same table)*
Basil	Stop! Halt! Sorry . . . I think there might be another one there. Excuse me . . . *(he collects it)* Ah, yes. Lucky guess.
Carnegie	Well, who's responsible for putting them there?
Basil	Er . . . Manuel, our Spanish waiter. *(turns to Manuel, who is just behind him, gives him the plates and slaps his head; to Mr Carnegie)* Now would you like to sit over here . . . please . . . ?
Carnegie	Well, does he do it often?
Sybil	Oh, no, no.
Basil	No, no, no, it's the first time, but he sometimes looks as though he's going to, but we always catch him of course. *(Polly enters carrying the veal)* Ah.
Polly	Here's your veal, Mr Carnegie. And one green salad.
Carnegie	Thank you.
Basil	Ah, good, *bon appétit. (he goes into the kitchen)* Well done, Terry.

He goes to the back door, opens it, and takes a deep relaxing breath. Then he sees the cat; it is throwing up. He turns and rushes back into the dining room and snatches the plate away from under Mr Carnegie's nose as Polly adds the vegetables.

Basil	Sorry. Not hot enough. *(the plate burns him)* Aaaagh! Not big enough. Sorry!
Carnegie	What . . .
Basil	Not big enough. Sorry . . . excuse me. Really, Polly! *(he hurries out with it; Polly, Sybil and Mr Carnegie stare after him)*

In the kitchen, Terry is already putting another veal in the pan. Basil throws his in the bin.

Basil	What are you doing?
Terry	Well, if that's the one . . . these are OK.
Basil	What?
Terry	If that's the poisoned one, these are all right.
Basil	. . . Brilliant. Great. Right. OK.

Polly and Sybil come in.

Sybil	Basil, what is going on?
Basil	That was the poisoned one. The cat had it.
Polly	The cat! . . . Oh! *(she dashes off towards the back yard)*

Sybil	Poisoned?
Basil	Yes . . . so that one must be OK. *(goes into dining room)*
Sybil	*(confused)* Basil . . .

In the dining room, Basil approaches Mr Carnegie.

Basil	Sorry, just getting you a proper sized one.
Carnegie	It was big enough. It was all I wanted.
Basil	Well, it could have been a bit hotter . . . Well, not much . . . but . . .
Carnegie	Look . . . *(he looks at his watch)*

Manuel comes into the room.

Basil	Yes, yes, just coming . . . won't be a sec . . . *(a young upper-class couple, Ronald and Quentina, have entered)* Ah, Manuel . . . would you . . . thank you. *(he exits to the kitchen; Manuel shows them to their table)*

In the kitchen, Basil comes in to find Polly holding the cat.

Basil	What?
Polly	Well, he's all right! Look!
Basil	He can't be!
Polly	Well, he is.
Terry	*(holding out a plate of veal)* Here you are, Poll.
Polly	Oh. *(she hands the cat to Basil and takes the plate)*
Basil	He can't be!
Sybil	What do you mean?
Basil	Well, he was vomiting.
Sybil	Vomiting? *(Basil demonstrates)* That's just fur balls, Basil.

Polly takes the plate into the dining room.

Basil	. . . What?
Sybil	That's just fur balls. He does that all the time in the summer. *(she takes the cat out through the back door)*
Basil	But . . . if he's all right . . . that one might . . . *(he realizes the plate has gone and flies after Polly)*

In the dining room, Polly is approaching Mr Carnegie with his veal. Basil comes in just as Polly puts the veal down on the table.

Basil	Polly . . . too much.
Carnegie	What?
Basil	Too much. *(he waves her back)* Too much of a good thing

	always leaves one wanting less, I always find.
Polly	Ohh! *(exits to kitchen with the veal)*
Carnegie	What is wrong *now?*
Basil	Well, we wouldn't want you to think that because you were one of Her Majesty's Civil Servants, that we were showing you any excess favouritism. I'm sure you wouldn't want that.
The Major	*(who is on the table behind, standing up)* Oh! So you're the rat inspector. *(Mr Carnegie stares at him; Basil cringes)* Sorry! Sorry Fawlty! Starling Inspector.
Carnegie	Starling Inspector?

Basil indicates the Major is mad. Basil exits and Manuel returns to the young couple's table with the menus. As he waits for them to choose he suddenly sees the rat nosing about by Quentina's feet. He freezes and stares. Ronald sees him and gives him a hard look, thinking Manuel is staring at Quentina's legs.

Ronald	Do you mind?
Manuel	*Qué?*
Ronald	We'll have one Windsor soup, one pâté, please. *(Manuel doesn't move)* One Windsor soup . . .
Manuel	Shh! *(he starts backing away slowly; Ronald is amazed)*

In the kitchen, Basil, Sybil, Polly and Terry are standing round the table considering the plate of veal.

Basil	No, no, if the cat's slice is all right, that might be the poisoned one.
Sybil	No, no.
Polly	Yes! Yes, he's right.
Terry	And if the cat's one is all right . . .
Polly	Which it **is**.
Terry	We can give him that, can't we. *(he goes to the bin and takes the cat's veal out)*
Basil	Right!
Manuel	*(coming in)* Mr Fawlty!
Basil	Shut up!!
Sybil	But Terry, that's got **things** on it.
Terry	Oh, that's all right, Mrs Fawlty. What the eye doesn't see the chef gets away with.
Manuel	Mr Fawlty.
Basil	What is it?

Manuel	Table seven!!
Basil	What?
Manuel	Basil! *(he pushes Basil through the door into the dining room)*

In the dining room, Ronald is getting annoyed. Basil and Manuel come in.

Basil	*(to Mr Carnegie)* Sorry, it's just coming.
Ronald	Excuse me.
Basil	*(going over to him)* Of course. Good afternoon, sir. Good afternoon, madam.
Ronald	Look, I was just trying to give an order to your waiter and he walked away while I was doing it.
Basil	*(looking down subtly)* Hmmm?
Ronald	Well, he wasn't paying attention at all.
Basil	I'm so sorry? What were you saying?
Ronald	. . . Your waiter wasn't listening when I was giving him our order. He seemed more interested in my fiancée's legs.
Basil	Really? May I? *(he has a look)* No, I don't think so. In fact I think there's a bread roll down there.
Ronald	May I give my order?
Basil	Oh please, of course.
Ronald	We'd like one Windsor soup and one pâté, and then . . .

Polly comes in. Basil is kneeling pretending to do up his shoe lace.

Basil	Just doing my shoe lace up.
Ronald	Are you going to take my order?
Basil	Er, yes . . . Polly, would you take the order here please, on this table . . .
Ronald	. . . We'd like one Windsor soup.
Polly	One Windsor.
Ronald	One pâté . . .
Basil	He's there. S'there.
Ronald	What?
Basil	There, there.
Ronald	What do you mean, 'There, there'?
Basil	It's all there. There, there, there and there. All there for your enjoyment.
Polly	And one pâté?
Basil	Manuel, would you get the bread roll, please . . . no, no, no, get the box. *(Ronald stares)* We have a box, a bread-

	box . . . for any bread that has gone past its prime.
Polly	And you'd both like the . . .
Ronald	The veal.
Polly	Oh! The veal's off, I'm afraid.
Ronald	How **can** it be? You've only just started.
Basil	Ssh. Ssh, sssh.
Ronald	Don't shush me.
Basil	I'm sorry. But the veal is in fact off, well it was never really on, quite honestly, that's a misprint.
Ronald	A misprint?
Basil	Yes, it should say . . . um . . . 'eel'.
Ronald	Eel escalope? *(to Manuel, who has gone under the table)* Stop it, will you. Just leave it. Wait till after the meal.
Basil	No, no, we have to get it now, I'm afraid. Health regulations. Before it moulds.
Ronald	Well, I'll get it, then. *(he starts looking down)*
Basil	*(restraining him)* No, no, no, no, please, please, allow us, please, all part of the service.
Polly	So that's one pâté and one Windsor . . . *(sees the rat in Quentina's handbag on the floor)* . . . **soup**!!! *(to Manuel)* Psst!

Sybil comes out of the kitchen carrying Mr Carnegie's latest veal.

Sybil	Here's your veal, Mr Carnegie. Sorry for the delay.
Ronald	He's been given veal!
Basil	Er, no, that's veal substitute.
Ronald	Veal **substitute?**
Basil	Yes, it's not very good, it got held up on the boat on the way over from . . .
Polly	Japan . . .
Basil	. . . Norway. It's a sort of Jappo-Scandinavian imitation veal substitute, but I'm afraid that's the last slice anyway.
Ronald	*(standing up)* We're leaving.
Basil	OK. If you insist.
Ronald	What?
Basil	By all means. Be my guest, thank you.
Ronald	I want a taxi.
Basil	Polly – would you arrange a taxi, please.

Ronald and Quentina go into the lobby.

Polly	*(to Basil)* It's in the bag.
Basil	*(nods, puts his finger at the side of his nose and winks, then, to*

	Mr Carnegie) Is your veal, er . . .
Polly	In **her** bag. *(she goes into the lobby)*
Basil	*(to Mr Carnegie)* In **her** bag?
Carnegie	What?
Basil	Excuse me. *(he exits rapidly into the lobby)*

In the lobby, Ronald and Quentina are standing at reception.

Polly	*(hurrying up to them)* Do you know where you're going?
Ronald	Can you recommend a restaurant?
Polly	*(dialling)* Yes, of course, what sort of a . . .

They both look at Basil who has come up behind them stealthily and is standing just behind Quentina's shoulder looking into the bag.

Basil	Yes, where is somewhere that serves really good veal, Polly? Somewhere in the . . .
Polly	*(energetically)* Oh, veal, yes! Of course. A really good restaurant . . . just a minute, because I do remember a place where I had some **really** good veal once . . . I just can't think of the name of it . . . it was . . . er . . . oh . . . *(does her Diane Keaton impression)* Lah de dah . . . did you see *Annie Hall?* . . . 'Lah de dah' . . .

Basil is groping very carefully in Quentina's bag.

Ronald	Annie **who?**

Quentina turns and sees Basil with his hand in her bag.

Quentina	What **are** you doing?
Basil	What . . . ?
Quentina	*(to Ronald)* He had his hand in my bag.
Ronald	*(stepping towards Basil)* What?
Basil	Er . . . no . . .
Ronald	You know something! You're getting my gander up, you grotty little man. You're asking for a bunch of fives!
Polly	Bomb scare!
Ronald	What?
Polly	There's been a bomb scare.
Ronald	A bomb scare?
Basil	Yes.
Polly	Yes – that's why he was searching in your bag – he didn't want to alarm you.
Basil	May I?

Quentina	Well, I don't . . .
Basil	Just one moment . . . thank you. *(he takes the bag and moves to the other end of the reception desk and rummages in it)*
Polly	We had a call, you see.
Ronald	Well, shouldn't you get everybody out?
Polly	Well, that's why we were looking under your table . . . we just didn't want to draw attention . . .

Basil lets out a howl and pulls his hand out of the bag very fast. He drops the bag, and the rat streaks across the lobby, into the dining room, past Manuel, who sees it, and under a table. Manuel looks round and disappears unnoticed under the table. A moment or two later he emerges, evidently holding the rat in his hands.

Carnegie	Waiter. *(Manuel freezes)* Waiter.
Manuel	One *momentito. (he moves quickly to the sweet trolley and puts the rat into the biscuit tin, then returns to Mr Carnegie) Si* . . . ?

The Major leans across and takes the tin off the trolley. He opens it and takes a biscuit out without noticing its inhabitant.

Carnegie	Some cheese and biscuits and a coffee, please.
Manuel	*Si, si.*

He hurries back to the trolley, but is amazed to find the tin missing. He looks round the room without noticing it on the Major's table, then disappears into the kitchen. Basil comes in with his hand wrapped in a handkerchief.

Basil	*(to Mr Carnegie)* Anything to follow?
Carnegie	I've ordered some cheese and a coffee.
Basil	Certainly. *(Sybil comes in from the kitchen)* Coffee please, Sybil.
Basil	*(bringing the trolley to Mr Carnegie)* Here we are, Mr Carnegie. *(Polly comes in from the lobby)* Polly, would you get the biscuits, please.
The Major	Here they are, Fawlty! *(he hands the tin to Polly)*
Basil	Cheddar, Danish Blue, Edam . . . ?
Carnegie	A little Danish Blue, please.
Basil	Certainly. Edam?
Carnegie	No, thank you.
Basil	Biscuits?

Basil puts the cheese in front of Mr Carnegie. Sybil comes over with the coffee pot. Polly takes the lid off the biscuit tin and offers it to Mr Carnegie without looking. In the tin sits the rat. Mr Carnegie looks at the rat; the rat looks at Mr Carnegie. Basil notices this first, then Polly and Sybil. They stare at Basil. Mr Carnegie is stunned and continues to stare at the rat.

Basil   . . . Would you care for a rat? Or . . . ? Just . . . just the biscuits then please, Polly.

Polly leaves with the tin. Carnegie continues to stare into space.

Sybil   . . . Black or white?
Carnegie   . . . Hmmm?
Sybil   Black or white?
Carnegie   . . . Black, please . . . was that a . . . ?
Sybil   There we are.
Polly   *(coming back)* Here are the biscuits.

She holds the tin out, now minus rat. Mr Carnegie stares at it. He takes a biscuit mechanically and just holds it. In the background Manuel is dragging an unconscious Basil by the heels out of the door into the lobby.

Sybil   *(conversationally)* I'm afraid it's started to rain again.